J. Silk

5/2021

Belief

Belief

A Pragmatic Picture

Aaron Z. Zimmerman

OXFORD
UNIVERSITY PRESS

OXFORD

UNIVERSITY PRESS

Great Clarendon Street, Oxford, OX2 6DP,
United Kingdom

Oxford University Press is a department of the University of Oxford.
It furthers the University's objective of excellence in research, scholarship,
and education by publishing worldwide. Oxford is a registered trade mark of
Oxford University Press in the UK and in certain other countries

First Edition published in 2018

Impression: 1

Published in the United States of America by Oxford University Press
198 Madison Avenue, New York, NY 10016, United States of America

British Library Cataloguing in Publication Data
Data available

Library of Congress Control Number: 2017958749

ISBN 978-0-19-880951-7

Printed and bound by
CPI Group (UK) Ltd, Croydon, CR0 4YY

For Max and Evie

All of the author's royalties will go to the Center for Cancer and Blood Disorders at Children's National in memory of Rakan Stormer, may his name be a blessing: זכרו לברכה :حياتك في البقية, *and to Children's Hospital Los Angeles, in appreciation of Mark Krieger, M.D., Division Chief, Neurosurgery.*

I quite agree that what mankind at large most lacks is criticism and caution, not faith. Its cardinal weakness is to let belief follow recklessly upon lively conception, especially when the conception has instinctive liking at its back. I admit, then, that were I addressing the Salvation Army or a miscellaneous popular crowd it would be a misuse of opportunity to preach the liberty of believing... What such audiences most need is that their faiths should be broken up and ventilated, that the northwest wind of science should get into them and blow their sickliness and barbarism away. But academic audiences, fed already on science, have a very different need. Paralysis of their native capacity for faith and timorous *abulia*... are their special forms of mental weakness, brought about by the notion, carefully instilled, that there is something called scientific evidence by waiting upon which they shall escape all danger of shipwreck in regard to truth. But there is really no scientific or other method by which men can steer safely between the opposite dangers of believing too little or of believing too much. To face such dangers is apparently our duty, and to hit the right channel between them is the measure of our wisdom as men.

(James, 1896/1912, x–xi)

Contents

Acknowledgments   xi
Preface: Some Initial Questions   xv

1. Defining the Nature of Belief   1
2. Alternative Measures and Taxonomies   22
3. Against Intellectualism: Animal Belief   42
4. Belief and Pretense   81
5. The Authority to Define "Belief"   97
6. Pragmatic Self-Deception   128

Cited Sources   141
Index   175

Acknowledgments

This relatively short book is an extension and defense of the conception of belief I defended in my 2002 Ph.D. dissertation "Directly in Mind: A Defense of First-Person Authority," and a subsequently published essay entitled "The Nature of Belief" (2007). These prior writings are indebted to frequent conversations with Carl Ginet and Sydney Shoemaker, who advised me throughout the dissertation process. I wish to thank them and all the students, teachers, and friends I have philosophized with over the years. I am especially grateful for the University of California, Santa Barbara where I have taught since 2002 thanks to the enlightened citizens of this great state of California; for Daniel C. Dennett, who introduced me to philosophical work on belief (and much else besides) when I studied philosophy of mind at Tufts University in the early 1990s; for Jason Stanley, who convinced me to remain in philosophy; for Branden Fitelson, for thirty years of philosophical friendship, for Joshua May, Neil Levy, Eric Schwitzgebel, Kenny Easwaran, Walter Sinnott-Armstrong, and three anonymous referees for comments on drafts of this manuscript; for Peter Momchiloff for his interest and guidance throughout; for the staff at Crave Café in Studio City where much of this book was written; and for my children's teachers at the Neighborhood School in Studio City and Colfax Charter Elementary School in Valley Village, who do an amazing job instructing their young students about their brains and behaviors. My greatest debt, though, is to my family: my son Max, daughter Evie, wife Kira, mother Hope, father Dan, sisters Mara and Rebecca, in-laws Laurie, Norman, Howard, Larry, Arie, Nina, Matt, Stephen, and all their families. I am grateful for all of you. Especially Kira. You're amazing.

When I wrote on these topics fifteen years ago, I had misleadingly labeled the present view of belief "neo-Cartesian," even though I had all along joined Hume in arguing that non-human animals and prelinguistic infants have beliefs, therein rejecting Descartes' view that sentential language is essential to the phenomenon. I had used the "neo-Cartesian" label to emphasize the theory's divergence from both behaviorism and the kinds of Turing machine functionalism then dominant within the philosophy of mind.[1] My guiding idea was that belief must be defined in terms of attention and control, and could not be fruitfully used to define these more fundamental elements of consciousness and agency.

But "neo-Carteisan" was a poor choice, and not only because it suggests Descartes' noxious claim that humans are the only animals who form beliefs and reason from them. The label also suggested Descartes' dualistic conception of the relation between mind and body, whereas I have long been convinced that a person's mind is nothing above or beyond her nervous system.

In the years that ran away from me after the 2007 publication of "The Nature of Belief," I spent some time researching the development of American philosophy from its origins in the liberalism articulated by Locke and his heirs. In graduate school, I had focused a great deal of my time on David Hume's philosophical work, and though I had read through the secondary literature on Hume's attempts to define belief— and his expressed dissatisfaction with these attempts—I had not read much on the subsequent work of a fellow Scot, the philosopher and anatomist Alexander Bain, who founded *Mind*, one of our preeminent journals in philosophy. When I did study Bain in earnest, a better label for the view immediately suggested itself. The clearest prior statement of the account of belief I defended in my dissertation was given by Bain when he concluded, "What we believe, we act upon" (Bain, 1868/1884, 372).[2]

According to C.S. Peirce, the school of thought we now know as "pragmatism" began at Harvard University, when Nicholas St. John Green urged the members of the ironically named Metaphysical Club— an august group including both William James and Oliver Wendell Holmes—to accept this very definition of "belief." Indeed, Peirce claimed

---

[1] See, e.g., Putnam (1975a) and Fodor (1975). See too the more relaxed conceptions of functionalism defended by Armstrong (1973), Shoemaker (1984), Stalnaker (1984/2003), and Lewis (1986).

[2] Cf. Bain (1859/1865) and Bain (1888). Admittedly, Bain claims, "It was an advance in correct thinking (by St Augustine and others in the 5th century) to declare in favour of the Unextended mind" (1859/65, 500), and "There is an alliance with matter, with the object, or extended world; but the thing allied, the mind proper, has itself no extension, and cannot be joined in local union" (Bain, 1873, 136). But this concession to dualistic thinking—and Bain's description of mind and brain as a "double faced unity" (1873, 196)—is not commonly evoked by "pragmatic," whereas "Cartesian" continues to bring *substance* dualism to mind, a philosophy of mind univocally rejected by both Bain and the heirs to his pragmatism.

in retrospect that the remaining tenets of pragmatism were "scarce more than a corollary" to Bain's account (Fisch, 1954). After assessing a wide body of historical evidence in favor of Peirce's assessment, M.H. Fisch, an esteemed intellectual historian (and the administrator of Peirce's papers) concluded,

> Prior to the genesis of pragmatism, all the members of The Metaphysical Club— Green, Fiske, James, Peirce, Holmes, Wright and Warner—were acquainted at first hand with works of Bain in which his theory of belief was expounded; Fiske, James and Wright had referred to the theory in their published writings; and Wright had made a significant application of it. Furthermore, at or before the time of his own and Peirce's first published formulations of pragmatism (1877–1879), James made a careful re-examination of the theory in Bain's final exposition of it in the third edition (1875) of *The Emotions and the Will*. It appears very likely, therefore, that whatever, as a matter of logic, pragmatism could have owed to Bain's theory of belief, it did, as a matter of fact, owe to it...I shall only add that Dewey's *Logic: The Theory of Inquiry* takes its start from the theory of inquiry which Peirce developed out of Bain's theory of belief, though Dewey, having forgotten his Bain, is obviously puzzled to account for Peirce's advance upon Hume and Mill. (1954, 434–42)[3]

After reading Fisch's history I realized that I had all along been defending a *pragmatic* definition of "belief." In effect, I had been advocating a return to the roots of this distinctively American philosophy on the grounds of its superiority to both its Lockean antecedents and its behaviorist descendants. I then began to grapple with the connections between Bain's pragmatic "picture" of the mind on the one hand, and evolutionary accounts

---

[3] Rorty's account is more charitable toward Dewey. "Taking his cue from Peirce's use of Bain's definition of belief, Dewey dismissed the idea that beliefs represent reality. He tried to substitute the idea that beliefs are tools for dealing with reality—maxims dictating the behavior of the organism that has the belief" (Rorty, 1990, 2). Cf. Wiener (1946), Fisch (July 1947), Fisch (1964), and Murphy (1990, 21–2). Fisch (1964) adds Berkeley and Mill to Bain as the primary influences on the members of the Metaphysical Club, but Mendell (1995) claims this is still too restrictive. All scholars acknowledge the effect of Kant on Peirce and Hegel on Dewey (see, e.g., Bernstein, 1971, 165–229). Menand's (2001) account of pragmatism's development by these and other American intellectuals focuses on the U.S. Civil War and the desire for compromise engendered by its horrors, and Brandom (2009) runs with this, arguing that the contemporary Anglo-American analysis of belief is superior to the pragmatist's conception without even mentioning Bain's influence. C. West plays up the poetry when he claims that "Emerson is the inventor of the American religion, Dewey is its Luther" (1989, 85), though his otherwise insightful history of pragmatism also fails to mention Bain.

of cognition (so influential among the pragmatists) and James's doctrine of the will to believe on the other.

The present work examines these connections and looks too at the consequences of adopting a pragmatist definition of belief for the reader's thinking on the relation between psychology and philosophy, the mind and brain, the nature of delusion, faith, pretense, racism, and more.[4] The essay will succeed in its own terms if the reader finds the package an attractive one and therein resolves to think of belief largely as Bain proposed so long ago.

Finally, a note on the text: Though it's not the most beautiful prose in existence, I've tried to make the body of this work relatively painless. Extended source quotes, discussion of a large body of connected literature, and the evaluation of several rival accounts have been banished to the footer. These notes are intended for those interested in pursuing the discussion further. Ignore them for a smoother, more pleasurable read. I just want to admit up front that my arguments for pragmatism aren't irresistible. The footnotes contain aid for the resistance.

[4] The pragmatists were not free from racism. See West (1989), Seigfried (1989), Eldridge (2004), Lawson and Koch (2004), Sullivan (2004), and Kim (2009), the last of whom describes pragmatism as, "a philosophy that sanctioned, in effect if not intent, reticence on the abolition of white supremacy" (2009, 49). But I believe that Bain's definition of belief was not directly implicated in these attitudes and their deleterious effects. As a preliminary, note that Bain's reflections on the race relations of his day were not entirely unenlightened. He debunked utilitarian and eugenic pretexts for racial segregation in the United States, approved of "making anti-slavery opinions a 'term of communion' [to] prohibit all inter-course with persons concerned in the practice," and argued that "there is probably no case of moral police more defensible" (Bain, 1859/1865, 277–8). See too H. Cormier's argument that James was led by his pragmatic view of belief's relation to the will to deny the reality of race "understood as a hierarchy among different human populations that is created and determined by natural conditions" (2009, 158) and J. Campbell's (2011) argument that pragmatism encourages and celebrates diversity. Pragmatic attitudes toward race and racism are discussed at length in chapter 5 of this volume.

Preface: Some Initial Questions

Do you believe in God? In life after death? In reincarnation? Prophesy? Karma? Or do you instead believe that the universe existed long before any intelligence evolved and that its origins must be entirely non-mental, lacking both purpose and thought?

Do you believe you are the object of real love: that some people already have an ultimate, non-instrumental concern for your wellbeing? Or do you think that the people you know are "ultimately" self-interested: helping and supporting you only when they think this will bring them something they want for themselves? Do you believe that people will do the right thing in the absence of strong incentives to do otherwise, or that we conform to the established rules of conduct because we fear the negative reactions of others?

What about your parents, children, siblings, or friends? How often do you immediately accept what they tell you? Do you only trust claims that confirm your prior thinking on some matter? Do you listen to dissent with an open mind or follow the weapons inspector's policy of "trust but verify"?

Do you believe that Germany will win the next World Cup? That the Dow Jones Average will drop over the next few months? That a regional war will be averted in the Ukraine or Syria? That a Democrat will win the next election for president of the United States? That humanity will eventually render the Earth unfit for life? How certain are you in these predictions?

Do you believe that humans have walked on the moon? That Booth assassinated Lincoln? That noodles were invented in China? How confident are you in the truth of historical reports?

Do you have beliefs about the town where you grew up, the teachers you've had, the friends you've made, and the various places you've visited? Do you have beliefs about your current location and the things you can now see, hear, smell, and feel?

Do you have beliefs about your own mind, your thoughts at present, your mood and its source? Do you have a take on the minds of others and their beliefs about you?

Do you have beliefs about your personality, your skills, your appearance, and your intelligence in comparison to the other people you know?

Do you believe "in yourself"? Do you have faith in your ability to accomplish your goals, even when what little evidence you have favors a bet against your success?

Is this seemingly endless string of questions growing tiresome? If so, and you're still interested in thinking about the nature of belief, skip to chapter 1. If, on the other hand, you haven't yet tired of these questions, read on. "Belief" denotes an incredibly rich frame of mind. And the quickest way to grasp its diversity is to settle on some understanding of what you do and don't believe.

So do you believe you have both friends and enemies? Supporters and detractors? Colleagues and pets? Assets and debts?

Do you believe that humanity evolved from some other primate species via "natural" mechanisms of selection, or that someone created us to accomplish a definite task? Do you believe that the observable universe was created by a Big Bang and is still expanding, or that it has always been around, fluctuating between each of its possible variations for time immemorial? Do you believe that $E=MC^2$? That simultaneity must be relativized to a frame of reference? That there are ineliminable indeterminacies in the location of certain fundamental particles? How much credence do you invest in the deliverances of science?

Do you believe that $2+2=4$? That when summed the square of the length of the hypotenuse of a right triangle is equal to the sum of the squares of its two other sides? That if one thing is inside of a second thing and that second thing is inside of a third, then the first must also be inside of the third? That no surface can be both wholly red and wholly blue in color? That no time can pass unless something changes? Do you believe in the necessity of these claims? That things couldn't have been otherwise?

Do you believe that Mozart and Monk wrote beautiful music? That Giacometti's sculptures and Lucian Freud's paintings are powerful beyond description? That Astaire and Kelly or Baryshnikov and Whelan are elegant dancers? That James Brown and Bootsy Collins or Jam Master Jay and DJ Premier created devastatingly funky rhythms? That Gilda Radner and Robin Williams were side-splittingly hilarious? Do you expect or encourage others to join you in these judgments?

Do you believe that everyone has a right to life, liberty, and the pursuit of what they define as happiness—so long as realizing this conception doesn't involve derogating the correlative rights of others? That wisdom is good and ignorance bad? That it is vicious to take pleasure in the suffering of an innocent person? That kindness and fairness are both essential virtues? That parents have obligations to their young children and that grown children have obligations to their aging parents? That everyone should do what she can to promote the happiness and mitigate the suffering of others when doing so doesn't cost that much?

Do you believe that guns should be limited to the police and military or that everyone has a right to bear arms? That marijuana is a relatively harmless drug that should be legalized or that its decriminalization would spell the death of ambition? That abortion deprives an unborn child of what she needs to survive and should be outlawed on this basis or that it is a relatively harmless form of birth control the state should provide to every woman who wants it? That a modicum of health care is a right to be provided free of charge to each person by her fellow citizens, an obligation justly mandated by the state, or a prerogative reasonably ignored by those who can tolerate the risk?

What *is* it to believe something anyway?

1

Defining the Nature of Belief

Preparedness to act upon what we affirm is admitted on all hands to
be the sole, the genuine, the unmistakable criterion of belief.

(Bain, 1888, 505)

The test of belief is willingness to act.

(James, 1896/1912, 90)

What is belief? This has all the marks of a classical "philosophical"
question: it's highly abstract, it's been around at least since Socrates, it
still has no widely accepted answer, and yet, despite its antiquity and
intractability, the responses we give to it strike us as highly relevant to
our daily concerns. In fact, our assumptions about what it is to believe
something impact our views of ourselves, our understanding of one
another, and the social interactions in which these conceptions issue.
The question is just as important as it seems.

I would argue that we can define "belief" in a reasonably succinct
fashion if we allow ourselves the use of sufficiently general terms. To
believe something at a given time is to be so disposed that you would use
that information to guide those relatively attentive and self-controlled
activities you might engage in at that time, whether these activities
involve bodily movement or not. Equivalently—given the rough equivalence of mind and brain—beliefs are those neural states or structures that
encode the information that is primed to shape our relatively attentive
and self-controlled actions, where, again, "actions" should be understood
to include purely mental achievements like drawing a conclusion or
imagining a scenario.

When it is defined in this way, "belief" marks a threshold with regard
to your use of information—a threshold imposed on a pair of quantifiable psychological phenomena: attention and control. You can direct

more or less attention to what you are doing when you are acting, reasoning, or computing, just as you can exercise more or less control over the imagery that you're conjuring when fantasizing or the movements that you're executing while dancing.

> Minding, in all its sorts, can vary in degree. A driver can drive a car with great care, reasonable care or slight care, and a student can concentrate hard or not very hard.   (Ryle, 1949, 136; cf. Peirce, 1931–5, 5.109, 69–70)

If you bring a given body of information to bear when paying full attention to the activity you're engaged in, we can say that you have at least *minimally assimilated* the information that guides you in that endeavor. Similarly, information is minimally assimilated when you bring it to bear when exercising complete control over the movement of your limbs though space or the progression of your thoughts over time.

In contrast, if you act or reason on that same information when your attention is fully diverted to other things (or is as diverted to other things as is compatible with your successfully acting or reasoning as you do), we can say that the information in question is *maximally assimilated*. Something similar is true if you bring that information to bear when exercising minimal control over your thoughts or movements, or as little control over your thoughts or movements as is compatible with your acting or reasoning as you are.

The qualitative definition of "belief" I introduced above is derived from this quantitative notion of "degree of assimilation" insofar as it equates your beliefs with representations that are *minimally* assimilated within your mind, brain, or nervous system. Note that degree of assimilation is *inversely* correlated with guidance by belief. The idea here is that focusing attention and exercising control are the means by which you bring your beliefs to bear on an activity. Insofar as the more fully assimilated information guiding your performance of an action does not accord with these beliefs, that information may be something you do not accept.

Of course, your instincts and habits do often accord with your beliefs. You may react to a stimulus precisely as you would act were you to focus your attention on it and exercise control over your response. For example, you can probably answer the medical staff's questions about your name, address, and occupation while your attention is largely diverted to your children, or your cellphone, or the crossword puzzle you've been working on while waiting patiently at the doctor's office. In this case, your beliefs align with your relatively automatic communicative dispositions: you instinctively or automatically or unthinkingly say exactly what you would say were your attention squarely focused on the nurse's queries.

Nevertheless, according to the pragmatic view propounded below, these happy states of concord are not definitive of belief. You can fully believe something long before you have fully assimilated it (cf. Schwitzgebel, 2001b). Suppose, to continue our example, that you recently moved from the leafy environs of 1132 Holly Drive to a lovely residence at 1123 River Walk. Mightn't you instinctively or automatically or unthinkingly respond to the medical staff's questions with your old address? Suppose you do. Does this mean that you still believe you live on Holly Drive? The pragmatic conception denies this implication: you might really believe, without contradiction, that your address is 1123 River Walk. Over time, this new information will become so fully integrated into your mind/brain that you will reason and act on it without the need for much in the way of attention and control. And when that happens, your more automatic assertions will agree with your beliefs, even if those assertions will then have relatively automatic linguistic habits—rather than beliefs—as their proximal source. But until that happy state of affairs is realized, you may continue to reflexively assert what you no longer believe: i.e., that you live at 1132 Holly Drive rather than your new digs by the river. "In the primitive aspect of volition, belief has no place" (Bain, 1859/1865, xviii; cf. Bain, 1888, 505).

Now why should we think of belief in this way? What follows is a book-length attempt at an answer. But consider, before we plunge into these waters, how different it would be were you to put down your crossword puzzle, shush your kids, turn off your cellphone, and focus entirely on the staff's request for information. Of course, silencing these external sources of distraction might not be enough; you might remain preoccupied with anxiety over a mounting pile of bills or a nagging fascination with the continuum hypothesis. But if you suppose a person's attention isn't divided in this way—if you suppose that she is wholly focused on the question of her residence—and you suppose that she still answers with her old address, don't you experience a much more pronounced inclination to say that she's forgotten about the move? If you answer "Holly Drive" when fully focused on the question and answering exactly as you intend, it would seem you really have forgotten your residence at River Walk, even if you immediately smack your head in recognition when corrected by your spouse, partner, or roommate. If these intuitions are to be trusted, paying attention and exercising control are the means we employ to bring our beliefs to bear on our activities.

Admittedly, the pragmatic definition does not provide us with a fully precise measure of belief. To perform sophisticated actions you must divide your attention and exert control in complex ways, and substantive judgment is required if we're to apply the definition to these behaviors to identify the beliefs behind them. There are a number of borderline cases: cases in which someone pays some middling level of attention to various aspects of what she is saying or doing and exercises a moderate amount of control over various components of her thoughts, utterances, or actions, where we cannot adjudicate in advance whether the information that guides her endeavors figures among the things she believes. And the simple scale of automaticity and control introduced above—the scale on which the pragmatist's threshold for belief is imposed—fails to accurately reflect the complexity of attention and self-control themselves: phenomena that are heterogeneous at both cognitive and biological levels of description. This complexity is hard to see when we look at assertions and other baldly semantic phenomena. But the pragmatists insisted that our beliefs are not limited to articulate thoughts. Belief is manifested in a wide variety of non-discursive behaviors, many of which involve the dissociation of attention from control within the execution of a task.[1]

For instance, in a classic experiment, P. Fourneret and M. Jeannerod (1998) highlighted the kind of control we can exercise over our limbs without paying attention to their movements through space.[2] Subjects directed a cursor on a computer screen by manipulating a stylus that was hidden from view so that they could neither see it nor their own hands. (Because they couldn't see their hands, subjects moved the stylus around while watching the coordinated movement of the cursor on the screen.)

---

[1] For investigation into the neural/computational correlates of these phenomena see Monsell and Driver (2000), Miller (2000), Koechlin and Summerfield (2007), and Sherman et al. (2008). For more philosophical overviews see Perner (2003) and Tibbets (August 2004).

[2] Cf. Pisella et al. (2000) and Jeannerod (2006). The work of Jeannerod and colleagues is reviewed in a special edition of the journal *Neuropsychologia*, 55 (2014). For related results see Goodale et al. (1986), Goodale and Humphrey (1998), and Humphreys and Riddoch (2003).

Unbeknownst to them, the motion of the cursor on the screen was systematically biased at various points in the exercise; subjects had to adjust the stylus toward the right or left to guide the cursor straight ahead to the target. Subjects successfully adjusted to account for the bias: their movement of the stylus was not rigidly or inflexibly fixed on the trajectory they established when they initiated the movement of the stylus in concert with their visual perception of the target. But when the bias was not too extreme ($x < 10°$), they were unaware of the adjustments they were making, focused, as they were, on the screen before them.

Clearly, "attention" and "control" are not different words for a simple phenomenon: agency or will or ego. Instead, control can be exerted over behavior while attention is diverted from it. More cautiously, you can exert a certain degree of control over your movements while your attention is largely diverted from them. And when your attention is largely diverted away from your actions in this way, you will lack the self-awareness necessary for an accurate verbal report of what you are doing. Action of any complexity requires the coordination of perception with responsive movement, not the undifferentiated "conscious willing" of a predetermined goal.[3]

---

[3] For this reason, "volition" and "will" are not to be found in the pragmatic analysis of belief defended in this book. These expressions seem to be associated with a vague composite of our feelings when acting, reasoning, or calculating (the experience of effort in terms of which Hume defined the will) and the kind of self-awareness we try to articulate when reporting our reasons for action in an attempt to justify what we're doing (our take on the "content" of the intentions manifested in our actions). Because of this, uncritical use of "will" and "volition" provide a gateway to confusion, an incitement to over simplify. As Ryle complains, "The concept of volition is in a different case. We do not know in daily life how to use it, for we do not use it in daily life and do not, consequently, learn by practice how to apply it, and how not to misapply it. It is an artificial concept. It does not, of course, follow from its being a technical concept that it is an illegitimate or useless concept. 'Ionization' and 'off-side' are technical concepts, but both are legitimate and useful. 'Phlogiston' and 'animal spirits' were technical concepts, though they have now no utility . . . the concept of volition belongs to the latter class . . . This refutation will not invalidate the distinctions which we all quite properly draw between voluntary and involuntary actions and between strong-willed and weak-willed persons. It will, on the contrary, make clearer what is meant by 'voluntary' and 'involuntary', by 'strong-willed' and 'weak-willed'" (Ryle, 1949, 62–3). This prohibition signals a break with one of our pragmatist protagonists in what follows, William James, who claimed, "Attention and effort are . . . but two names for the same psychic fact" (1890/1950, 126) and "volition is nothing but attention" (1890/1950, 424). Sartre embraced a similar claim, which led him to mistakenly read choice into instinctive fear and other seemingly automatic reactions to stimuli. "One must be conscious in order to choose, and one must choose in order to be conscious. Choice and consciousness are one and the same thing" (1943/1956, 462). For an account of James's thinking on the relation between control,

Still, we must take care not to over-interpret Jeannerod's findings. Noted psychologist and philosopher W. Prinz says they undermine "the folk psychology notion that act follows will" (Prinz, 2003, 26). The psychologist C.D. Frith (2014) agrees with this assessment. And the late D. Wegner (2002) was an even more most strident advocate for "will-skepticism" in its various forms (Levy and Bayne, 2004; Bayne and Levy, 2006).

It seems to each of us that we have conscious will. It seems we have selves. It seems we have minds. It seems we are agents. It seems we cause what we do . . . it is sobering and ultimately accurate to call all this an illusion.   (Wegner, 2002, 342)

Wegner's skepticism was premised not only on Jeannerod's experiments, but on his own related work with "illusions of control" and the seminal investigations of physiologist B. Libet (1916–2007), who famously discovered a lag in time—of about 400 milliseconds—between the neural origins of a movement and the kind of self-awareness a person would need to report that she'd initiated the act.

The brain 'decides' to initiate, or at least prepare to initiate the act before there is any reportable subjective awareness that such a decision has taken place.
(Libet, 1985, 36)[4]

Libet was not himself as a "will skeptic," but Wegner is not the only neuroscientist to embrace this label. Indeed, while Jeanerrod's analysis of the relevant body of research is somewhat more cautious that Wegner's, he too concludes that consciousness "reads behavior rather than starting it; consciousness represents a background mechanism for the cognitive rearrangement after the action is completed, e.g. for justifying its results" (2006, 65). Has cognitive neuroscience refuted the will, and with it Bain's attempt to define belief as a volitional state?

Now as a matter of definition, a skeptic rejects a commonly held belief or concept. So if we're going to assess whether skepticism is the just response to the precedence of movement to awareness made salient by

attention, and belief see Gale (March 1999). For intriguing contemporary accounts of the representations operative when we coordinate perception and movement see Campbell (2002), Engel et al. (2013), and Nanay (2013).

[4] H. Lau (2009) traces Libet's findings to results reported by H. Kornhuber and L. Deecke in the 1960s. For a more extensive evaluation of neuroscience-based skepticism with regard to autonomy see Mele (2009).

contemporary neuroscience, we need to know precisely which beliefs and concepts the phenomenon is supposed to overturn. As E. Pacherie puts it, "Will-skepticism may rest in part on too simplistic a view of the phenomenology of agency" (2008, 180; cf. Bayne and Levy, 2006). In fact, I think this is more than just a possibility. For Bain and James also highlighted the relatively unconscious nature of many of our purposive behaviors; they just didn't view this family of phenomena as cause for skepticism. Witness Bain's discussion of walking, turning a wheel, and stitching a garment:

The Habitual, or routine actions, which make up the acquired ability and skill of men and animals . . . are performed almost unconsciously; that is to say, the more thoroughly they attain the character of routine, or habit, the less is the feeling that attends their exercise. Such actions as walking, turning a wheel, stitching, may be sustained without giving rise to any but a feeble conscious impression, so as to leave the mind free for other exercises or emotions.   (Bain, 1859/1865)

James goes on in a similar vein, quoting G.H. Schneider with approval,

Knitting appears altogether mechanical, and the knitter keeps up her knitting even while she reads or is engaged in lively talk. But if we ask her how this be possible, she will hardly reply that the knitting goes on of itself. She will rather say that she has a feeling of it, that she feels in her hands that she knits and how she must knit, and that therefore the movements of knitting are called forth and regulated by the sensations associated therewithal, even when the attention is called away.   (James, 1890/1950, 119)

He then goes on to embrace the infamous Dr. H. Maudsley's more general claim,

If the careful direction of consciousness were necessary to its accomplishment on each occasion, it is evident that the whole activity of a lifetime might be confined to one or two deeds.   (James, 1890/1950, 114)

So let's return to Jeannerod and his stylus. To be sure, you had to apply yourself to learn to write. You had to focus your attention on your dominant hand to better control your grip, your pressure on the pencil, and its lateral movements as you traced the forms you were instructed to reproduce. But this is now all "wrote." You can now take notes while maintaining eye contact with your professor, or sign a check for services while discussing the terms of a contract. Perhaps you must still pay some small level of attention to your writing hand on such occasions, and this gives rise to that "feeble conscious impression" of its progress that Bain references above. But is it surprising that you are not sufficiently "keyed in" to notice the relatively small adjustments you've been making to surmount minor topological irregularities?

In our first attempts to write, to cipher, to play on an instrument, to speak, or in any other work of mechanical skill,—the inward sense of labor and difficulty is corresponded to by the number of awkward and irrelevant gesticulations. On the other hand, in the last stage of consummated facility and routine, the consciousness is almost nothing; and the general quietude of the body demonstrates that the course of power has now become narrowed to the one channel necessary for the exact movements required.   (Bain, 1873, 56)

If you're writing an argumentative essay, and you're thinking hard about the best way to make your point, you might "find yourself" rising from your desk to pace around the room (Searle, 1983). Is it surprising that you might return to write before training your attention on the mechanics of your standing up and then sitting down? And if your attention is occupied by the argument, do you have the information you need to accurately describe your bodily mechanics?

And it's not just your movements through space that often pass without your notice. As Bain recognized, common experience provides ample evidence of similar dissociations between the focus of attention and the execution of distinctively mental actions.

The routine operations sustained by mere contiguity evolve no feeling; the more perfect the intellectual habits, the less consciousness is associated with them. A practiced accountant approaches to a calculating machine.   (Bain, 1859/1865, 38)

You can control your body without consciousness of doing so, and if you "think on your feet" you can execute a similar number of inferences or calculations without reflecting on these movements in thought. But if you're going to answer questions about what you've been thinking or doing, you're going to have to turn your attention to these processes and do your best to describe what then becomes salient (Nielsen, 1963, Nielsen et al., 1965, Nielsen, 1978, Berry and Broadbent, 1984). As Pacherie concludes, "Some but not all of the processes of action production and control depend on conscious experiences" (2007, 214). Is this a shocking conclusion? Is it cause for "will-skepticism"?

As we'll see in what follows, Bain's account of belief anticipates contemporary cognitive neuroscience in emphasizing the priority of movement to both self-awareness and self-control. But Bain defends his assertion of this priority thesis with common observations of human infants and other animals (1888, 321–30). Our children are born sucking and swallowing. But it takes time for them to focus their attention on nursing so as to exercise greater control over the process. Is it surprising that infants move their lips, tongues, and jaws before they are aware of doing so? Is it surprising that their movements prefigure the kind of self-awareness they utilize to develop more sophisticated forms of consumption? Observant parents began to report on this developmental trajectory long before the advent of cognitive neuroscience. Cognitive neuroscience hasn't overturned our common understanding of the relationship between self-awareness and self-control; it has deepened it.[5]

Admittedly, most of us "folk" think that we are at least frequently conscious of our more deliberate thoughts and behaviors; and we think that turning attention to our actions allows us to control them in ways we otherwise could not. As we've noted, we typically need to focus our attention on what we're doing if we're to describe our behavior in any detail. And the heightened self-awareness that results doesn't seem to be "merely" observational. Instead, reflecting on our own actions seems to affect them, for better or for worse. Does contemporary science impugn these assumptions and those concepts of agency we premise upon them?

Notice, first, that we often exercise self-control by dividing our attention between our bodies and various objects of interest we encounter on our travels. (As stated above, action is typically the coordination of perception with responsive movement: "sensorimotor coupling" in its varying manifestations.) And it would seem that as long as our attention is not divided any further than this, the more articulate among us often can say what we are doing with a relatively high degree of accuracy. For instance, in Jeannerod's experiments described above, significant biases of the cursor's movement on the screen ($x>14°$) required similarly dramatic corrections of the stylus: corrections which were invariably salient to the subjects making them (Slachewsky et al., 2001).[6] So while these

[5] According to J. Bruer, "Michael Gazzaniga and George A. Miller coined the name cognitive neuroscience in 1976, over martinis at the Rockefeller University Faculty Club" (Bruer, 2009, 1221). Our observation holds whether we use this event to date "contemporary cognitive neuroscience," or instead use the publication of James's *Principles of Psychology* in 1890 or even something much earlier.

[6] Cf. Knoblich and Kircher (2004). Note, though, that neurotypical subjects underestimate the degree to which they are compensating for the bias, and a deafferented subject G.L.

experiments provide evidence of minimal self-control without self-awareness, they also provide ample evidence of the importance of self-awareness to more significant levels of self-control. A pronounced response to stimuli captures your attention so you can better direct that response. You can correct for a little bias while your mind is elsewhere, but you're not going to deliver a serviceable sketch of your dream home without looking at your drawing. You might even erase and redraw a line or two. This is indeed common sense.[7]

Now it may turn out that we folk regularly overestimate the degree to which we are aware of what we are doing. Cognitive scientists may reach consensus that awareness of self-control—or at least articulate awareness of self-control—is over reported. But even if this understanding continues to gain steam, we will still have no difficulty identifying the various components of agency in terms of which the pragmatists define "belief." For these are the very components of our "wills" that the neuroscientists are disentangling with their clever experimental designs. We will always distinguish the graceful gestures of a ballerina from the uncontrolled spasms that bedevil those suffering from epilepsy. We will never have a problem differentiating an absent-minded interlocutor who has "tuned us out" from someone who is hanging on our every word. And we are not about to stop criticizing the unrepentant agent of destruction who confabulates self-serving accounts of the damage she has have wrought on friends and family. Attention, control, and self-awareness are all the materials we need to construct a coherent conception of the evolution and operation of even the most sophisticated forms of autonomy. And it is precisely these forms of autonomy we assume when holding each other responsible for our actions. When you tell me that I shouldn't be doing what I am doing—or you insist that what I am doing is immoral or wrong—you assume that I can attend to my actions and alter their course from my appreciation of their more destructive features and consequences. Need you assume the "unity of my will" in any further sense than this?

(who suffers a pathological loss of haptic information) did not become aware (nor verbally report) her compensation for the bias. See Fourneret et al. (2002).

[7] It is compatible with this that self-consciousness can often impair performance. Sexual intercourse is the example most frequently cited by neurotics in the 1960s when complaining about their "hang ups," but athletic prowess is also vulnerable when undue attention is paid to an otherwise habituated mechanics. See Beilock (2010) and Papineau (2015).

Bain's traditional taxonomy divides the mind's functions into three: feeling, will, and intellect (Bain, 1859/1865). And though Bain classified belief under the category of will rather than intellect or feeling, and therein inaugurated a pragmatic revolution in the philosophy of mind, he did not conceive of the will as a "simple" faculty or phenomenon. Instead, Bain devoted thirteen chapters to the will's components and operations—thirteen chapters on the science of his day that he interpreted with the aid of common sense and careful reflection. Our more succinct treatment of belief follows Bain in this. If you naively think of the will as simple or unanalyzable in a Platonic sense, you should be worried about the science that informs the pragmatic treatment that follows. But science has yet to provide reason for rejecting the more sophisticated conception of agency it assumes.[8]

Importantly, for those who would join the pragmatist in defining belief in terms of relatively autonomous thought and action, attention and control are not best conceptualized as elements of your cognitive "scaffolding": capacities you must use to learn a skill, which can then be thrown away once mastery is achieved (Stanley, 2011). Since you can walk without paying attention to your legs, you can see what's happening in front of you and pay attention to it (James, 1890/1950, 114). And if you ever get your footwork down, and hone your responsiveness to pass rushers, you'll be able to focus your attention on the receivers down field and find the seam through which to deliver one a tight spiral. Similarly, if you didn't have to focus on your bowing and fingering, you would be able to pay more attention to the conductor and your collaborators on stage. There can be no serious suggestion that execution of these skilled activities might unfold just as successfully while attention was diverted from the task altogether, as it would were our quarterback or violinist calculating the decimal expansion of pi in her head in the midst of her performance.

---

[8] Though Bain offers a volitional theory of belief, he assigns conception to intellect and grants it an essential role. "The state of mind called Belief, Expectation, Confidence, Trust, Assurance, Conviction, involves obviously our intellect or ideas: we must know or conceive the fact that we believe in" (1888, 505). "I have here regarded belief as a primitive disposition to follow out any sequence that has once been experienced, and to expect the result. It is thus an incident of our intellectual constitution; for it shapes and forecasts the order of the world; and then proceeds upon that, till a check occurs" (1888, 536). Cf. Bain (1859/1865, 524).

Thus, while she defines "belief" in terms of attention and control, the pragmatist doesn't restrict belief to the frame of mind you're in when carefully choosing your words for an apology or gingerly navigating a more literal minefield. Communication and locomotion are never the discrete effects of thought; they are its concomitant. Indeed, according to the pragmatists, thought is itself a form of action: mental (and so neural) action of a certain kind.[9] And a healthy animal normally performs a host of these mental actions whenever she speaks or moves her body through space. The pragmatists claim that your beliefs are "brought to bear" on both your more controlled, attentive transitions in thought and your more controlled, attentive movements through space, even as your transitions in thought respond to your movements through space, and your movements through space respond to your transitions in thought. So it is at best misleading to speak of a person's beliefs and desires "causing" her decisions, which are then supposed to generate those intentions that sculpt her movements. You don't experience physical paralysis when deliberating, and then unconsciousness when moving, and then physical paralysis when evaluating how your movements are progressing, and then unconsciousness when adapting your trajectory to this self-critique. Instead, action is typically an amalgam of movement, perception of self and environment, ingrained response to these stimuli, calculation of means and ends, varied concentration on both process and interim result, somatic feelings, mood, background concern, a desire for something better, satisfaction with what is, or some unstable vacillation between the two. Everything happens at the same time. And belief is intertwined with it all.

Consider, for instance, your most basic mode of transport. Instinct led you to move your limbs in your mother's womb and to squirm soon after delivery. She could feel your legs kick and your arms swing as you practiced your motor routines. According to Bain, there was no belief in this. He reiterates, "In the primitive aspect of volition . . . there is no place for belief" (Bain, 1859/1865, 524–5). But soon after birth you had to learn to turn yourself over, to crawl, and to walk. And to learn how to do these things, you had to acquire beliefs about how they are done. You had

---

[9] "Thought is not preparatory to action but a function within action which seeks out an intelligent response to a difficulty encountered or anticipated" (Lawson and Koch, 2004). "Cognition is action" (Engel et al. 2013, 203).

to record your successes, to remember your errors, and draw the requisite lessons from the two. This was a conscious, all-consuming effort to acquire the crucial knowledge.

Although most people would assume that infants walk and fall a lot, few would guess that the average toddler takes 2368 steps, travels 701 meters—the length of 7.7 American football fields—and falls 17 times per hour. Hourly rates provide only a tantalizing window into the amounts of practice that likely accumulate over a day. For example, a multiplier of 6 hours (approximately half of infants' waking day) would indicate a daily rate of about 14,000 steps, 46 football fields, and 100 falls.   (Adolph et al., 2012, 1392–3)

It took some doing, but if you now know how to walk, you can probably do it without really trying or concentrating on the matter. If so, you don't need to bring your beliefs to bear on this activity. But you would need to focus attention and act from your hard-won knowledge of bipedal locomotion were you recovering from an injury. And even if your legs are fairly functional right now, if you want to move as best you can, you must quit your reveries and focus attention to consciously regulate your gait, an activity that requires the acquisition and deployment of a host of beliefs about yourself and the terrain over which you traverse. Someone coaching your efforts to sprint 200 meters orders you to "dig, dig, dig" out of the blocks, to "chop, chop, chop" into the turn and then "open up" your stride. When you hear "Open it up!" as you exit the turn, you form beliefs about how your coach wants you to move, and you utilize your awareness of your own stride to bring these directions to bear. If you hear a competitor approach from behind and adjust your stride to keep pace, your beliefs and knowledge seem equally in evidence. You might tell yourself "she's coming" and urge yourself to "pick it up." But you needn't. As will become clear in what follows, your beliefs can guide your movements in the absence of any propositional frame. You can draw directly on perception in the service of motion (cf. Millikan, 1995; Chemero, 2009).

Thus, while the pragmatist defines belief in terms of attention and control, she finds these phenomena intertwined with automatic, relatively uncontrolled processes in the performance of most of those actions that make up our daily lives. Belief is ubiquitous. It plays a number of different roles in the rapid verbal repartee of political pundits, the improvisational rhymes of freestyle rappers, and the fast-speak of auctioneers. It is manifested in the highly polished dexterity of artisans, surgeons, athletes, and musicians. It's not that the pragmatists are Platonists. We do not claim that virtue and social skill are themselves forms of knowledge, or that belief is sufficient for the comparably complex motor abilities of those who work with their hands for a living. Far from it. As Dr. Maudsely says above, if we had to think it all through, we'd get very little done. But belief in its various forms and modalities remains an essential *component* of almost all that we do.

True, when one component of a skill is routinized, we no longer need to employ our beliefs to guide that component (Dickinson 1985, 1989). (When an agent has fully assimilated a body of information, it will directly shape her reactive thinking and movement without the need for the attentive, controlled application of information to action that we pragmatists equate with guidance by belief.) But an agent's beliefs are not, then, irrelevant to an explanation of her actions. Instead, if her behavior has any complexity to it, she will bring her beliefs to bear on distinct, non-routinized components of the activity in which she is engaged and her efforts to coordinate these components with various "subroutines" guided by bodies of information she has more fully assimilated. Because of this, "Automaticity is a concept best applied to components of complex behaviors rather than to behaviors as a whole" (Jonides et al., 1985).[10] The actions of the quarterback and violinist described above bear this out. These actions are complex. Some of the components involved are automatic and others not. According to the pragmatists, the less automatic a component, the greater the role of belief in its execution, though, again, an agent's ingrained behavior may still accord with her beliefs when it unfolds precisely as it would were she bringing her full cognitive resources to bear on that aspect of her performance.[11]

In sum, our pragmatic definition acknowledges the distinct contributions of attention and control to the kind of action and thought that flow from a person's beliefs, and it acknowledges that these capacities are intertwined in ways that need to be elaborated, even if it fails to advance a

---

[10] "Habit diminishes the conscious attention with which our acts are performed" (James, 1890/1950, 114). Cf. Wu (2015).

[11] Of course, skillful performance requires rhythm, which mitigates effort while enhancing regularity in movement. And distraction is itself a component of certain skills. If a triathlete can better run through her pain by letting her mind wander, her coach might advise that she "zone out to zone in." This may be a case in which "the less belief the better," until adaptation to an obstacle proves necessary.

fully general proposal on how to classify cases in which they are exercised at cross-purposes with respect to the actions they shape.

Still, some dissociations are easy to adjudicate. In *The Diving Bell and the Butterfly*, journalist Jean-Dominique Bauby (1997) describes his experience with "locked-in syndrome" (LIS). The book was communicated by Bauby with the use of his left eyelid: the only body part he was able to control after suffering a massive stroke. Patients with "total" locked-in syndrome cannot even blink, though their mental lives continue unabated (Bauer, Gerstenbrand, and Rumpl, 1979). To describe and measure the beliefs of a patient with total LIS, we must consult her thought and reasoning. Intuitively, her inability to act and communicate does not imply that she lacks beliefs, nor even that she believes "less" than those capable of movement through space. Of course, our patient isn't moving. So she isn't gaining the beliefs we do when we explore. But as she lays immobile in bed, thinking, fantasizing, lamenting her fate and praying for a recovery, she will figure some new things out. She may even gain novel imaginative and cognitive skills. She may begin to fantasize in more detail or develop the ability to imagine a wider range of objects and events. Will the new beliefs she then brings to bear in thought compensate for the beliefs she has lost? Insofar as beliefs can be counted and compared, her disability will likely induce a net reduction in information. But this result is uncertain because of the "offsets" we've identified. Much will depend on the development of the patient's imagination and intellect prior to paralysis.

As the converse of this, we might imagine someone with fully "locked-out" syndrome who is entirely incapable of the kind of mental action that can be executed without bodily movement. The patient never engages in detached reasoning or planning; she doesn't hold forth with silent soliloquies or imagined conversations; she neither dreams about the future nor computes figures in her head; she spends no time reminiscing or interpreting the words and deeds of those she knows. But she does retain her external or physical agency: a suite of abilities, encoded in her nervous system, that she engages by moving elegantly through space in response to threats and opportunities, obstacles, and affordances. Though this hypothetical "locked-out" patient's actions are neither preceded nor accompanied by deliberation, we can suppose that they would not be what they are were she not controlling her body and paying attention to various macro-level features of the somewhat unpredictable environment through which she navigates (Ouellette and Wood, 1998). By hypothesis, the contemplative and communicative life of a fully locked-out agent is irrelevant to an assessment of her beliefs, which can be entirely determined by the information that guides her relatively non-instinctual, non-habitual, non-reactive behavior.

But mightn't the two distinct spheres in which we exercise attention and control—and the correlative elements of our definition of "belief"—come apart from one another? What if a person regularly uses a piece of information to guide her thinking, but never brings it to bear in bodily action: Does she believe it? And what should we say about those pieces of information that do guide her physical movements, if they never feature as premises or assumptions in her reasoning: Does she believe them? Clearly, these cases are difficult to conceptualize until they are specified in more detail. If we knew the agent's thoughts as well as her actions, it would seem to us as though she had fallen prey to an extreme dissociation of inner and outer: a full-blown epiphenomenalism that would leave us wondering whether there was a single mind there to assess. Mightn't we have imagined a person with two minds: one "intellectual," the other "animal"?[12]

Again, the pragmatist definition of "belief" articulated above provides no resolution to these speculations. When controlled, attentive thought and behavior belie an agent's instincts, habits, associations, and relatively automatic reactions to stimuli, the pragmatist definition councils us to limit our focus to the former when assessing the agent's beliefs. But were an agent's more directed thinking to become radically dissociated from her similarly controlled or deliberate actions, all bets would be off.[13]

---

[12] This sort of diagnosis is taken seriously when used to explain the behavior of some of those patients who have received brain bisection surgery: the severing of the corpus callosum and with it many of the connections between the right and left hemispheres of the patient's brain. See Gazzaniga (1995) and for an insightful philosophical analysis Nagel (1979). Anarchic hand syndrome—in which a patient disavows the seemingly intentional movements of one of her own hands—may result from a less thoroughgoing dissociation. See Della Sala et al. (1991), Riddoch et al. (1998), and Riddoch et al. (2001).

[13] Cf. Bain, who cites Sterne, Byron, and Wordsworth as poets who were "tender" in writing and imagination but "hard-hearted toward real persons," and contrasts them with Southey whose, "indignation was wholly imaginative; the man being singularly free from bitterness or antipathy, even such as his opinions made him think were right and becoming. Such men live in two distinct worlds, their behavior in one being no clue to their behavior in the other. In meditation, and in composition, they enter their ideal sphere, and converse with imagined beings; in real life, they encounter totally different elements, and are affected accordingly" (1859/1865, 208–9).

Some readers will object to my use of "self-control" to describe the actions of a "locked out" agent.[14] To see why, consider a person with advanced Parkinson's disease who has lost a great deal of control over the movement of her body through space. Suppose that these impairments don't compromise her command over her thoughts. After all, Parkinson's disease needn't engender thought insertion, obsession, or any of those symptoms associated with diagnoses of paranoid schizophrenia. We can suppose, too, that our patient's mastery over her feelings, drives, and appetites remains typical. After all, Parkinson's needn't make one overly prone to rage, or pathological gambling, or compulsive consumption of food and drugs. Though the patient we have described has lost control over her body, her mastery over her own mind remains intact. And some would say, because of this, that her self-control is in no way diminished. On this way of thinking, the body lies outside the self; motor control is not a form of self-control, but something wholly other.

And yet, while it is not uncommon to identify the mind and self, this way of thinking is ultimately problematic, as it lies in tension with the Aristotelian realization that people are animals of a complicated sort. Since you are the animal that you see in the mirror each morning, its visible parts—the arms and legs you see, the hands and feet, head and toes, eyes and nose—are all parts of you. When you flex and relax the muscular components of your body—when you reach and grab, turn and glare, stride and twirl, crouch and leap—you are controlling yourself. Might you control *yourself* without controlling your *self*? Might you control *yourself* without deploying your capacity for *self*-control? No, come on, that makes no sense.

The proper meaning of self can be nothing more than my corporeal existence, coupled with my sensations, thoughts, emotions, and volitions, supposing the classification exhaustive, and the sum of these in the past, present and future. Everything of the nature of a moving power belonging to this totality is a part of self. The action of the lungs, the movement of the heart, are self-determined; and when I go to the fire to get warm, lie down under fatigue, ascend a height for the sake of a prospect, the actions are as much self-determined as it is possible for actions to be. (Bain, 1859/1865, 509)

---

[14] I thank Joshua May and Neil Levy for raising this concern.

You are an animal, not an animal part.[15] You are a human being, not a human's brain, mind, or personality. When you direct the movement of your body, you are manifesting one component of your more general capacity for self-control. Importantly, motor control is a form of self-control that many non-human animals possess, even those who cannot suspend judgment on an issue, or ignore temptation to make good on a promise, or adopt a "persona" in order to be seen by others as they want to be seen.

> The control of feelings generally is among the hardest of our voluntary acquisitions; and although in education it ought to be commenced as soon as at all practicable, we must not reckon it among the first or most elementary.
>
> (Bain, 1859/1865, 330)

It would be wrong to say that young children—and those animals who cannot delay gratification of their appetites—are entirely incapable of controlling themselves, and it would be similarly wrong to say they lack all capacity for self-control, for this would mark a pernicious tightening of the expression's usage: pernicious in its encouraging the efforts of those who seek to distance adult humans from children and other animals.[16] The desire to discourage this tendency seems to me a good one. At any rate, it was mirrored by the pragmatists' acceptance of Darwin's account of the evolution of human psychology from that of other primate species. And it justifies the bloody-minded, literal uses of "self" and "self-determination" articulated by Bain above. Any being animated by something beyond instinct and habit—any animal who deploys her capacities for thought or movement in service of her goals—therein controls herself.

---

[15] I should say that you are a whole animal unless you are a conjoined twin or a cognitively distinct part of a brain bisection patient. If you could survive being conjoined to another person (and sharing most of a single body with her) or you could survive as one of two minds inhabiting a brain bisection patient, then you are currently a whole animal that could survive as a more or less integrated part of one. I take no stand in what follows on the metaphysical question of whether you are "essentially" a whole animal, but (for what it's worth) I favor meta-level pragmatism and object-level mentalism on the issue: the metaphysical question of what you are "essentially" transcends all possible evidence, but we are best served by thinking of ourselves as animals whose only essential parts are our minds or nervous systems. For recent discussion see George and Lee (2008).

[16] This isn't to claim that willpower is unique to humans. F. De Waal takes philosophers to task for this claim, citing and explicating Beran (2002), Evans and Beran (2007), Hillemann et al. (2014), and other studies. For de Waal's criticism of P. Kitcher and H. Frankfurt on this score see De Waal (2016, 221–9). Cf. Peirce (1931–5, 5.533–4, 371–2).

According to the pragmatists, these beings are all guided by their beliefs in the execution of their actions.[17]

* * *

Despite its attractions, the pragmatic picture of belief I have begun to paint has largely slipped from academic debate.[18] So I begin the following brief on its behalf by contrasting pragmatism with more popular conceptions of the mind. Those advancing formal models of rational choice, action, and judgment tend to follow F. Ramsey (1931) in defining degrees of belief in terms of a person's willingness to risk money, happiness, and other "good stuff" on the truth of a sentence or proposition. The dominant paradigm in cognitive psychology—introduced by D. Kahneman (2011) and colleagues—distinguishes "two systems" of cognition, and some theorists—e.g. K. Frankish (2004)—have tried to define "belief" in terms of these two systems. L.J. Cohen (1992) defines "belief" phenomenologically, in terms of feelings of conviction. The pragmatic conception of belief differs from all of these approaches. My aim in chapter 2 is to demonstrate this divergence and begin taking a new look at the old story.

Chapter 3 turns to the evolution of belief. According to Bain—and the pragmatist philosophers who found common ground in his theories—belief co-evolved with various capacities for self-control. Field ethologists report wolves, dolphins, and scrub jays acting in many of the ways we do when we are more than willing to describe each other as acting on our beliefs. Non-human animals are capable of reflection and planning, teaching and learning, loving and forgiving. It is a mark in favor of pragmatism that it allows us to understand these behaviors as manifestations of complex bodies of animal belief. My stalking horse throughout this discussion is the "intellectualist" whose theory of belief emphasizes uniquely human psychological traits. Descartes was a "über intellectualist" in this sense. The other animals fail to construct sentences, and

---

[17] This is a thoroughly contemporary perspective on the matter. "Self-agency is part of every action that an animal—any animal—undertakes" (de Waal, 2016, 241). Cf. Bekoff and Sherman (2003), Keijzer, van Duijn and Lyon (2013), and Fridland (2014). Note that there is also some evidence of neurological unity in the anatomical substrates of self-control and self-awareness in its various forms. On the unity of self-control see Cohen and Lieberman (2010); on the unity of self-awareness see Chua and Bliss-Moreau (2016).

[18] See, however, the pragmatic approach to cognition identified and defended by Engel et al. (2013).

Descartes inferred from this that they entirely lack beliefs. In partial contrast, contemporary intellectualists—e.g. B. Williams (1973) and D. Velleman (2000)—allow non-human animals beliefs in an "impoverished" sense of the term, while advancing accounts of belief that emphasize the importance of an animal's "possessing concepts" in one sense or another, or her "aiming at the truth" when constructing representations of her environment. The pragmatists reject these criteria as undermotivated. Of course, humans use sentences to attribute beliefs to themselves and other animals. But there is no further sense in which belief is itself a "propositional attitude." In advancing this thesis, the pragmatist account breaks with current orthodoxy among analytic philosophers. The pragmatist also rejects the philosophical status quo in another way, by analyzing desire as a complex class consisting of both evaluative beliefs and non-doxastic "construals."

Some intellectualists argue that concern for the truth must be essential to belief. "If we don't say that a desire for accuracy is necessary for belief," they worry, "we won't be able to distinguish belief from pretense. And if we could believe without regard to the truth," they continue, "we'd be capable of believing at will, which is something we manifestly cannot do." In response to these objections, I turn to the Aristotelian idea of potentiality that Bain deployed when framing his account of belief. Beliefs are "poised" to inform a wider range of behaviors than states of pretense.

The same difference allows pragmatists to distinguish belief from acceptance for the sake of argument or inquiry. When acceptance falls short of belief, a limit has intentionally been placed on the influence of some information. But these are differences in degree, not kind. As Hume pointed out, when a provisional assumption or state of imagination comes to inform an uncommonly wide range of behaviors, it can transform itself into a state of belief. Delusions provide an interesting instance of this phenomenon: the typical Capgras patient believes that one of her family members has been replaced with an impostor. But if she fails to act or reason on that information in all of the contexts in which she acknowledges its relevance, the pragmatist definition classifies her belief as incomplete.

These first four chapters paint a pragmatist picture of belief. Chapter 5 features my main argument for preferring this conceptualization to the other ones in play. And it is here that I introduce a second thesis about the question to which this book is addressed. The nature of belief cannot be determined by scientific theorizing alone, but must be relativized to a set of theoretically underdetermined taxonomic choices. Though we must consult the results of various sciences to arrive at a satisfactory theory, our questions about the nature of belief are not wholly scientific. In support of this claim, I focus on racial cognition and the various ways in which "belief" might be integrated into our understanding of racism. My aim here is to highlight the enormous social consequences that attend the adoption of a given conception of belief. I conclude that the stakes are sufficiently high to render blind deference to the stipulations of scientists unwise. Acceptance of the pragmatist definition of "belief" is best seen as a philosophical choice among empirically equivalent but socially divergent alternatives. This is the sense in which pragmatism is not itself an article of science. If we adopt Bain's definition, we are choosing a picture to live by. The pragmatist confesses to this without embarrassment. She simply insists on a similar admission from those advancing various forms of behaviorism, intellectualism, machine functionalism, and the like.

To conclude the discussion, I turn to James's defense of the will to believe. Philosophers have tended to focus on the normative question of whether it is ever OK to adopt beliefs for pragmatic reasons. The "evidentialists" are prepared to criticize those who would resort to this sort of thing, and the intellectualists go further to argue that we pragmatists are all self-deceived. I argue against these epistemic scolds. The social science of "positive illusions" confirms the coherence of James's doctrine and provides an evidential basis for Bain's theory of belief. Sometimes, we can ignore the evidence and believe what we want to believe knowing full well that this is what we are doing. The will to believe is real. Within limits, it can even be a good thing.

2

Alternative Measures and Taxonomies

> We generally know when we wish to ask a question and when we wish to pronounce a judgment, for there is a dissimilarity between the sensation of doubting and that of believing. But this is not all which distinguishes doubt from belief. There is a practical difference. Our beliefs guide our desires and shape our actions. The Assassins, or followers of the Old Man of the Mountain, used to rush into death at his least command, because they believed that obedience to him would insure everlasting felicity. Had they doubted this, they would not have acted as they did. So it is with every belief, according to its degree. The feeling of believing is a more or less sure indication of there being established in our nature some habit which will determine our actions. Doubt never has such an effect.
>
> (Peirce, 1877, 4)

Recall the more central components of our pragmatic definition of belief: (1) You believe the information poised to guide your controlled and attentive actions. (2) "Assimilating" information allows you to act on that information without bringing your beliefs to bear. (3) The operation of highly assimilated information is in evidence when your attention and capacities for self-control are largely diverted away from a given action to other components of your overall activity.

When it is understood in this way, degree of assimilation is not well correlated with "degree of belief" or "degree of credence" in the ordinary sense of these familiar expressions. Indeed, in cases of absent-mindedness, maximal assimilation can exist alongside minimal conviction. For example, in the case described above, you are not at all convinced that you still live on Holly Drive, even if you assert or act on this information when distracted. But maximal conviction in the truth of a proposition is not invariably correlated with minimal assimilation either. In the states of "happy concord" that we've discussed, an agent is fully convinced of a body of information that she doesn't have to consider precisely because it has been "offloaded" to habits and other relatively automatic dispositions of response. To indulge in a hackneyed example, you are fully convinced that a turn of the wheel will yield a corresponding alteration of your car's trajectory, though you haven't had to focus on these correlations since you first learned to drive.

So how does the pragmatist definition relate to more traditional measures theorists have employed to quantify our beliefs? The most common approach has been to measure degree of belief in terms of risk.[1] Consider the assassins Peirce discusses above, who willingly risk their lives for the Old Man on the Mountain because they believe the prospect is "win-win." Honor greets them if they succeed, but paradise awaits death on the Old Man's order. The assassins so described bet their lives on the claims made by the Old Man of the Mountain. If the bet in question were monetary, and if we could assume each assassin a "miser" whose hopes and dreams are entirely trained upon the accumulation of cash, and we could ignore the diminishing "marginal utility" of money to them—and so on and so forth—we could equate the degree to which each assassin believes what the Old Man tells him with the amount of money said assassin would bet on the truth of the Old Man's claims.[2] As with degree of assimilation, willingness to bet is a descriptive, non-normative, or "causal" measure of belief. Both measures answer Frank Ramsey's famous characterization of the class. "The degree of a belief" Ramsey said, "is a causal property of it, which we can express vaguely as the extent to which we are prepared to act on it" (1931, 169).[3]

----

[1] More precisely, classical decision-theoretic accounts measure degree of belief in terms of some "operationalization" of risk: e.g. a subject's dispositions to gamble money, time, or some other quantifiable resource on the truth of a claim. Without an operationalization of this sort, circularity is a real worry. Mightn't "risk" itself require definition in terms of belief? See, e.g., "Risk... is exposure to a proposition of which one is uncertain" (Holton, 2004, 22). You can call it "holism" instead of circularity, but when the circle is that tight it fails to provide much insight.

[2] For this use of "miser" see Joyce (Dec 1998).

[3] See too, Ramsey's claim, "Some beliefs can be measured more accurately than others; and, secondly, the measurement of beliefs is almost certainly an ambiguous process leading to a variable answer depending on how exactly the measurement is conducted. The degree of a belief is in this respect like the time interval between two events; before Einstein it was supposed that all the ordinary ways of measuring a time interval would lead to the same

That degree of assimilation differs from willingness to bet seems fairly clear on reflection.[4] Consider two assassins: A and B. Both are ready to gamble everything they have on whichever horse the Old Man picks. But A has been picking horses since childhood and B is new to the task. Assassin A easily remembers the Old Man's pick—Scarlet Sunshine— and places her wager on the mare while playing Minecraft on her cell phone throughout the transaction. But when B tries to follow suit, she winds up betting on the wrong steed: Crimson Rain. Each assassin is just as confident as the other in the truth of what the Old Man has said. Indeed, we can stipulate that if B hadn't been playing Minecraft, she would have successfully bet all she had on Scarlet Sunshine. It's just that A has more fully assimilated the relevant degree of credence in the target proposition than has B. Degree of belief—as classically measured in terms of risk—does not determine degree of assimilation.

We can decouple degree of assimilation from degree of risk in the other direction too. A given piece of information can be assimilated to a high degree without this entailing a similarly elevated willingness to risk money or happiness or wellbeing on its truth. For example, your typical American consumer of Chinese food may assume, without doubt, that Chinese immigrants introduced fortune cookies into American cuisine. She may reason on this premise and assert it without hesitation. And yet, if asked to bet a measly $1 on the proposition, she might balk and reconsider her conviction. Might this clever dessert have an entirely domestic origin? Mightn't Japanese immigrants deserve the credit? (Mikkleson, 2016) Though Ramsey liked the metaphor, we are *not* constantly betting on the truth of the assumptions on which we act. Some of our most well-integrated beliefs concern matters of little consequence. We act on them without risk.

Nor can we equate degree of assimilation with phenomenological measures that are equally important to acknowledge. Recall Peirce's

---

result if properly performed. Einstein showed that this was not the case; and time interval can no longer be regarded as an exact notion...the degree of a belief is just like a time interval; it has no precise meaning unless we specify more exactly how it is to be measured" (1931, 168). Ramsey's numerically precise approach to measuring belief in terms of behavior is nicely developed and situated among the alternatives by Halpern (2000); see especially pp. 20–4.

[4] For a contrary opinion see Rowbottom (2007). Cf. Mellor (1977–78) and Mellor (1991).

claim above that "there is a dissimilarity between the sensation of doubting and that of believing."[5] Surely, there is something right about this, though we'd go too far were we to conceive of degrees of belief in the way we do degrees of pain. As W. Kneale quips, "When we realize that $2 + 2 = 4$, we do not sweat with any feeling of supreme intensity" (Kneale 1949, 15). Instead, the relevant question asks, "What was it like for A and B when they first came to believe in the Old Man's infallibility?" Did the realization slowly dawn on them, or did it come in a flash? And how did they feel when the Old Man told them to pick Scarlet Sunshine?

Without getting into the details, let us imagine that their experiences were the same in relevant respects. A and B felt equally convinced of the Old Man's pick when he shared it with them. And let us also suppose that when Crimson Rain actually nosed out Scarlet Sunshine at the wire—as you, dear reader, suspected would happen—A and B felt equally surprised at this event, even while A cursed her gullibility in trusting the Old Man and B thanked the universe for her good luck. If we make these assumptions, haven't we therein described a case in which A and B have the same phenomenal degrees of belief, the same cognitive "sensations" with respect to the Old Man's prediction, while differing in the degree to which they have assimilated it? If so, the degree to which one feels convinced of the truth of a proposition does not determine the degree to which it has "sunk in."

---

[5] For a more recent and better developed analysis of belief's characteristic phenomenology see Cohen (1992). According to Cohen, to believe that p is to be disposed to "feel" that p when the question of whether p arises. Cohen distinguishes a number of experiences into which such "creedal" feelings enter: despair, incredulity, disbelief, doubt, uncertainty, suspicion, faith, confidence, and conviction (1992, 11). And people can vary a great deal in the degree to which their creedal feelings are reflected in their actions, which, on Cohen's account, are more directly influenced by "states of acceptance" than beliefs (1992, 8–11). Belief, as the pragmatist thinks of it, is similar in some ways to what Cohen calls "acceptance," but in others ways not. (E.g., in contrast with what Cohen insists is true of acceptance, belief needn't involve sentential language or contents judged true.) Ramsey's account of the limits to phenomenological analyses remains trenchant. "We can, in the first place, suppose that the degree of a belief is something perceptible by its owner; for instance that beliefs differ in the intensity of a feeling by which they are accompanied, which might be called a belief-feeling or feeling of conviction, and that by the degree of belief we mean the intensity of this feeling... This view seems to me observably false, for the beliefs which we hold most strongly are often accompanied by practically no feeling at all; no one feels strongly about things he takes for granted" (1931, 169). For an alternative (non-propositional) analysis see Proust (2015a).

And there is yet another notion of degree of belief worth mentioning here: the degree to which a given body of information is *entrenched* within the mind/brain of a given person or animal, where degree of entrenchment might be equated with the amount of evidence, argument or "doxastic force" necessary to dislodge the relevant representation. To verify that degree of entrenchment (so understood) is indeed a distinct measure of belief, we might imagine a superstitious gambler who approaches a race between horse X and horse Y willing to bet everything on X if the wind is blowing east and everything on Y if the wind is blowing west. If the wind is blowing east, the gambler will be rightly said to have a "high degree of belief" in X's winning, so long as degree of belief is measured by risk, but the mental state in question will only be weakly entrenched—and so believed to a "low degree" in this distinct sense—insofar as it would be immediately abandoned were the wind to change direction. Similar stories might be told to distinguish degree of entrenchment from the intensity of the gambler's feelings of conviction, and the "depth" to which her representation of the putative winner of the race between X and Y has been assimilated within her mind/brain.

I invoke these varying classical conceptions of "degree of belief" only to put them aside. My primary aim in what follows is to fill in the conception of belief I have defined in terms of degree of assimilation; to describe its relation to work in academic philosophy and psychology; and to assess the relevance of academic theories of belief so defined to our "folk" psychology: the body of information we bring to bear when explaining ourselves to one another in the course of our social inter-actions. I only mention these more traditional concepts here to distin-guish them from the topic at hand.

If, as I have suggested, "belief" is best analyzed in terms of information and its role in shaping the attentive, controlled thoughts and behaviors of humans and other animals, articulating a full understanding of belief would require the statement and defense of definitions, theories, or accounts of "information," "guidance by information," "attention," and "self-control." But each of these concepts applies to an enormously complex phenomenon about which many thousands of journal articles and books have been written.[6] Since I cannot pretend to have read and

---

[6] For instance, readers might be familiar with accounts of information transfer and recovery in physics; debates about the nature of computation that lie at the foundations of

digested most of this material, the analysis I am presenting is both parochial and partial in its reliance on the reader's more or less intuitive grasp of the concepts I use to define "belief." To be sure, I will continue to discuss various forms of attention and self-control in what follows, and further clarify what it means for someone to be "guided" by information when acting. And I will commit myself to a view of "information" on which it can be carried by a wide variety of neurological structures, many of which have little to do with communication or the use of sentential language. But there is no distinctively pragmatic theory of neurological representation. Bain's conception of belief implies nothing about the means by which our nervous systems encode the kind of information we utilize when thinking and acting. Similarly, we pragmatists assume that there is some neurological reality to those phenomena colloquially described as "focusing attention," "dividing attention," and the like; and a similar neurological reality to polished mechanics, self-restraint, and other forms of self-control. If we didn't think of these as real phenomena, we wouldn't define belief in their terms. But our definition is silent on the nature of the neurological correlates or essences to which we are committed. It has nothing to say on how and where attention and control are realized in our brains. The reader must turn to contemporary neuroscience for proposals on these matters. I'm only making one real stab at a definition in this book, and the above definition of "belief" is it. As Peirce observed, it is pragmatism's axiom. What remains are its corollaries.

computer science; the extensive semantics literature advancing different models of sentence meaning and the extraction of "semantic content" from standing meaning and an appreciation of context; debates within the philosophy of language and logic over the nature of propositions understood as objects of assertion, affirmation, inference, or debate; literature that lies at the intersection of philosophy of mind and biology defending or attacking various biological, computational, or otherwise reductive theories of reference and representation; the cognitive science literature on different modes and processes of mental representation and computation (sensory vs. non-sensory, discursive v. non-discursive, sentential v. connectionist); the sophisticated literature in aesthetics on the distinction between belief and pretense; the enormous and endlessly expanding literature on consciousness (which is conceptually connected to both attention and control); and the historically important literature in ethics, political philosophy, and moral psychology on freedom of action, will power, prudence, the assumption of moral responsibility, and other forms of self-regulation. The relevance of all of these incredibly rich discussions to the nature of belief is one of the reasons the question, "What is belief?" remains so intractable. Though this book contains a limited number of references to work on these subjects, I direct the unsatiated reader to the Stanford Encyclopedia of Philosophy, which is a free, online resource with entries on all of these topics.

I've been asserting that our minds are more or less our nervous systems.[7] And those who study our nervous systems—e.g. the growing population of cognitive neuroscientists—invariably employ "attention," "self-control," or variations on these folk psychological concepts when framing and evaluating their hypotheses about the sources, effects, and contours of what they observe happening within our skulls. The most common such variations are "central executive," which purports to name the computational and/or neural correlate of attention and self-control, and "executive function," which denotes the phenomena themselves.[8] As a result, there are a number of neurocognitive theories of attention and self-control that have been published, reviewed, and critiqued. And yet, these key psychological concepts still lack widely accepted neurological analyses or definitions.[9]

Doesn't this present an insurmountable obstacle for those of us bent on conducting an investigation into the nature of belief? Doesn't it imply that our definition of belief is vulnerable to those gross forms of misunderstanding that result when we use "information," "attention," and "self-control" to explain ourselves to one another without first fixing definitions of these terms? Perhaps it does. But despite this failing, the definition is still useful. For one thing, the difficulties that arise when scientists try to successfully define "attention" and "self-control" differ from those that attend our attempts to define "belief." Attempts to identify neurological systems and processes of attention and self-regulation do not generate the political, social, and ethical controversies that come to the fore when we consider the ramifications of adopting

---

[7] I say "more or less" to avoid confronting philosophically popular forms of "externalism" that view beliefs as psychosocial relations, and to steer clear of debates about the correct specification of the relation between mind and body. Is it identity? Constitution? Supervenience of causal powers? I suspect that more than one such conceptualization can be reconciled with both science and social interaction. In any event, the mind is nothing "over and above" the nervous system. For further discussion see Bernstein and Wilson (May 2016).

[8] These are the terms used by those writing about "working memory." See, e.g., Baddeley and Hitch (1974) and Baddeley (1996). Norman and Shallice (1986) introduced the concept of a "supervisory attentional system" (or SAS) to much the same effect.

[9] On attention see Peterson and Posner (2012), Mole (2013), Wu (2014), and the nine essays on attention that together constitute section III of Gazzaniga (2009). Mole's definition of attention as cognitive unison meshes well with the pragmatic conception of belief, but is clearly independent of it. On self-control see Kellet, Wagner, and Heatherton (2015). On the "exogenous" nature of a great deal of attention see Ransom et al. (2016).

various conceptions of belief. And this lends philosophical substance to the pragmatic definition: it analyzes the more controversial in terms of the less.

Now, as we've just admitted, those of us who endorse the pragmatic conception of belief are committed to the neurological realty of attention and self-control. And this means we are betting that neuroscientists won't wind up rejecting these concepts altogether. Instead, though cognitive science isn't there yet, we (pragmatists) are betting that best practices will eventually generate consensus around an "explanatory theory" of how attention and control are realized in our nervous systems, rather than an "error theory" of how we came to falsely represent their manifestations to ourselves. And this bet is based on little beyond optimistic introspection. We did our best to answer some of the existing arguments for "will skepticism" in chapter 1, but we can't rule out the emergence of novel grounds for doubt. That's the price we pay for the substance of our claims.

Not that this book has all that much substance. If it's successful, it shows how a pragmatic theory of belief might be integrated with whatever (non-skeptical) theories of information, attention, and self-control come to attract the support of cognitive neuroscientists. The resulting theory would provide those who grasp it with a relatively deep understanding of the evolution and operation of their own minds. In contrast, the present work is comparatively shallow in its reach. As usual, the philosophers leave the hard work for the scientists.

Still, while it has fallen out of fashion, the pragmatist's definition of "belief" is not entirely unrepresented in today's academy. Indeed, it bears some resemblance to the dominant paradigm: a "two systems" model of judgment that currently enjoys fairly widespread support among cognitive scientists. The pragmatists define belief in terms of attention and control. And those theorists who distinguish two systems of cognition typically use associated concepts when explicating their hypotheses.[10]

---

[10] For accounts of the emergence and development of these models see Smith and DeCoster (2000), Osman (2004), Evans and Frankish (2009), Kruglansk and Orehek (2007), and Gawronski and Creighton (2013). Evans and Frankish trace the modern history of dual process theories to three independent developments: (i) Arthur Reber's experimental studies of implicit learning in the 1960s as summarized in Reber (1993), (ii) publication of Schneider and Shiffrin (1977a) and (1977b), and (iii) collaborative studies of reasoning conducted in the 1970s by Peter Wason and Jonathan Evans, who introduced the terms

Perhaps the most common choice is to divide the mind into "automatic" processes executed by system 1 and "effortful" processes executed by system 2. But some theorists go on to describe system 1 as "experiential" and system 2 as "rational"; some claim system 1 is "associationist" in its operations whereas system 2 is "rule-governed"; some posit an "affective" or emotionally "hot" system 1 which is distinct from a "deliberative" or relatively "cool" system 2; some argue that system 1 operates in an "unconscious" manner whereas the operations of system 2 are introspectively accessible to those in whom they unfold, and so on. After cataloging this diversity in defining characteristics, G. Keren and Y. Schul (2009) argue that almost all self-described two systems theories identify system 1 by the *automaticity* of the processes it executes, the *inaccessibility* to introspection of these processes, their *associationist* character, and the *emotional salience* of their products. In contrast, almost all such theories identify system 2's characteristic processes with their *effortfulness*, their conscious *accessibility*, their *rationality* or rule-governed nature, and the *emotional quietude* of their products. On this basis, Keren and Schul propose to use "system 1" to refer to a hypothesized cognitive system that is "intuitive, associative, experiential, and affectively hot," while reserving "system 2" for a purportedly distinct cognitive module that is "rational, rule-based, reflective, and cold."[11]

If we adopt this understanding we can ask a more well-defined question about the connection between philosophical pragmatism and the relevant research program in contemporary cognitive science: What is the relationship between positing two systems of cognition distinguished, at least in part, by the attention and control necessary to

---

"type 1" and "type 2" processing. Introduction of the terms "system 1" and "system 2" is attributed to Stanovich (1999). We might add the distinction between "automatic" and "attentional" mental processes as drawn by Posner and Snyder (1975). As Evans and Frankish note (2009, 2), a more expansive conception of dual or multi-systems theories would trace their (Western) origins at least as far back as Plato's doctrine of the "division of the soul," as the failures of self-control Plato crafted his theory to explain remain among the data motivating multi-systems approaches. See, e.g., Metcalfe and Mischel (1999) and more recently Levy (2011).

[11] See too Newstead (2000). T. Gendler's bifurcation of the mind into beliefs and aliefs posits similar correlations. See her claim, "Alief is associative, automatic, and arational. As a class, aliefs are states that we share with nonhuman animals; they are developmentally and conceptually antecedent to other cognitive attitudes that the creature may go on to develop. And they are typically also affect-laden and action generating" (2008a, 641).

execute their characteristic processes, and defining "belief" in terms of
the information we utilize when thinking or acting in an attentive and
self-controlled manner? Can we adopt the pragmatist definition of
"belief" articulated above without taking a stand on the utility, fecundity,
or tenability of distinguishing our minds into these two distinct systems?
And which taxonomy provides a better means for integrating our common-
sense understanding of belief with substantive (neurological) explanations
of attention and control: pragmatism or the dual systems view?

It should be relatively clear that dual systems theories—as defined by
Keren and Schul—are committed to psychological clusters that are not
implicated by our pragmatic conception of belief. Are automaticity,
inaccessibility, and emotional salience more highly correlated with each
other than they are with effortfulness, accessibility, and quietude? Are
effortfulness, accessibility, and quietude more highly correlated with one
another than they are with automaticity, inaccessibility, and emotional
salience? Keren and Schul argue that we lack the evidence we would need
to make this determination.[12] No two systems theorist has yet to present
evidence against the existence, regularity, or normalcy of automatic
judgments unaccompanied by high emotion (i.e. bare intuitions),[13] or
states of high emotion that result from bouts of fantasy or imagination
that are directly accessible to those who experience them (e.g. mastur-
batory fantasies), or the unconscious and affectively barren knowledge
we seemingly employ when interpreting the syntax and meaning of
sentences spoken to us in our native languages (e.g. my knowledge that

---

[12] See Keren and Schul (2009, 538). Cf. Newstead (2000, 691) and Gigerenzer and Reiger
(1996).

[13] Of course, intuitions are often affective. The most famous demonstration of this is the
Iowa Gambling Task, where neuro-typical subjects have "feelings" as to which of the four
decks from which they are selecting cards are better than the others without an articulate
knowledge of the relative frequencies with which they have pulled good and bad cards from
the decks in question. But these results don't imply that intuitions are invariably affect-
laden, nor that they are more robustly felt in general than judgments gleaned from
inference. Intuitively, the content of a judgment and the importance of its truth or falsity
to the subject have a greater impact on its emotional salience than does its relation to
inference. For a more detailed account of the Iowa Gambling Task and the "somatic marker
hypothesis" the experiment has been used to support, see Bechara et al. (1994), A. Bechara
et al. (1996), and Bechara et al. (1997). For criticism see Maia and McClelland (2004) and
(2005) and Dunn et al. (2006). Some defenders of the somatic marker hypothesis have
responded to criticism by dropping the claim that learning on the Iowa Gambling Task is
genuinely "unconscious" or implicit. See Bechara et al. (2005).

you are using "I" to refer to you). Are these examples best conceptualized as exceptions to the general rule posited by the two systems theorist? Or have cognitive scientists posited a fissure in our "mental architecture" where none exists? The pragmatist would do well to remain agnostic on these issues.

But some theorists are not so reticent. In contrast with the pragmatist's studied ambivalence, a number of philosophers of mind have embraced two systems hypotheses that posit correlations among seemingly diverse sets of cognitive characteristics. And some have tried to integrate debates over the nature of belief within this conceptual space. K. Frankish's (2004) distinction between our "minds" and our "superminds" is perhaps the best developed of these proposals.

Frankish begins his account by joining R. de Sousa (1971) in embracing an ambiguity thesis: there are two different kinds of mental state we denote when using "belief" outside the laboratory. One of these states is what de Sousa calls "belief in the proper sense."[14] Belief in this sense is *acceptance* of some information or, as Frankish puts it, "highly confident reliance [on it] in deliberations which are truth-critical with respect to their premises" (2004, 38). To link this ambiguity thesis to the two systems framework, Frankish supposes that the state of mind in question is "conscious, subject to occurrent activation, flat-out, capable of being actively formed, often language involving, and consequently, unique to humans and other language users" (2004, 4–5). According to Frankish (again following de Sousa) the other kind of mental state we commonly denote with "belief" is *subjective probability* or credence as depicted by formal epistemologists.[15] Belief in this sense is supposed to

---

[14]   As Frankish notes when describing the evolution of his view, D. Dennett (1978/1981) calls the state, or a similar state, "opinion." (Dennett's (1978/1981) essay is a reply to Baier (1979).) Frankish joins L.J. Cohen (1992) in using "acceptance" to define uniquely human belief or what de Sousa calls belief in the "proper" sense.

[15]   De Sousa cites R. Jeffrey (1970). In that essay, Jeffrey accepts the conception of credence as defined in terms of risk by Ramsey and his heirs, citing Savage (1954) and Raiffa (1968). But the explicit analysis Jeffrey then offers exhibits a worrisome circularity insofar as it defines "degree of belief" in terms of one's *judgments* about the fairness of various gambles. "'Belief' here is understood as an attribute toward various risks. In particular, in terms of your attitudes toward various gambles in which only small gains and losses are possible (so that your utility curve is fairly linear) your degree of belief in a proposition A is p if and only if you *think it fair* to bet on A at odds of 1-p: p (e.g. to pay $p to get $1 if A is true and lose your $p if A is false)" (emphasis added, 1970, 161). Jeffrey is also unduly dismissive of the philosophical questions that arise when we compare

be, "non-conscious, possibly not subject to occurrent activation, partial, passively formed, probably non-verbal, and common to both humans and animals" (2004, 23–4). Frankish then further integrates this view of belief with the two systems framework by equating the two different referents of "belief" with the states of two different cognitive systems. According to Frankish, non-conscious, passively formed, (probably) non-verbal degrees of belief constitute an animal's (or person's) "mind." In contrast, each person's "supermind" is constituted by her conscious, actively formed, (often) linguistically articulated, flat-out doxastic commitments.

Note that Frankish's "supermind" lumps together the sources of spontaneous assertion, conscious, effortful reasoning, introspection, and self-characterization. The "mind" also joins together several seem-ingly distinct phenomena: degrees of confidence as measured in terms of willingness to risk, inarticulate opinions, sensory expectations, memories of distal features of one's environment to which one plans to return, instinctive responses to perceived threats and affordances, and various dispositions to affective response. And Frankish's attempt to read unity into this diversity raises questions comparable to those articulated above. For example, should language be associated with conscious states that are actively formed? Widespread evidence of verbal priming with stimuli that are presented too rapidly to be consciously processed tells against such a move.[16] Consider, too, verbal slips (Freudian and otherwise), sleep talking, and the linguistic manifestations of Tourette's syndrome. Because of these phenomena, common sense countenances linguistic habits, associations, and mechanisms that do not constitute beliefs, alongside articulable beliefs that are acquired, stored, and expressed without conscious effort (cf. Proust, 2015, 722). And are conscious,

Ramsey-style risk-based analyses of degree of belief with other measures of the same phenomenon and compare these academic efforts to measure our minds with the ways in which we use "belief" to explain ourselves to one another in the course of social interactions. "This notion of degree of belief accords well enough with one strand in our talk about belief, but it is not intended as a bit of ordinary language analysis or a bit of phenomenology. This notion is the theorist's and need not be the agent's" (1970, 161–2). "Nor am I disturbed by the fact that our ordinary notion of *belief* is only vestigially present in the notion of degree of belief. I am inclined to think Ramsey sucked the marrow out of the ordinary notion, and used it nourish a more adequate view. But maybe there is more there of value. I hope so. Show me. I have not seen it at all clearly, but it may be there for all that" (1970, 171–2).

[16] See, e.g. Hutchison (2003) and Pickering and Ferreira (2008).

effortful beliefs typically flat-out or all-or-nothing as Frankish suggests? Consider, as a counterexample, a jurist who thinks long and hard about the purported guilt of the party on trial and finds herself, at the end of this process, leaning more toward guilt than innocence, but not by much. Isn't the jurist's frame of mind here best characterized as an effortful credence? Or should we say, with de Sousa, Dennett, and Frankish, that she has tried and failed to accept a verdict or tried and failed to commit herself to the truth or falsity of the allegations on hand, and that her minimally-greater-than-0.5 credence in guilt is the result of passive, non-conscious processes distinct from her more articulate deliberations? Again, no evidence of any kind has been presented to buttress so radical a reinterpretation of our self-conceptions.

In more recent work, Frankish identifies system 2 with processes that *people* (or animals) undergo when taken as unified, whole organisms and the states that enter into such processes. Correlatively, Frankish now identifies system 1 with various sub-personal processes and the states of such. Beliefs are consequently divided into the "personal" and "sub-personal."[17] But this taxonomy has challenges of its own. It is the subject herself who discovers, to her embarrassment, that she has been absent-mindedly picking her nose in public. She is embarrassed because *she* has been picking her nose; this is not a vicarious form of shame that she feels on behalf of her disgusting sub-personal grooming mechanisms. But this kind of activity is automatic, habitual, and unconscious in the relevant sense. It is the white subject herself who struggles with the Implicit Association Test, taking longer to pair good words with black faces and bad words with white than good words with white faces and bad words with black. She is ashamed of herself—of *her* vulnerability to stereotypes—and yet, the performance of a self-described racial egalitarian is inhibited on this task by precisely the kind of introspectively inaccessible affective association still thought to characterize

---

[17] See Frankish (2009, 89–107). Frankish is aware of some of the problems with this taxonomy as he warns that what he calls "sub-personal beliefs" are still attributable to the person as a whole. "There is a sense in which all beliefs are personal; it is people who believe things, not their brains. The proposed terminology is designed to underscore the claim that there are two very different ways in which a person can believe something, defined by the relative roles of subpersonal and personal factors in the processing of the belief in question" (2009, 103). But this is hard to parse. Automatic processes are often attributable to people (rather than their parts). There is, it would seem, no natural mapping of the personal–subpersonal distinction onto the system 1–system 2 distinction.

system 1.[18] Moreover, Frankish continues to distinguish personal from sub-personal beliefs in much the way he distinguished states of mind from states of super-mind in his previous work: personal beliefs are supposed to be flat-out, effortful, and "entertained as premises in episodes of conscious reasoning" whereas sub-personal beliefs are supposed to be unconscious, automatic, and admit of degree (2009, 103–4). Frankish's new conceptual scheme therefore inherits the controversial commitments of its predecessor.[19]

Of course, a two systems theorist can eschew commitment to the posited correlations and focus on just one or two of the dichotomies that have been proposed. Since D. Kahneman's (2011) recent work adopts this approach—and it is perhaps the most influential two systems account elaborated to date—it is worth considering whether it is subject to a similar critique.[20] As is typical among such theorists, system 2 processes are supposed by Kahneman to be effortful and require greater attention than system 1 processes, which are in turn supposed to be more automatic and require less focus and exertion. And yet, in contrast to what is typically maintained by psychologists working within this framework, Kahneman now asserts that his talk of two systems is supposed to be entirely *metaphorical* (2011, 28–30).[21] So understood, Kahneman

---

[18] I will have more to say about implicit associations below. See Greenwald, McGhee, and Schwartz (1998), and for overviews Wittenbrink and Schwarz (2007), Petty et al. (2009) and Bodenhausen and Richeson (2010).

[19] Frankish (2009, 104, fn. 7) allows that personal beliefs can be "ungraded" and "all-or-nothing" even if they are not "certainties" and subjects are not fully "attached" to them. But he does not say anything positive about what would make a state of uncertainty to which one is only weakly attached "ungraded" or "all-or-nothing."

[20] Evans and Stanovich (2013) have also hedged their commitment to the clusters they posited. Accessible overviews of this body of work include Kahneman (2003) and (2011). See too H. Kornblith (2012), who misleadingly equates system 1 with processing that does not utilize consciousness and system 2 with processing that does require consciousness.

[21] " 'System 2 calculates products' . . . is intended as a description, not an explanation . . . It is shorthand for the following: 'Mental arithmetic is a voluntary activity that requires effort, should not be performed while making a left turn, and is associated with dilated pupils and an accelerated heart rate' " (2011, 30; cf. 77–8). "The two systems do not really exist in the brain or anywhere else. 'System 1 does X' is a shortcut for 'X occurs automatically.' And 'System 2 is mobilized to do Y' is a shortcut for 'arousal increases, pupils dilate, attention is focused, and activity Y is performed' " (2011, 415). Cf. "These terms ['system 1' and 'system 2'] may suggest the image of autonomous homunculi, but such a meaning is not intended. We use the term 'systems' as a label for collections of processes that are distinguished by their speed, their controllability, and the contents on which they operate" (Kahneman and Frederick, 2002, 51). In this, Kahneman appears to have abandoned a more realistic

claims no more than that we can usefully distinguish those mental processes that require more attention and effort from those that require less, as dividing large numbers with other large numbers is more effortful than dividing small even numbers in half. According to his avowed interpretation of his two systems theory, then, Kahneman is not committed to the surgical dissociability of effortful from effortless processes, nor to the evolutionary or developmental priority of effortless processes, nor to the relative ease with which effortful processes can be introspectively accessed in comparison to relatively effortless processes, nor to correlations between effort, conscious accessibility, and emotional salience. Indeed, if we restrict the literal content of Kahneman's account to the postulation of degrees of attentiveness and self-control, its truth *is* entailed by the pragmatist's definition of belief.

Nevertheless, even if we follow Kahneman's instruction to interpret his talk of "two systems" in an entirely metaphorical way, his project cannot be fully reconciled with various *meta-level* aspects of the pragmatic picture of belief I will sketch in what follows. That different cognitive processes evolved at different times, emerge at different stages in an animal's development, and yield states of mind that are differently related to introspection or language or affect are all substantive, relatively "extra-conceptual" theses. But the claim that belief, habit, instinct, emotion, effort, language, introspection, and attention are related to these dissociable processes in the manner envisaged by such theories is as much a claim about the concepts we associate with "belief," "habit," "instinct," "effort," "language," "introspection," and "attention," as it is about the reality we use these concepts to describe, categorize, predict, and explain. What should we say about Kahneman's metaphor? Is it offered as a "true claim," or a recommended reform to our ordinary ways of describing one another? And how should we interpret the pragmatic

interpretation of "two systems" language. See Kahneman and Fredrick (2007), which concludes, "Behavioral and brain imaging data are required to understand how best to conceptualize the susceptibility to framing effects and the ability to resist them...serious theorizing in the domains of judgment and decision making can be informed by imaging results and the integration of concepts from both lines of research is necessary and feasible." According to J. Evans, "Dual-process accounts...cannot be architectural, if they posit a continuum between one form of thinking and another." Thus, according to Evans' taxonomy, Kahneman's latest iteration of his theory is not an "architectural" form of the view. See Evans (2009, 35). For an alternative taxonomy that would include Kahneman's theory within the intended class see Fiske, Lin, and Neuberg (1999).

definition of "belief" we advanced above? What is its purpose? From what does it derive its authority?

Since Kahneman is a Nobel Prize–winning scientist, it is surprising to read that his avowed goals when presenting his view are more normative than descriptive. He is less interested in integrating our folk psychological concepts with the relevant science than he is with "introduc[ing] a language for thinking and talking about the mind" (2011, 13). Indeed, each chapter of Kahneman's popular presentation of his view in *Thinking, Fast and Slow* ends with sentences intended to instruct the reader as to how she can incorporate the "system 1"-"system 2" vocabulary into her lexicon. E.g., "He didn't bother to check whether what he said made sense. Does he usually have a lazy system 2 or was he unusually tired?" (Kahneman, 2011, 49).

In contrast, the pragmatist picture I develop in what follows would reject Kahneman's use of his epistemic authority to advance this frankly normative project as presumptuous if not anti-democratic. Normative proposals to reform our speech should be advanced without the imprimatur of science. We should not pretend that they "fall out" of experimental work or academic reflection upon it. For this reason, the pragmatist must offer her definition of "belief" as a piece of philosophy, not science.

I think this is an important point. We, philosophers, should follow Hume's advice to articulate transitions from "is" to "ought," to evaluate them in clear prose, and to limit deference to the premises of these transitions when they are propounded by experts. But let me dull the argument's critical edge: Kahneman is a great scientist and a good philosopher. My request is just that he clarify for his audience where his science ends and his philosophy begins. I will argue in what follows that acceptance of a pragmatic definition of "belief" is in some ways incompatible with deference to the authority of academic psychologists to adopt and enforce definitions. But deference to pragmatist philosophers would be almost as bad.

Admittedly, there are passages in which Kahneman does try to integrate his proposal with our more "folkish" conception of our own minds. These are passages in which Kahneman suggests that our *beliefs* are typically system 2 products. System 1 is thought to produce sub-doxastic or pre-doxastic states—impressions or intuitions—which can only be converted into belief through a system 2 process that Kahneman labels "endorsement."

System 1 continuously generates suggestions for system 2: impressions, intuitions, intentions and feelings. If endorsed by system 2, impressions and intuitions turn into beliefs, and impulses turn into voluntary actions.   (2011, 24)[22]

And this claim, couched as it is, in folk psychological terms including "belief," would allow us to directly compare Kahneman's two systems approach to the pragmatist account of "belief" articulated above.

But the resulting interpretation jars so radically with folk psychology it cannot be taken to seriously represent Kahneman's considered view.[23] First, unless a person is plagued by radical skeptical doubt, her acceptance of the products of system 1 processes of perception and intuition is more often than not a passive or effortless affair. (E.g., in most cases we just believe what we see.)

We are all faith at the outset; we become sceptics by experience, that is, by encountering checks and exceptions. We begin with unbounded credulity, and are gradually educated into a more limited reliance.   (Bain, 1868/1884, 382)

Often we suppose and then believe... But these cases are none of them primitive cases. They only occur in minds long schooled to doubt by the contradictions of experience.   (James, 1890/1950, 946)

Thus, given Kahneman's considered taxonomy, acceptance is itself a system 1 process. But then those mental states that arise through passive acceptance of the contents of perception and intuition must either be described as system 1 states of belief—contrary to the passage excerpted above—or we must instead say that they are not beliefs at all.

How might Kahneman best clear things up? Other features of his two systems approach are instructive. For instance, because ordinary conversation or "small talk" is effortless—and so doesn't dilate a speaker's pupils—Kahneman attributes the phenomenon to system 1 processes

---

[22] I'm not being uncharitable here: Kahneman often repeats this characterization (see, e.g., 2011, 105). We might compare Kahneman's talk of "system 2 endorsement" with C. Peacocke's (1999) idea of a person taking the content of one of her perceptual experiences "at face value." For a more in-depth discussion see Lyons (2009).

[23] It also lies in tension with Kahneman's (2011, 80–1) endorsement of D. Gilbert's (1991) "anti-Cartesian" and "pro-Spinozan" theory, according to which all representations constitute beliefs unless they are prevented from this by self-conscious monitoring, or what Kahneman would call "system 2 processes" of critical appraisal and consequent doubt. On Spinoza's view see Della Rocca (2003). The pragmatists also endorsed this theory of "primitive credulity." See Bain (1888, 526–7), Fisch (1951) and Kauber (Jan 1974). For a more recent attack on accounts of belief that require substantive epistemic agency see Kornblith (2012, 73–107).

(2011, 34).[24] But, if folk psychology is to be trusted at all, small talk regularly involves the expression and relatively passive acquisition of beliefs.

Q: "How's your day going?"
A: "Fine, I just got back from the park."
Q: "Lovely, I had a great time there yesterday."

Here Q comes to believe that A just went to the park, and expresses her belief—either "based in" or "constituted by" memory—that she (i.e. Q) went to the park the previous day. But it is consistent with this that Q and A are not expending much effort in speaking to one another and that their attention is almost entirely occupied by their children, or their dogs, or their knitting, or whatever else they are doing while chatting away. Communicative processes needn't be any more system 2-ish than other psychosocial processes.

It seems, then, that the best interpretation of Kahneman's theory would countenance both system 1 and system 2 beliefs.[25] Indeed, though instincts are perhaps invariably automatic and so always attributable to Kahneman's system 1, those habits that partially constitute hard-won skills are invariably the result of Kahneman's system 2. After all, it's hard to figure out how to do most of the things worth doing, and this knowledge can be difficult to sustain. Effortful, attention-consuming, belief-guided movement and thought continues to play an important role in the maintenance and greater perfection of almost all our mechanical skills.[26]

---

[24] See too, "System 1 understands language, of course, and understanding depends on the basic assessments that are routinely carried out as part of the perception of events and the comprehension of messages" (2011, 91). For the distinction between tacit and explicit processes of grammar acquisition see Reber (1993), and for the neurological differences between automatic and effortful uses of language see Jeon and Friederici (2015). On the intermingling of fear and language comprehension see Olsson, Nearing, and Phelps (2007).

[25] Cf. Kornblith (2012) who, because he adopts the same system 1/system 2 taxonomy as Kahneman, concludes that, "Reasoning which is carried out by System 2 is always influenced by System 1 as well. There can be no wholly autonomous System 2 reasoning" (2012, 152).

[26] Kahneman seemingly denies this when he attributes all skill to system 1: "The acquisition of skills requires a regular environment, an adequate opportunity to practice, and rapid and univocal feedback about the correctness of thoughts and actions. When these conditions are fulfilled, skill eventually develops, and the intuitive judgments and choices that quickly come to mind will mostly be accurate. All this is the work of System 1, which means it occurs automatically and fast" (2011, 416). For more nuanced accounts of the interrelation between skill and propositional knowledge see Stanley and Krakauer (2013) and Christensen, Sutton, and McIlwain (Feb 2016).

We have already made the case for this understanding of skill in chapter 1. But it is worth reiterating in this context, as two systems theorists have been particularly prone toward underselling the role of reflection in action. Consider their metaphors, which seem expressly designed to undermine our pretentions to autonomy. We're told that we shouldn't think of system 1 as an elephant and system 2 as its rider. Instead, your system 1 is the big dog in the room and your system 2 its tiny little tail (Haidt, 2001, 2006). Science journalists then magnify these images of subjugation to the cognitive unconscious by reporting on the "flow" that characterizes supposedly "effortless" expertise. We're subjected to a seemingly endless stream of dumb jock quotes from amazing athletes who have little insight into their graceful mechanics. We're told the most successful performers don't really know what they are doing. They don't think; they just do (Dreyfus, 2002). Their mechanics can only be explained from the "outside" by computational models of motor control that few of us can understand, much less formulate (Beilock, 2010; cf. Papineau, 2015).

And yet, while laypeople cannot describe their motor processes in mathematical detail, reflection on the practice of learning, mastering, and teaching a skill lies at variance with the dominant image of reason enslaved to passion. Reflective examination and critical thinking remain important in all domains of activity, even after someone's expertise is widely acknowledged. The star athlete's inarticulate responses to reporters are really beside the point. Our beliefs are often difficult to articulate. So even a relentless regimen of reflective study needn't yield eloquence on the topic at hand.

"My strength" says Albert Pujols, the great MLB slugger, "is that I'm a smart player. If someone tells me to do something, I change it quickly. If there's something wrong with my hitting, tell me what's wrong and I'll pick it up right away. That's the best thing I have—my ability to listen to a coach and fix what I'm doing wrong." (Tejada and Shenolikar, 2012)

Pujols is not a novice. He is one of the most successful hitters in MLB history. And he is telling us that his expertise is in large part constituted by his responsiveness to criticism; the faith he places in his instructors and his efforts to do what he believes he must to incorporate their instructions into his swing. Pujols excels in his ability to weave his "two systems" together as the world watches him adjust his bat to a fast-moving hardball flung along an uncertain trajectory. It's almost as if he has just one system of control: his mind.

And if this is true of hitting, how much more does it apply to carpentry or music or math or dance? We are constantly stopping, looking, criticizing, evaluating, doing, and redoing with the aid and advice that make these practices possible. Effortless expertise? Come on. The development and manifestation of skill invariably intermingles automatic and controlled, attentive processes.

And so does the experience and manifestation of emotion. Though an instinctive fear of snakes or spiders is surely the provenance of system 1, when a person forces herself to feel grudging admiration for the well-deserved victory of an opponent, system 2-ish processes are in play. The polished athlete doesn't vacillate between rage and admiration. A defeat that was once an incitement to crazed jealousy or sour grapes is now processed through an ideological commitment to fair play and sportsmanship. Disappointment is less complete from the get-go. The competitor's cognitive set insures as much.

> The mental tone of the individual is to a certain degree within the limits of voluntary control; by an effort of resolution, we often resist or stave off depression, and keep up a degree of cheerfulness not at all in accordance with surrounding circumstances. Some minds have this power to a surprising degree, and there are few cases where the natural strength of the will is brought to a severer proof.
>
> (Bain, 1859/1865, 201fn)

The stoic and Confucian philosophies of self-command are supposed to yield *mature* passions—positive, useful, and well-regulated feelings—not apathy in the contemporary sense of the term. They wouldn't have proven so popular otherwise.[27]

In sum, while there are interesting conceptual connections between attention, cognitive effort, introspective awareness, and affect, standard ways of delimiting our supposed two systems of cognition cut across the folk psychological categories in terms of which the pragmatist situates our beliefs. It may be time to table the "two systems" talk in favor of a more holistic view.

---

[27] On the Stoics see Sorabji (2000). On Confucius see Reber and Slingerland (2011). For related work in cognitive neuroscience see Barrett, Ochsner, and Gross (2007) and Huijding and de Jong (2006).

3

Against Intellectualism
Animal Belief

"What is it, Polynesia?" asked the Doctor, looking up from his book.

"I was just thinking," said the parrot; and she went on looking at the leaves.

"What were you thinking?"

"I was thinking about people," said Polynesia. "People make me sick. They think they're so wonderful. The world has been going on now for thousands of years, hasn't it? And the only thing in animal-language that PEOPLE have learned to understand is that when a dog wags his tail he means 'I'm glad!'—It's funny, isn't it? You are the very first man to talk like us. Oh, sometimes people annoy me dreadfully—such airs they put on—talking about 'the dumb animals.' DUMB!—Huh! Why I knew a macaw once who could say 'Good morning!' in seven different ways without once opening his mouth. He could talk every language—and Greek. An old professor with a gray beard bought him. But he didn't stay. He said the old man didn't talk Greek right, and he couldn't stand listening to him teach the language wrong. I often wonder what's become of him. That bird knew more geography than people will ever know.— PEOPLE, Golly! I suppose if people ever learn to fly—like any common hedge-sparrow—we shall never hear the end of it!"

"You're a wise old bird," said the Doctor.

(Lofting, 1920/2004, 9)

Even though I won't attempt to define "attention," "self-control," and "information guidance" in biological or computational terms—and the pragmatic definition of "belief" I've proposed is therefore non-reductive— the account has real teeth insofar as it conflicts with other at-least-halfway-plausible accounts that philosophers and cognitive scientists continue to defend. Perhaps the most important such difference derives from the kind of control the pragmatic conception grants us over many of our beliefs. In fact, several of the most widely discussed philosophical accounts of belief distinguish belief from pretense, supposition, and acceptance on the basis of control. The irresistibility or passivity of belief is supposed to provide some basis for defining it in terms of accurate representation. Belief is supposed to be an impression or an image or a depiction generated from without: the effect of "the world" on us, rather than a component of our effect on it.[1]

For example, Bernard Williams (1970/1973), Donald Davidson (1980, 1984), Michael Bratman (1992), and J. David Velleman (2000) all premise their accounts on the intuition that people cannot believe at will, and for this reason—among others—they define belief as something like acceptance for the sake of truth.[2] If your goal or intended aim in premising your actions and deliberations on a piece of information is not accuracy, you do not count as believing it. According to the intellectualists, the best explanation of this purported datum is that "belief" is limited in meaning to information "regarded as true." In Velleman's words,

> The norm of correctness for belief is not open to question because it is internal to the nature of belief itself. The concept of belief just is the concept of an attitude for which there is such a thing as correctness or incorrectness, consisting in truth or falsity... If a cognitive state isn't regulated by mechanisms designed to track the truth, then it isn't belief: it's some other kind of cognition.   (2000, 16–17)

> The aim with which a proposition must be regarded as true in order to be believed is the aim of getting its truth-value right, by regarding it as true only if it really is.   (2000, 246)[3]

---

[1] Of course, one might agree that belief is essentially passive without attempting to support or explain its passivity with a definition centered on its aiming at truth. Indeed, at least one theorist—Owens (2003)—argues that the passivity of belief is incompatible with viewing it as cognition aimed at truth. Cf. Shah (2003) and Reisner (2009).

[2] Williams (1970), Davidson (1980) and (1984), Bratman (1992), and Velleman (2000); see especially Velleman, "On the Aim of Belief" (2000, 244–81). Cf. Evans (1963), Mayo (1963–4), Price (1969), Kelly (2002), Hieronymi (2006), Petersen-Steglich (2006), and Vahid (2006). Vahid (2010) argues that Davidson's intellectualism is incompatible with acknowledging pragmatic grounds for belief.

[3] Note, however, that Velleman equates intentions with self-fulfilling prophesies (e.g. the belief supposedly expressed when someone says, "I'll have the club sandwich"), which he excludes both from the traditional denial of belief at will and from Clifford's normative dictum that we ought to restrict our beliefs to what is adequately supported by the evidence we have at the time of judgment (Velleman, 2000, 52, esp. fn. 17). Williams's rejection of "doxastic voluntarism" is perhaps the best known. "If I could acquire a belief at will, I could

I reject these definitions on several grounds, the most compelling being their overly intellectualist character. Non-human animals have beliefs. This is an obvious truth: a datum on which we can premise our inquiries into the evolution of our own minds. In the famous words of the philosopher, historian and essayist David Hume (1711–76),

Next to the ridicule of denying an evident truth, is that of taking much pains to defend it; and no truth appears to me more evident, than that beasts are endowed with thought and reason as well as men. The arguments are in this case so obvious, that they never escape the most stupid and ignorant.

(1740/2000, 1.3.16.1)[4]

Indeed, it would seem that many so-called "beasts" have "meta-cognitions": beliefs about the beliefs of the other animals with whom they interact (Cheney and Seyfarth, 2007).

But though many animals represent each other's representations, only humans construct sentences and sort them into truths and falsehoods. So an analysis of belief in terms of propositions "regarded" as true or accurate starts off on the entirely wrong foot. Belief is neither essentially nor invariably propositional.

Consider just one representative anecdote from the tenure of "O-six," a matriarch in the population of wolves that scientists have reintroduced into the American West (Smith and Ferguson, 2005; Safina, 2015). A group of coyotes had been accosting wolves returning with food to

---

acquire it whether it was true or not; moreover I would know that I could acquire it whether it was true or not. If in full consciousness I could will to acquire a 'belief' irrespective of its truth, it is unclear that before the event I could seriously think of it as a belief, i.e. as something purporting to represent reality" (1973, 148). Cf. Bennett (1990).

[4] Cf. Malcolm (1973) and Bennett (1976). According to Malcolm, Descartes mistakenly equated cognition with "thinking of propositions" and "when we see the enormity of this exaggeration of the propositional in human life, our unwillingness to ascribe propositional thinking to animals ought no longer to make us refuse to attribute to them a panoply of forms of feeling, of perception, of realization, of recognition, that are, more often than not, nonpropositional in the human case. Their nonpropositional character does not mark them as something less than real forms of consciousness" (1973, 16). But Malcolm hypothesized that the other animals don't engage in the kind of conscious thinking or reasoning we do when solving problems, an admittedly mitigated form of Cartesian skepticism that is nevertheless placed in doubt by the steady stream of YouTube videos showing apes, elephants, crows, and honey badgers solving complex problems without leaning on trial and error. "Chimpanzees, like all apes, think before they act. The most deliberate ape is perhaps the orangutan, but chimps and bonobos, despite their emotional excitability, also judge a situation before tackling it, weighing the effects of their actions. They often find solutions in their heads rather than having to try things out" (de Waal, 2016, 84). For early observations of these phenomena see Yerkes (1925).

the den where O-six was waiting with her pups. The coyotes would surround a solitary wolf and force him or her to regurgitate meat intended for the pups' supper. ("Coyote extortion," as the ecologist Carl Safina calls it.) One day, O-six tired of the missing meals and left her den for the coyote encampment, bringing the rest of her wolf pack in tow. She turned up her nose at the coyotes harassing her, dug into their den, pulled out their pups one by one, and shook them all to death. Then, in front of all the coyotes assembled, she proceeded to eat the pups she had killed. According to Rick McIntyre, a scientist who has been observing these wolves for many years, "O-six turned and trotted back toward her waiting family as if to say, 'And that's how it's done.'"

Note that this was an entirely novel behavior: *an innovation in intimidation.*[5] As McIntryre reports, "That's the only time we've ever seen a wolf eat coyotes." Writing eloquently about this episode, and a wide variety of similarly striking deployments of psychological understanding on the part of non-human animals, Safina concludes, "These creatures—in their ancestral homelands or a reasonable facsimile—know what they are doing." If that's right, to know what one is doing, one needn't be acting under a "description" of one's actions (Anscombe, 1957/2000). One need only be acting under some representation of one's deeds. And the wolf mind/brain appears to contain representations of the relevantly unarticulated variety.[6]

Did O-six *know* and hence *believe* that she was eating the children of the coyotes who had robbed food from the mouths of her own brood? As long as we are willing to allow that this is an overly precise description of her frame of mind, I think we have to answer "yes." But does this mean

---

[5] O-Six's recently published biography (Blakeslee, 2017) provides further evidence of her creative ferocity. For more formal studies of animal innovation informed by databases constructed from similar observations see the various contributions to Reader and Laland (2003).

[6] Cf. Safina (2015, 164). The kind of awareness of what one is doing that sustains one's doing it—the "intention in action" as it is described by Searle (1983, 83–98)—involves a relatively sophisticated form of belief, the causal relevance of which is revealed when an animal's awareness of what she is doing "breaks down," as when, lost in thought, you forget your objective. (For example, my knowledge or belief that I am looking for my phone guides me into the kitchen, but it is often then "lost" or "blocked," leading me to stop and ask myself what I was looking for.) Action grinds to a halt when the intention-in-action is lost to memory. See Radvansky and Copeland (2006) and Radvansky et al. (2011). For reviews of pathologies in action awareness see Blakemore and Frith (2003), Blakemore, Wolpert, and Frith (2002) and Jeannerod (2006). Cf. Levy and Bayne (2004) and Bayne and Levy (2006).

that O-six entertained, endorsed, or believed to be true the proposition we express when describing her frame of mind? The answer is "no." Despite widespread opinion to the contrary, belief is not an exclusively propositional attitude.[7]

What about culture? Safina's reports from the Institute for Marine Mammal Studies in Mississippi capture its culture: the ways in which dolphins not only innovate, but transmit these innovations to kin. The institute's workers had managed to train the dolphins to clean their own pools by trading garbage for food. Afterward,

A dolphin named Kelly realized that she got the same size fish for bringing in a big sheet of paper as for a small piece. So, under a weight at the bottom of the pool she hid any paper that blew in. When a trainer passed, she tore off a piece of paper to trade for a fish. Then she tore off another piece, got another fish. Into the economy of litter, she'd rigged a kind of trash inflation rate that kept the food coming. Similarly, in California, a dolphin named Spock got busted for tearing pieces off a paper bag he'd stuffed behind one of the pool's underwater pipes, using each shred to buy another fish.

One day, a gull flew into Kelly's pool, and she grabbed it and waited for the trainers. The humans seemed to really like birds; they traded her several fish for it. This gave Kelly a new insight, and a plan. During her next meal, she took the fish and hid it. When the humans left, she brought the fish up and baited more

---

[7] I'm unsure of the folk, but the view that belief is a "propositional attitude" is widespread among contemporary analytic philosophers. Some trace it to (founding father) B. Russell's (1921) account. But (i) Russell's analysis countenances non-discursive beliefs whose contents are entirely composed of sensations and images; (ii) Russell follows James in countenancing content-free feelings of belief, and (iii) Russell merely proposes *for the sake of discussion* to use "proposition" in a non-classical sense to encompass images, sentences, and various combinations of them. So Russell (1921) does not advocate what is currently accepted as the propositional attitude analysis of belief. Alternatively, some cite Gottlob Frege as the originator of the propositional attitude analysis, and Frege was indeed a neo-Cartesian of some sort insofar as he thought language necessary for thoughts about the past and future. See, e.g., Frege (1972). But it has been argued that Frege's notion of thought does not conform to standard uses of "proposition" in logic, philosophy of language, and epistemology, and that Frege's construct plays several roles which cannot be satisfied by a unitary phenomenon. See, e.g., Burge (1979) and (2005). Whatever its origins, the impact of "the" propositional attitude analysis on contemporary theorizing about belief cannot be doubted. Velleman is an influential case in point: "From the fact that believing entails believing-true we have now derived two features of belief: Belief always takes a propositional object, and it regards that object as true" (Velleman, 2000, 249). On the contrary, from the "fact" that belief does not always have a propositional object, and from the "fact" that believers needn't regard anything as true in holding their beliefs, we have derived the conclusion that believing does not entail believing-true. As it so often goes in philosophy, one theorist's modus ponens is another's modus tollens.

gulls, to get even more fish. After all, why wait to scrounge an occasional piece of accidental paper when you could become a wealthy commercial bird-fishing dolphin? She taught this to her youngster, and so the dolphins there became professional gull baiters.   (Safina, 2015, 338)

Dolphins figure things out for themselves. They represent their ends— e.g. eating fish—and form conjectures as to how these ends might be more easily met. They improve upon entrained practices, recognize these improvements for what they are, and share their innovations with peers and kin. These are paradigmatic processes of belief formation and transmission, and we're not the only apes to employ them.

It takes years of practice to place one of the hardest nuts in the world on a level surface, find a good-sized hammer stone, and hit the nut with the right speed while keeping one's fingers out of the way. The Japanese primatologist Tetsuro Matsuzawa tracked the development of this skill at the "factory," an open space where apes bring their nuts to anvil stones and fill the jungle with a steady rhythm of banging noise. Youngsters hang around the hardworking adults, occasionally pilfering kernels from their mothers. This way they learn the taste of nuts as well as the connection with stones. They make hundreds of futile attempts, hitting the nuts with their hands and feet, or aimlessly pushing nuts and stones around. That they still learn the skill is a great testament to the irrelevance of reinforcement, because none of these activities is rewarded until, by about three years of age, the juvenile starts to coordinate to the point that a nut is occasionally cracked. It is only by the age of six or seven that their skill reaches adult level.   (de Waal, 2016, 80)[8]

Chimpanzees, wolves, and dolphins are social animals who construct families and live in congresses, packs, or pods. The same might be said of those birds who live in flocks and the primates from whom we've evolved, who clearly understand what others in their troops expect of them.[9] Apes know who can mate with whom without invoking a challenge, and when copulation will provoke punishment. And they achieve

---

[8] See too the spread of sweet potato washing among macaques reported by Imanishi (1952) and Matsuzawa (1994). Further examples include Inoue-Nakamura and Matsuzawa (1997), Noad et al. (2000), Rendell and Whitehead (2001), Whiten et al. (2005), Sapolsky (2006), van de Waal et al. (2013), and van Leeuwen et al. (2014).

[9] On birds see, e.g., Dally (2006), and "Scrub jays with prior experience of stealing another bird's caches subsequently reached food in new sites during recovery trials, but only when they had been observed caching. Naïve birds did not... experienced pilferers had formed a belief that observers will pilfer caches they have seen, and recache food in new sites to fulfill their desire to protect their caches," Clayton, Emery, and Dickinson (2006, 197). Cf. Taylor et al. (2007).

this understanding by reading each other's behavior, comportment, facial expressions, smells, grunts, gestures, and postures. The language they use to these ends is not our own, as scientists are at pains to explain to uninitiated observers.

Ethologists mostly interpret behavior within the wider context of species' habits and natural history. They thus avoid uninformed interpretations, such as that a grinning rhesus monkey must be delighted, or that a chimpanzee running toward another with loud grunts must be in an aggressive mood. Anyone who has watched these animals for the amount of time that primatologists typically devote to their work knows that rhesus monkeys bare their teeth when intimidated, and that chimpanzees often grunt when they meet and embrace. In other words, a grinning rhesus monkey signals submission, and grunting by a chimpanzee usually serves as a greeting. Hence, the careful observer may arrive at insights that are at odds with extrapolations from human behavior.

(de Waal, 1999, 264; cf. de Waal, 2016, 140–9)

Apes don't just express their thoughts and emotions without prior processing. Many display a kind of Machiavellian intelligence in deceiving each other so as to avoid the negative consequences of transgressing the expectations of other apes (Goodall, 1971; Kummer and Goodall, 1985, chapter 10; Byrne and Whiten, 1990, 1992; and Hare et al. 2001). Often enough, two or more individuals join together to defeat a third (Harcourt and de Waal, 1992). Large groups of chimpanzees are known to coordinate a hunt, chasing their monkey prey into the dense jungle where conspiring chimps wait in ambush (Boesch and Boesch-Achermann, 2000). Even in contrived experimental contexts, chimpanzees show a remarkable ability for instrumental and "abductive" reasoning (Camp, 2009). If they know grapes are hidden in one of two covered cups, and the empty cup is shaken, they immediately infer that the grapes are in the other vessel (Call, 2004).[10] Indeed, a recent overview of the evidence by J. Call and M. Tomasello (2009) concludes that chimpanzees have an almost fully human-like understanding of each other's minds, though the jury is still out on whether they attribute false beliefs to one another.

But my money's on the chimps. Consider, as preliminary evidence, an anecdote F.B.M. de Waal relates of his days as a student in Utrecht, when two young chimpanzees escaped during the night to frolic through the

---

[10] For a report of similar inferential abilities in sea lions see Schusterman, Kastak, and Kastak (2003).

building, "only to return to their cage, carefully closing its door behind them before going to sleep" (de Waal, 2016, 33).[11] Weren't these naughty chimps trying to conceal their escapade? Weren't they trying to induce false beliefs in de Waal and his colleagues? Perhaps even more impressive, are the touching gestures of Lolita, the proud mother of a newborn chimpanzee baby who de Waal asked to see.

I called Lolita out of her grooming huddle, high up in the climbing frame, and pointed at her belly as soon as she sat down in front of me. Looking at me, she took the infant's right hand in her right hand and its left hand in her left hand. It sounds simple, but given that the baby was ventrally clinging to her, she had to cross her arms to do so. The movement resembled that of people crossing their arms when grabbing a T-shirt by its hems in order to take it off. She then slowly lifted the baby in the air while turning it around on its axis, unfolding it in front of me. Suspended from its mother's hands, the baby now faced me instead of her. After it made a few grimaces and whimpers—infants hate to lose touch with a warm belly—Lolita quickly tucked it back into her lap.

With this elegant motion, Lolita demonstrated that she realized I would find the front of her newborn more interesting than its back. To take someone else's perspective represents a huge leap in social evolution.   (2016, 148–9)

Note that human children were also thought to lack an understanding of false belief prior to four years of age, but this hypothesis has recently been disconfirmed and the evidence in its favor adequately explained away.[12] (The parents I know have always doubted it. A three-year-old knows when she is lying.) It is reasonable to wonder whether expert opinion on ape cognition will soon follow suit. And yet, though these social animals use systems of communication to express their beliefs to one another, they do not construct sentences, propositions, or other representations that they then evaluate for truth or falsity. So belief is often more basic—in both a phylogenetic and ontogenetic sense—than acceptance for the sake of truth.[13]

---

[11] Professor de Waal also relates the story of Dandy, a lower-ranked ape, who hid grapefruits from higher-ranked males for future consumption (2016, 62). Didn't Dandy try to mislead the other apes into thinking the grapefruits were all gone?

[12] See Baillargeon, Scott, and He (2010), Rubio-Fernández and Geurts (2013), and Helming, Strickland, and Jacob (2014). In response, Apperly and Butterfill (2009) defend a "two systems" theory of belief attribution built on an analogy with our two systems for representing the number of things in a collection.

[13] The only known exceptions to this generalization are those primates who have learned language from humans. For a first-person account of ape language research (APL) coupled with an assessment of its philosophical significance see Savage-Rumbaugh, Shanker, and

The most famous figure in modern biology, Charles Darwin, had no compunction attributing high-level mentality to other social animals. In *The Descent of Man* he argued that all such animals are capable of love, sympathy, reciprocation, and self-command.[14] But if other animals know what they are doing and know what we are doing to them, what distinguishes them from us? What, if anything entitles us to hunt, kill, and eat them when we would be unjustified in treating our fellows in this way? After a century of failed attempts to supply the needed rationale, many philosophers and ecologists would now answer "Nothing" (Cavalieri and Singer, 1993).

Of course, psychologists have long warned against what Ruskin (1856) called the "pathetic fallacy" of projecting one's emotions onto nature. And C. Lloyd Morgan (1894) insisted that no animal behavior should be understood as "the exercise of a higher psychical faculty, if it can be interpreted as the outcome of the exercise of one which stands lower in the psychological scale."[15] But what came to be called "Morgan's canon" employs ill-defined concepts of "higher" and "lower." A more accurate phylogeny—or graphic representation of the descent and differentiation of species—would dispense with talk of a linear scale in favor of a branching

Taylor (1998). Kanzi, the bonobo most extensively trained and studied by Savage-Rumbaugh, developed an ability to understand novel sentences that compared favorably with that of a normal two-and-a-half-year-old human child. Cf. I.M. Pepperberg's experiments with Alex and other African grey parrots: Pepperberg and Gordon (2005), Pepperberg (2006a), Pepperberg (2006b), and Pepperberg et al. (2013). Since researchers are still studying the languages of birds, dolphins, killer whales, and other highly communicative animals, it remains to be seen whether contemporary humans and their ancestors will always have whatever status we choose to award them for constructing, understanding, and evaluating sentences.

[14] Indeed, Darwin thought other-regarding concern evolved in many different animal species. "Parental affection, or some feeling which replaces it, has been developed in certain animals extremely low in the scale, for example, in star-fishes and spiders. It is also occasionally present in a few members alone in a whole group of animals, as in the genus Forficula, or earwigs" (1871/1982, 73). Recent studies with fish (groupers) and birds (corvids) confirm Darwin's general stance. See Bshary et al. (2006), Vail et al. (2014), and Clayton et al. (2007). Darwin's mistake was in describing these animals as "lower" rather than "other," as a more accurate phylogeny would warrant. See, e.g., Hodos and Campbell (1969).

[15] "It is extremely difficult to obtain true observations of the instincts of animals from the disposition to make them subjects of marvel and astonishment. Many people take delight in storing up tales of the extraordinary sagacity of dogs, cats, horses, birds, &c. in doing things quite incomprehensible and inexplicable on any law of nature whatsoever. It is nearly as impossible to acquire a knowledge of animals from popular stories and anecdotes, as it would be to obtain a knowledge of human nature from the narratives of parental fondness and friendly partiality," W. and R. Chambers (1854); quoted in Bain (1859/1865, 48).

structure. For this reason, modern interpreters construe Morgan as counseling us to explain animal behavior with instincts, habits, and associations unless these prove inadequate and we are "forced" to credit animals with beliefs and plans (Bermudez, 2003, 6–9).[16]

Now scientists who insist that we can *never* know whether other animals make plans and formulate beliefs, might be likened to those "climate skeptics" who insist that we do not yet know whether human activity is responsible for the rise in global temperatures (Conway and Oreskes, 2010). If anthropomorphism is an epistemic vice, so is the kind of "anthropodenial" de Waal first described twenty years ago (1997, 1999).

One may also ask why zoo visitors are always joking about the primates, whereas the antelopes, lions, reptiles, and elephants fail to elicit hilarity. People stand in front of the monkey rock hooting and yelling, scratching themselves in an exaggerated manner, and pointing at the animals while shouting pleasantries like: "I had to look twice, Larry, I thought it was you!" More than other animals, primates place a question mark behind the dichotomy between the visitors and the visited. In my mind, the laughing reflects anthropodenial: it is a nervous reaction caused by an uncomfortable resemblance.

(de Waal, 1999, 260; cf. Sheets-Johnstone, 1992)

Contemporary researchers now argue that "the goal of comparative research should be understanding the cognitive mechanisms underlying animal behavior in their full variety and complexity" rather than partitioning them into the rational vs. the non-rational or the associative vs. the rule-governed (Shettleworth, 2010, 19; cf. Papineau and Heyes, 2006).

Correlatively, most moral philosophers now recommend that we ignore species distinctions entirely, and instead justify our treatment of each individual animal (human or otherwise) on the basis of its "morally relevant" psychosocial features. If an animal is sensate, it is wrong to strike it, pinch it, or cause it pain. But if an animal is insensate, or anesthetized, these activities might be just fine. More seriously, since only some animals value proximity to parents or offspring, or their

---

[16] Though Morgan advanced this rather skeptical methodological suggestion, he was willing to acknowledge the beliefs and designs of non-human animals when prolonged observation seemed to warrant it. See Sober (2005) and de Waal (2016, 41–3). But a continued emphasis on "formal parsimony" (Dacey, 2016a) retains its dangers. For example, Bermudez is led by his neo-Morganian methodology to conclude that human language is necessary for meta-cognition (2003, 150–88) contrary to the ethological observations reported above.

freedom to migrate across long distances, only some animals are unjustly restrained or separated from kin without good reason. An ethically mature judge proceeds on a case-by-case basis (Rachels, 1990; Savage-Rumbaugh, Shanker, and Taylor, 1998; cf. Singer, 1990 and Francione, 2007).

Still, even those scientists and philosophers who bemoan man's treatment of the rest of nature continue to speculate on the important differences between humans and other animals: those features that are supposed to account for the extraordinary diversity in human culture, the "advance" of human technologies, and the enormous changes humans have wrought on the Earth's ecology when these are compared to the contributions of other animals. In sketching *A Brief History of the Human Mind*, the neuroscientist W. Calvin (2004) signs on to one hundred such distinctions, citing everything from sentential language and other "structured stuff," to the distinctive kinds of motor planning implicated in launching a spear from a distance.[17] Even de Waal countenances a "few dozen differences" (2016, 125).

This ambivalence has a storied history. Though Darwin built his theory of natural selection on psychologically rich explanations of animal behavior, he also drew a distinction in kind between "us" and "them." For Darwin, "Fully subscribed to the judgment of those writers who maintain that of all the differences between man and the lower animals, the moral sense or conscience is by far the most important" (1871/1982, 120). According to Darwin, though other animals are appropriate objects of moral *concern*, they are inappropriate objects of moral *judgment*. In this respect, animals are like human children who have a right not to be tortured, while being too young and uncomprehending to be punished by the state, blamed in full by their parents, or held "morally responsible" for any torturous actions they might perform in turn. Among the animals of which we are aware, Darwin thought, only (relatively) mature humans are proper targets of moral appraisal.[18]

But what distinguishes a mature human's moral sense from that of a non-human animal? We will blame a person for stealing from us, or

---

[17] For a more nuanced and systematic overview see Shettleworth (2012). Cf. Kagan (2004), Premack (2007), Suddendorf (2013), and Millikan (2006). Millikan argues (against the Fodorians) that humans are unique in our capacity for propositional thought, which is in turn necessary for knowledge of "dead facts."

[18] For recent discussion see Humphrey (2002).

lying to us, or harming us physically. And though we discourage similar behavior in our pets, many of us think it is inappropriate to blame a dog for stealing a roast, or to express disappointment with a cat for scratching a stranger, and we find it similarly jarring to hear these animals described as acting "immorally" in the cases on hand. What, if anything, justifies this difference in our attitudes? "Reflection," was Darwin's answer.

Man, from the activity of his mental faculties, cannot avoid reflection: past impressions and images are incessantly and clearly passing through his mind.
(1871/1982, 136)

A moral being is one who is capable of comparing his past and future actions or motives, and of approving or disapproving of them. We have no reason to suppose that any of the lower animals have this capacity.   (1871/1982, 135)

Indeed, if the other social animals had the ability to reflect on their deeds and the consequences of their actions, they would have as great a moral sense as our own, albeit one suited to their characteristic patterns of social organization and means of reproduction.

Whilst the mother-bird is feeding, or brooding over her nestlings, the maternal instinct is probably stronger than the migratory; but the instinct which is the more persistent gains the victory, and at last, at a moment when her young ones are not in sight, she takes flight and deserts them. When arrived at the end of her long journey, and the migratory instinct has ceased to act, what an agony of remorse the bird would feel, if, from being endowed with great mental activity, she could not prevent the image constantly passing through her mind, of her young ones perishing in the bleak north from cold and hunger.   (1871/1982, 137)

Note that Darwin uses "reflection" to denote both introspection of what one currently thinks, feels and wants, and episodic, first-person memories as to what one has thought, felt, and desired in the past.[19] If the mother bird could reflect in this sense, she would not just realize that her babies were likely perishing in the bleak north, she would recall, from the "inside," that she left them to that fate when her maternal instinct proved weaker than her migratory. If she were capable of introspective thought, Darwin reasoned, she would blame herself and experience guilt and remorse because her settled (non-instinctive) preferences—the ones

---

[19] Contemporary psychologists have found that these capacities are neurologically linked to "prospection" wherein we imagine various seemingly possible futures in the course of deciding what to do. See Suddendorf and Corballis (1997), Suddendorf, Addis, and Corballis (2009), Hassabis and Maguire (2009), and Maguire and Hassabis (2011).

that come to the fore when she reflects on her past behavior—rank the wellbeing of her children above her own survival.

In sum, if Darwin is right, guilt and remorse set us apart from the other primates, allowed us to regulate emotionally violent responses to one another to form large tribes and intertribal coalitions, to generate a division of labor, to develop languages and other symbolic systems, to inaugurate incredible artistic transformations to celebrate those we love, and to eventually brainstorm those technological advances that now enable us to more effectively maim, kill, and disenfranchise those we hate. We domesticated ourselves, for better or for worse.[20]

But is Darwin right? We subject our dogs to punishment for their bad behaviors and reward them for doing what we wish. Does their memory of transgressing our expectations ever lead them to experience remorse or regret? It is not a priori obvious that human language is necessary for these emotions, nor the pained reminiscence that Darwin's migratory mother birds seem to lack. To the contrary, non-verbal practices of transgression, punishment, regret, repentance, and forgiveness seem to undergird our distinctively human need to verbally confess our sins and reconcile with those we've harmed.

To this end, de Waal describes an ordinary event in the lives of the chimpanzees living together in the Arnhem Zoo, an event that was to prove important to the subsequent development of primatology.

When the alpha male fiercely attacked a female, other apes came to her defense, causing prolonged screaming and chasing in the group. After the chimpanzees had calmed down, a tense silence followed, broken when the entire colony burst out hooting. In the midst of this pandemonium, two chimpanzees kissed with their arms wrapped around each other. These two chimpanzees turned out to be the same male and female central in the previous fight.

(2000, 586; cf. de Waal, 1982/2007)

Defining "reconciliation" as a friendly reunion between former opponents not long after a fight, de Waal and A. van Roosmalen (1979) went on to record regular occurrences of the phenomenon in the Arnhem colony. And subsequent study has identified more than thirty non-human primate species in which reconciliation regularly takes place (Arnold and Aureli, 2006).

---

[20] See Hare et al. (2012) and the related work of M. Tomasello (2014), who emphasizes cooperative activity and the forms of communication it requires.

But aren't we the only species to recruit neutral parties to adjudicate a dispute? Not according to de Waal, who describes the chimpanzee Mama as a "mediator par excellence" (2016, 184).

Two female chimps were sitting in the sun, with their children rolling around in the sand in front of them. When the play turned into a screaming, hair-pulling fight, neither mother knew what to do because if one of them tried to break up the fight, it was guaranteed that the other would protect her offspring, since mothers are never impartial... Noticing the alpha female, Mama, asleep nearby, one of them went over to poke her in the ribs. As the old matriarch got up, the mother pointed at the fight by swinging an arm in its direction. Mama needed only one glance to grasp what was going on and took a step forward with a threatening grunt. Her authority was such that this shut up the youngsters.   (de Waal, 2016, 67)

After reviewing a number of comparative studies of peacemaking among non-human primates and human school children, the ethologist P. Verbeek now concludes, "Evidence from ethological studies on young children suggests that peacemaking is a natural tendency that we share with other primates and, possibly, with any number of other social mammals as well" (2008, 1518; cf. Silk, 2002). Perhaps Darwin was ahead of his time, but behind our own. Perhaps there really is no difference "in kind" between them and us. Kumbaya.

Of course, the intellectualists invariably consider this objection from the minds of animals. For example, Williams grants that other animals believe things in an "impoverished" sense of the term (1973, 138).[21] In

---

[21] Dummett (1993) calls these impoverished beliefs "proto-thoughts." There are some notable exceptions to this grudging acceptance of the "quasi-beliefs" of non-humans. Famously, the Stoics, Descartes, Malebranche, and the Cartesians seem to have denied other animals cognitions of any kind. "For we see that magpies and parrots can utter words as we do, and yet they cannot speak as we do: that is, they cannot show that they are thinking what they are saying. On the other hand, men born deaf and dumb, and thus deprived of speech-organs as much as the other beasts or even more so, normally invent their own signs to make themselves understood by those who, being regularly in their company, have the time to learn their language. This shows not merely that the beasts have less reason than men, but that they have no reason at all"; Descartes (1637/1998, 140). For discussion of Descartes' motivations see Cottingham (1997), who excerpts Descartes' letter to Henry More on February 5, 1649 where Descartes writes, "It has never been observed that any brute animal has attained the perfection of using real speech, that is to say, of indicating by word or sign something relating to thought alone and not to natural impulse. Such speech is the only sure sign of thought hidden within a body. All human beings use it, however stupid and insane they may be, even though they may have no tongue and organs of voice; but no animals do. Consequently this can be taken as a real specific difference between humans and animals." Malcolm notes some conflicting evidence in Descartes'

what sense "impoverished"? According to Williams, the main obstacle to assimilating animal minds to our own is a matter of *determinacy*: there seems to be no fact of the matter as to how other animals conceptualize the objects of their fear or the sources of their satisfaction, and this prevents us from arriving at a well-articulated description of their beliefs (cf. Davidson, 1980, 164).[22]

The contents of a person's beliefs—the information a person uses to guide her actions and deliberations—would seem to stand in some relatively close systematic relation to her assertions. When you're ready to speak honestly, and you aren't lost for words, you can pretty much say what you think. Though R. Moran (2005) doesn't endorse this conception of the matter, he expresses it eloquently.

> The smile, if sincere, takes us to the pleasure of the other person, and the statements he makes, if sincere, take us to his genuine beliefs about some matter we are interested in. And since the other person's words are only of interest to us insofar as they are a reliable guide to his beliefs, we would do just as well, and

letters (1973, 41). Cf. N. Malebranche (1674–5/1997), especially sections 2.3.5, 5.3, and 6.2.7. For an historical overview of Western philosophical writing on animal minds see Steiner (2005).

[22] Velleman allows that other animals have beliefs (despite lacking the capacity for action) because the "cognitive mechanisms" responsible for their activity-guiding representations are "designed" to track the truth; the imputation of the desire for truth is a "personification" of aims that are in fact "subpersonal" (2000, 19; 184–8 and 253). My response to this conception of belief is threefold: (i) Sub-personal "truth tracking" is insufficient for belief—as pre-doxastic perceptual mechanisms track truth if anything does and these mechanisms can deliver up experiences and construals that, when disavowed and suppressed, persist for some time in the absence of any belief in what is represented. (ii) Truth-tracking is only necessary for belief if truth is understood in a sufficiently "thin" way so as to admit sensibility-relative truths about beauty, funniness, deliciousness, and so on: socially constructed phenomena that have no place in the theories advanced by academic scientists, but which are nevertheless "tracked" by cognitive mechanisms when they are deployed to render judgment in these domains. (As an interpretive matter, Velleman appears to be invoking a more "objective" sense of "truth" in his work, as when he argues that our color attributions are all false because things don't "really and truly" have colors.) (iii) There are several kinds of belief that are produced and regulated by mechanisms that do not track the "truth" even when truth is relativized to a subject's sensibility: self-affirmations, religious creeds, and philosophical codes are central examples. Of course, these considerations are not decisive. One might say that self-affirmations and value judgments are not expressions of belief and make comparable "moves" in response to criticisms (i) and (ii). As per our pragmatic meta-level thesis: the choice between Velleman's intellectualism, Bain's pragmatism, and the other plausible conceptions of belief discussed in this book is a "free" one and so radically undetermined by anything we might judge to be the "evidence" without controversy.

perhaps better, if we had more immediate access to those beliefs, dispensing with the need for verbal expression and all of its risks and inadequacies.

(Moran, 2005, 326)[23]

The problem is that the other animals we encounter either don't assert what they believe or we can't easily decode the postures, mannerisms, barks, whistles, rumbles, and chirps they use to express themselves. (Which is just to point out, once more, that the other animals don't utter sentences.) Thus, the vexed relation between language and thought poses a seemingly unanswerable philosophical question: Do other animals have beliefs they can't easily express, or do they have feelings, sensations, and experiences without thoughts?

It is clear that other animals perceive things, remember things, and expect certain things to happen (Clayton and Dickinson, 1998). And we regularly infer a person's beliefs from our knowledge of these perceptions, memories, and expectations. So if you want to maintain a skeptical attitude toward the minds of the "brutes," you're going to have to work hard at it.[24]

To take one of Hume's examples: when you hear a voice in the hall you will immediately infer that there is someone out there; and were you to open the door to the hall you would expect to see someone standing there (Hume, 1740/2000, 1.4.2.20; cf. Piaget, 1954). Wouldn't a dog similarly expect to see her master upon hearing or smelling the same? Of course

---

[23] Moran notes that assertion incurs responsibilities for a claim in ways non-verbal (especially non-intentional) expression of it need not. But these social and legal consequences of assertion flow from lies as surely as they do from sincere speech. Perjury is a paradigmatic example.

[24] Neurotypical people automatically distinguish biological motion from artificial mechanics and infer an animal's expectations from its (biologically natural) postures and movements. This contrasts (to some extent) with "deafferented" patients like G.L. (mentioned in chapter 1) who lack haptic or proprioceptive information about their own movements and are consequently impaired in their "mindreading" abilities, providing evidence that an observer's "simulation" of an animal's actions plays some role in her understanding of its mind. On the first point see Fox and McDaniel (1982). On the second, see Bosbach et al. (2005). On the third, see Iacoboni et al. (2004). Thus, if we doubt that animals have the expectations they seem to have, we are indulging in "Cartesian skepticism" in a broad sense of that term. Though skepticism about animal belief needn't involve distrust of the "senses" (narrowly construed), it does mean doubting the deliverances of a relatively automatic, relatively innate faculty, which functions to represent the minds of others: a capacity for social understanding. However, unlike Cartesian skepticism with regard to the external world, Cartesian analyses of belief cannot be dismissed a priori. We must instead address the grounds on which intellectualists "valorize" or prioritize sentential language.

she would (Ashton and De Lillo, 2011).[25] So why must we extol the riches of our own expectations in contrast with her "impoverished" simulacrum of belief?

The problems arise when we try to say precisely *what* the dog believes. Does she really believe that her "master" is in the hall? Doesn't this imply that the dog has a determinate conception of masters, servants, and other social hierarchies? Do dogs understand these relations in the way a child must before we are willing to say that she adequately understands the word "master" or some synonym? In the course of his examination, Williams dismisses the possibility that animals might possess such concepts.

Suppose there is a dog whose master is the President of the United States; a certain figure comes to the door, and this dog wakes up and pricks up his ears when he hears the person crossing the step—we say 'this dog took the person who was coming up the drive for his master'... we would hardly say that the dog had taken this figure for the President of the United States. Is this because it is a better shot to say that the dog has got the concept 'master' than it is to say that the dog has got the concept 'President of the United States'? Why? The concept 'master' is as much a concept that embodies elaborate knowledge about human conventions, society, and so forth as does the concept 'President of the United States'. There seems to be as much conventionality or artificiality in ascribing to a dog the concept 'master' as there is in ascribing to a dog the concept 'President of the United States'. So why are we happier to say that a dog takes a certain figure for his master than we are to say that the dog takes a certain figure for the President of the United States? I think the answer to this has something to do with the fact, not that the dog really has got an effective concept 'master', which would be an absurd notion, but that so much of the dog's behavior is in fact conditioned by situations which involve somebody's being his master, whereas very little of the dog's behavior is conditioned by situations which essentially involve someone's being the President of the United States.   (1973, 139)[26]

And yet, despite Williams's confident assertion that dogs lack an understanding of one animal's mastery over others, it is clear to most of those who study them that the wolves from whom our dogs descend understand

---

[25] It is also well known that dolphins recognize each other's signature whistles. See King and Janik (2013), and King et al. (April 2013), where is it is concluded, "This use of vocal copying is similar to its use in human language, where the maintenance of social bonds seems to be more important than the immediate defense of resources" (2013, 1). See too Barrett-Lennard (2000) and Ford (2002) who observe different call types among different populations. Dolphins and killer whales seem to maintain their group identities without sentential communication (Vincent, Ring, and Andrews, forthcoming).

[26] Cf. Davidson (1984, 163) and Armstrong (1973, 25), critically discussed by Stich (1978).

the social hierarchies in which they live.[27] Since properly trained dogs also evince some understanding of "who's the boss," the suggestion is not incredible.[28] If a dog does grasp its dependence on some human for love, nourishment, and freedom from punishment, and relates emotionally to that person in the ways we do when we interact with those on whom we depend for these things, we are warranted in saying, without emendation, that the dog believes its *guardian* or its *master* or its *owner* or its *leader* is nearby. If the dog could talk, she could help us discriminate between these subtly different formulations, but she can't, so she won't.[29] As H. J. Glock explains,

Although the sentences we use in ascribing thoughts have components, our ascriptions do not presuppose a prior ascription of these components. Instead, they are based on the subject manifesting certain perceptual capacities, attitudes and emotions. In the non-linguistic case, these manifestations will obviously not include assent to sentences. But they will include forms of behavior, postures and facial expressions which higher animals share with human beings.   (Glock, 2010, 20)[30]

---

[27] See Smith and Ferguson (2005) and Safina (2015) quoted above.

[28] Williams is also mistaken in asserting the oddity or infelicity of attributions of beliefs to dogs that employ terms associated with sophisticated political concepts like "the President of the United States." Suppose former President Barak Obama had stayed out late, but lent his coat to the first lady. And suppose that when Michelle Obama approached the door wearing the coat in question, the Obamas' dog Bo caught the scent and began to bark and furiously wag his tail with a vigor he reserves for the former president. One secret service agent might have then said to another, "Bo thinks the president is home." There is nothing infelicitous about such attributions, as is noted by all those who reject naively "Fregean" analyses of belief reports. See, e.g., T. Burge's example, "If Alfie says, 'The most powerful man on Earth in 1970 (whoever he is) is a crook,' not having the slightest idea who the most powerful man is, a friend of the potentate may say to him, 'Alfie believes that you are a crook'"; Burge (2007, 50). Beliefs with indeterminate contents are "incompletely conceptualized" and so "de re" in the sense Burge there defines, though Burge is right to characterize his example as a "de re ascription of a de dicto belief" (2007, 66).

[29] Davidson (1985) and Dummett (1993) both claim that an animal must possess the concepts we use in attributing a belief to her if she is to be credited with the belief we therein ascribe, and they claim, further, that animals cannot possess concepts without possessing an indefinite number of general beliefs. See Davidson (1985, 473–80) and Dummett (1993). Cf. McDowell (1994) and Steiner (2008, 1–29). Thus, Williams's dog cannot believe that his master is home unless said dog possesses the concept expressed by "master" which would require the belief that masters have rights over those whom they rule and so on and so forth. But both proposals are under-motivated. Why not instead retain our intuitive attributions and drop these supposedly necessary criteria for belief possession?

[30] Contra Armstrong (1973, 26–7). Cf. Wilkes (1997) and Camp (2009). Camp requires that animal's possess "general representational abilities" but not linguistic or quasilinguistic "vehicles" if they are to possess the concepts we associate with the terms we use to attribute beliefs to them. Though Camp accepts the propositional attitude analysis of belief, she

This line of reasoning would allow that beliefs are often indeterminate between various possible interpretations of their contents. When the Founding Fathers of the United States said, "All men are created equal," did they express the judgment that *all* men are created equal? Or did they mean that all European men, or all white men, or all literate men, or all men who are armed, dangerous, and willing to assert their equality with violent action must have been granted their equality by a creator? Who can say? The great Fredrick Douglass was right to be curious when he asked on behalf of his people, "Are the great principles of political freedom and natural justice embodied in that declaration extended to us?"[31] Even if we focus our assessment on, say, Thomas Jefferson's mind at the time at which he articulated the Declaration, there may be no fact of the matter. There may be no precise population of people such that Jefferson believed of its members that they (and only they) were created equal (White, 1978; Goodman, 2015). And the intended extension of "men" is the easiest part of the inscription to specify. Who or what is the implied creator? And what was the intended sense of "equality"? Since human utterances—and the beliefs they frame—are often indeterminate between their more plausible interpretations, indeterminacy fails to motivate a difference in kind between "us" and "them."[32] K. Wilkes nicely states the point.

---

emphasizes the importance of control or spontaneity in her analysis of concept possession and allows that the measure admits of degree. She therein embraces two important elements of the pragmatic account of belief.

[31] See Douglass (2014). Cf. Douglass and Jacobs (2004).

[32] For the realities of African-American attitudes toward the American Revolution see Horne (2012). Williams's own (1962) reflections on "all men are created equal" acknowledge its indeterminacy and nicely articulate the inscription's more substantive meanings. White (1978), Gates (2003), and Goodman (2015) offer detailed analyses of Jefferson's thinking about equality and slavery that nevertheless fail to attribute much determinacy on these matters. "In the 'Declaration' [Jefferson] holds that 'all men are created equal,' and in the *Notes on the State of Virginia* he writes eloquently about the evils of slavery. Yet he owned between one and two hundred slaves throughout his adult life, and fathered a slave family with his slave Sally Hemings. Compounding his inconsistencies, he argues in the Notes that 'the blacks' are an inferior race, the members of which should be expelled from America, lest they mix with 'the whites'" (Goodman, 2015, 101). For an interesting example of the indeterminacy of various relatively value-neutral judgments see H. Field's (1973) claim that Sir Isaac's Newton's beliefs about mass were indeterminate as between the contemporary concepts "relativistic mass" and "'real' mass." W.V.O. Quine's (1960/2015) more radical, more famous, and in some ways less interesting claim is that a hypothetical native's use of "gavagai" might be indeterminate in reference as between rabbits and "undetached rabbit parts."

I am... untroubled by the difficulty of specifying (with our linguistic categories) the contents of a cat's, rat's or bat's mind. The difficulty is no worse, or better, than that of pinning down the content of the thoughts and anticipations of a composer or an artist, or of a non-scientist about abstruse or difficult theoretical entities. There will be a huge spectrum between vagueness and precision amongst our ascriptions of what is said to be thought, believed or felt.

(Wilkes, 1997, 180)

In an equally ecumenical passage, the august philosopher D.J. O'Connor draws our attention to the indeterminacy lurking in our deepest convictions and creeds.

It is perfectly possible to believe a proposition of whose meaning we are uncertain or completely ignorant. It is said that some distinguished Roman Catholic philosophers profess to believe the propositions of their Church's creed 'whatever they may mean.' This is not so absurd a position as it can be made to sound.

(1968–9, 13; cf. Newman, 1870/1992)

The cognitive scientist, D. Sperber (1982, 1997) calls these beliefs "semi-propositional" or "half-understood" and effectively argues for the unnaturalness of those psychological taxonomies that exclude them. Many semi-propositional beliefs cannot be subjected to empirical testing without further elaboration. Why? Because it's unclear exactly what they entail with regard to future experience. And this is so even when they are conjoined with more fully propositional background beliefs. The most rabid positivists or "verificationists" asserted, on these grounds alone, that the Church's creed and similarly obscure dicta lack meaning altogether. But these words aren't epiphenomenal. Though frankly ideological, the beliefs acquired when we truly accept a religion guide substantive swaths of our thought and behavior. The indeterminacy of a belief's content is no argument against its psychological reality.[33]

---

[33] Endorsement of barely articulate (highly vague) language raises psycho-semantic and logical issues suitable for a book-length analysis or two. Conceptual understanding is a heterogeneous collection of abilities each one of which admits of degree, and full understanding is an ideal imposed upon these continua. As we move from acknowledged expertise with a concept—and familiarity with the phenomena it encompasses—to deferential usage of technical terms, we tend to uncover beliefs that are increasingly partial in their action-guiding profiles. (My beliefs about quarks don't inform much of what I think and do; my beliefs about my parental obligations are much more extensive in effect, and this is because I have a much better understanding of the relevance of the latter to what I'm doing or planning to do.) It would seem that we cannot help reasoning and acting on claims we barely understand despite the risks involved. "Half-understood representations such as the dogma of

To stick with O'Connor's example: Only the most curious Catholic children will ask for a coherent conceptualization of the trinity. Are the three divine beings really just parts of the one and only God? Or are they truly distinct in nature and only unified by our thinking of them as a single entity? Kids who ask these questions can be sent to the clergy, who can offer metaphysically coherent doctrines, or romantic readings, or attractive mixtures of the two. Perhaps inspiration can be found in the image of love between father and son freely exchanged within God's divine body. (Though this same scene assumes a sinister cast if our congregant discovers that a priest has molested her boy.) The believer who has "internalized" the Church's creed in this way thinks of her love for family as qualitatively similar to God's internal structure. And if her rituals reflect this way of thinking, if it informs her interactions with clergy and the other members of her church, it is not wrong to say that she is guided by the belief that God is both one and three.

It was said by Jeremy Taylor, 'Believe and you shall love'; he should have said rather, 'Love and you shall believe'; or, still better, 'learn to love, and you will learn to believe'. Religious truth cannot, therefore, be imparted, as has sometimes been supposed, by an intellectual medium of verbal exposition and theological demonstration. Being an affair of the feelings, a method must be sought adapted to heighten the intensity of these. Still, we must make allowance for a man thoroughly practiced in metaphysical and other reasonings, and fully convinced of his conclusions on their intellectual grounds. Doubtless, Aquinas, Calvin, and Butler, had a considerable amount of comfort from their intellectual convictions, apart altogether from their emotional culture, in which probably they were much below many Christians that could give no reason at all for the faith that is in them.   (Bain, 1888, 532)

Of course, "belief in the trinity" is an extremely coarse measure of these Catholic "life orientations" (Zackariasson, 2010). But from a pragmatic perspective, it is the life orientation that matters, not its inchoate linguistic expression.

---

the Holy Trinity can be objects of belief. However, disquoting such half-understood representations and using them unrestrictedly as premises in inference, on a par with well-understood representations, would be...hazardous. For instance, contradictions could arise undetected. Half-understood information may be epistemically useful, but only if it is treated with cognitive caution" (Sperber, 1997, 74). And this danger isn't merely discursive. A believer can be guided by an image in practice even while she acknowledges in discourse that it is inaccurate in certain respects. Sentences can be inconsistent and pictures incompatible. Do we feel less pressure to revise inconsistent beliefs when the conflict is intermodal (as it often is in the religious case)? Cf. Recanati (1997) and Bain (1859/1865, 552–3).

There are some who feel pretty sure that those who adhere, for instance, to the nihilistic monism of the Vedanta, or to the Athanasian doctrine of the Trinity, never really conceive together the elements of the propositions that they affirm; but no one can deny that, out of the maintenance of the posture of belief towards these propositions, believers derive highly distinctive and vivid experiences, which they could scarcely have in any other way.   (Lovejoy, 1908, 10)

Other examples arise from our reluctance to contemplate the abhorrent. For instance, you probably believe that infanticide is immoral insofar as you would describe it as such if asked. But suppose your ethics professor asks you to imagine you're a Jew hiding from the Nazis and that you must suffocate your crying baby to save everyone in your party from a trip to the gas chamber. Do you believe that infanticide is always immoral or that it is wrong unless necessary to prevent some greater evil? There are good reasons you haven't given the matter much thought and would have to work out the admissible exceptions to a fully general prohibition on the fly. But if that's so, there may be no fact of the matter as to how to best specify the belief you express when answering "yes" to "Is infanticide wrong?" As E. Durkheim (1912) argues, radically under-specified beliefs are often maintained by a meta-level belief in the "sacred" nature of their topic, a status that helps seal them off from critical investigation. Indeed, the intellectual conservatism of a society might be measured by the use of sanctity concepts by parents, teachers, and other authorities to limit inquiry into its "foundational" assump-tions. In the most liberal societies, children are allowed to press for definitions of everything, and nothing is sacred in the intended sense. Socratic philosophy is the epitome of this kind of intellectual liberalism. After all, Socrates, that great "gadfly" of Western philosophy, was sen-tenced to death for pressing the authorities to define terms—like "piety" and "justice"—that could not be made precise without embarrassment to accepted institutions.[34]

Deference to expert usage of technical terms is not the primary source of vague conception. Though our thoughts gain precision as we mature (McClelland et al. 2009), politics, religion, and morality are all sources of

---

[34] It is telling that in his rough draft of the U.S. Declaration of Independence, Jefferson called the equality of man a "sacred and undeniable" truth, and only later substituted the claim of "self-evidence" (White, 1978, 14).

irremediable indeterminacy in belief.[35] For instance, normative philosophies of judicial practice differ on the importance they assign to discerning the intended meaning of a statute or opinion. Which beliefs were legislators and judges trying to articulate when drafting the legislation in question or writing up their opinions? And how much weight ought a judge give to the discernible communicative intentions of the framers of our Constitution when she is trying to render judgment on a case to which they seem relevant?

These questions raise subtle philosophical issues. Surely, we are right to insist that people interpret us charitably. If I say something that seems inane, foolish, or obviously false, you should ask for clarification. And if you can discern more than one possible meaning my utterance might be naturally taken to have, and you are genuinely unsure which of these propositions I intended to assert, charity again demands you consult with me throughout your attempts at disambiguation.[36] But what if the conversation is no longer a "live" one and the speaker is dead or is otherwise incapable of helping us decide between genuinely different, equally reasonable takes on what she has written? When we've arrived at this juncture, are we justified in dropping the hermeneutic enterprise altogether and narrowing our focus to the differing consequences that would attend our adopting the varying interpretations on offer?

This is a characteristically pragmatist stance to take. We aren't forced by nature or government to give interpretive fidelity paramount importance in such cases, so we should only do so when we judge that this is the best course "all things considered." As the pragmatic Justice Oliver Wendell Holmes Jr. so memorably wrote, "The life of the law has not been logic; it has been experience" (1881, 5). But a much more modest proposal is relevant to the pragmatic philosophy of mind advanced here: There is a conceptual limit on the entire enterprise of charitable interpretation. A justice's efforts to determine the beliefs behind a legal utterance or inscription are limited by genuinely irresolvable indeterminacies in the thoughts she is attempting to discern. To think

---

[35] "As children grow, they cease to lump together concepts that older children (and adults) pull apart" McClelland et al. (2009, 1048).

[36] Charity makes more subtle demands when the speaker is prevented from properly conceptualizing her experience because of inadequacies in the language to which she's been exposed. For examples of these "hermeneutical injustices" see Nelson (1990), Code (1995), and Fricker (2007).

otherwise is to assume a preconceptual "given" that resembles our sensations and feelings in being non-linguistic in nature, but which is nevertheless already as sharply discriminated as the most exact verbal report. And this is a myth. There is no brain or mind code, with a unique, fully determinate interpretation, which might be discovered within a speaker's brain or mind. If we assume, as I do, that an animal's psychology is its neurology, we must also assume that a legislator's thoughts are themselves neurological phenomena. But a high-resolution picture of Thomas Jefferson's nervous system isn't going to help us disambiguate his declaration. The contents of his mind cannot be directly gleaned from its neurological constitution.

> How can one identify a population of neurons in a way that might identify it as the constituent of a sentence in the language of thought? How can one tell, amid the chaos of simultaneously firing neurons in the brain, which neurons are firing together to provide a vector coding? The only way to identify a population of neurons is to work out how particular tasks are being performed. That is to say, by working backward from the particular processing tasks being performed... But this, of course requires starting at the semantic level.   (Bermudez, 2003, 30)

No doubt, there are times when a person has a more or less precise thought that she struggles to put into language. But articulation brings shape to our thoughts just as often as it reveals conceptual, logical, or inferential structure already latent within them.[37]

Most philosophers are now willing to attribute beliefs to other animals, albeit beliefs with vague contents that admit of multiple incompatible specifications.[38] Even Ramsey, who narrowed his focus to the verbalized

---

[37] Thus Oliver Wendell Holmes Jr.—the famous pragmatist jurist—scoffed at the studied naïveté of the infamous Dred Scott decision rendered by the US Supreme Court in 1857, a judgment grounded in what Chief Justice R.B. Taney claimed to be the uniquely correct interpretation of our Constitution, "not only in the same words but with the same meaning and intent with which it spoke when it came from the hands of its framers." No doubt, the U.S. Constitution and its early interpretations do evince a great deal of racism. It's not Taney's interpretation of the meaning and intent of the founders that is justly deplored, but his racist attempt to deploy originalism in defense of slavery. For a nuanced discussion see Finkleman (2013, 49–74); cf. Thayer (1981). Though the young Holmes was an abolitionist who broke with his father on this point, there is some question as to whether the younger Holmes "succumbed to the increasingly legitimated racism that marked post-Reconstruction America," as suggested by E. A. Purcell Jr. (2002, 978). Cf. E.G. White's (1993) analysis.

[38] See Kenny (1989, 36–7), Glock (2000), Glock (2009), and Glock (2010). Bermudez initially claims complete determinacy essential to propositional thinking (2003, 39) but falls back to allowing "the type of localized indeterminacy that we are happy to accept in our

credences we might extract from a gambler's bets, acknowledged the precedence of animal thought to language. Ramsey considered a chicken's aversion to a species of caterpillar that made it sick.[39] Does the chicken believe the caterpillar is poisonous? Ruth Barcan Marcus, the ground-breaking modal logician, balked at this attribution, but she was willing to allow a range of less sophisticated interpretations. "We surely cannot attribute to the chicken the belief that the caterpillar is *poisonous*," she writes, "but surely we will not go too far afield if we attribute the belief that the caterpillar is not for eating." The chicken's behavior and neurology may be utilized to argue that one conceptualization is more appropriate than another, but without the chicken's verbal participation, this is des-tined to remain an imprecise art, highly indeterminate at the limit.[40]

ordinary social interactions" (2003, 198). I have also shifted view on this issue. I used to think that a person can't believe a claim when she knows that it's indeterminate between a true and false interpretation (Zimmerman, 2007b). But I now see that this is a normative judgment. The classical conception of a proposition is derived from an *ideal* of inquiry. The concept we need for classical truth-functional logic is the concept of a fully interpreted claim, which is either true or false "full-stop" at the actual world.

[39] "In order to proceed further, we must now consider the mental factors in a belief. Their nature will depend on the sense in which we are using the ambiguous term belief: it is, for instance, possible to say that a chicken believes a certain sort of caterpillar to be poisonous, and mean by that merely that it abstains from eating such caterpillars on account of unpleasant experiences connected with them. The mental factors in such a belief would be parts of the chicken's behavior, which are somehow related to the objective factors, viz., the kind of caterpillars and poisonousness. An exact analysis of this relation would be very difficult, but it might well be held that in regard to this kind of belief the pragmatist view was correct, i.e. that the relation between the chicken's behavior and the objective factors was that the actions were such as to be useful if, and only if, the caterpillars were actually poisonous. Thus any actions for whose utility p is a necessary and sufficient condition might be called a belief that p, and so would be true if p, i.e. if they are useful. But without wishing to depreciate the importance of this kind of belief, it is not what I wish to discuss here. I prefer to deal with those beliefs which are expressed in words, or possibly images or other symbols, consciously asserted or denied; for these, in my view, are the most proper subject for logical criticism"; Ramsey (1927, 159).

[40] Marcus continues, "The pre-verbal child hears familiar footsteps and believes a person known to her is approaching, a person who perhaps elicits behavior anticipatory of pleasure. It may not be the anticipated person, and when the child sees this, her behavior will mark the mistake. But must there be some linguistic obligato in the child to attribute to her a mistaken belief, or a disappointment? Must an agent have the concept of a mistake to be mistaken? The important kernel of truth in such a linguistic view is that arriving at a precise verbal description of another's beliefs and desires is difficult, and especially so when the attribution cannot be verbally confirmed by the subject"; Marcus (1990, 135). M. Richard (2013) nicely describes how Marcus's dispositionalist analysis of belief prevents her from countenancing belief in impossibilities. So much the worse for (reductive) dispositionalist analyses of belief that attempt to make do without a concept of encoded information.

Human beliefs can be distinguished from one another as finely as the sentences we use to express and report them to one another.[41] As the logician Gottlob Frege (1848–1925) famously argued, the belief that Hesperus is the evening star differs from the belief that Phosphorus is the evening star insofar as ancient peoples accepted the first claim while denying the second. And this is so even though Hesperus just is Phosphorus. (In fact, "Hesperus" and "Phosphorus" both name the planet Venus rather than a star or two.) Similarly, someone who reads the collected works of Mark Twain can't help concluding that Mr. Twain was clever. But a reader might still deny that Samuel Clemens was wicked smart if she doesn't know that "Mark Twain" was Samuel Clemens's pen name.

It would be a mistake, however, to infer from this, as Rudolph Carnap (1891–1975) once did, that belief is invariably a matter of taking a sentence to express a truth (1956, 62).[42] Intellectualism is not the inevitable result of so-called "Frege cases." Consider, in this regard, R. Richard's tale of Rin Tin Wrong, a riff on one of Aesop's fables.

Recall the fable of the dog who, carrying a piece of meat, crosses a stream and sees a dog holding a piece of meat. The dog wants the extra meat, snaps at it and, of course, loses the meat it's carrying. And since what the dog saw was its own reflection, it lost substance for shadow. In this case, the dog certainly knew, and thus believed, of itself and a piece M of meat, that it had M in its mouth. It also believed of itself and M, that it didn't have M in its mouth.   (Richard, 2013, 412)

Rin Tin Wrong believes under a visual "mode of presentation" that a given object, a hunk of meat, is down below him in the stream, not in his mouth. But he also believes, under a tactile mode of presentation, of that same piece of meat, that it is securely grasped within his jaws. So we must distinguish between Rin Tin Wrong's visually generated beliefs about the meat in question from those of his beliefs about it that are generated by his tactile impressions. These beliefs are all representations: we can assess them for truth or accuracy or verisimilitude. And we can lament those occasions when they conflict with one another to tragic effect as in Aesop's tale of that species of woe that follows so closely upon greed.

---

[41] Indeed, they can be distinguished even more finely than this when a person mistakenly believes that a single person's actions are attributable to two different people with the same name. See S. Kripke's (1979/1988) "Paderewski puzzle."

[42] See Carnap (1956). Cf. Russell (1971) and Kvart (1986).

But the beliefs in question are non-linguistic in nature: they are neither assertions nor inner affirmations nor "judgings true." They are not "attempts" at arriving at the truth in any sense save the most metaphorical. And the perceptual mechanisms responsible for them were not "designed" at all, much less designed to track the truth. They are the results of eons of natural selection; not artificial selection. What mattered was their contribution to the survival and reproduction of the perceiving organism and her kin. Their accuracy played no role beyond this.

The intellectualist adopts an alternative proposal toward all this indeterminacy insofar as she treats our power to use assertions and self-reports to fix a determinate interpretation of our minds as essential to belief itself. Sentential language allows us to commit ourselves to some specifications of our thinking and reject others. And as we establish and retain our memories of these commitments, we form a new kind of mental state: a doxastic commitment or "belief" in the supposedly true and proper sense of that term. In the absence of assertion and self-report, we are left gesturing toward a range of differing interpretations without the possibility of deciding amongst them. According to the intellectualist, these incompletely conceptualized representations are decidedly second-class.[43]

Surely, intellectualism contains deep and important insights. The effects of human language on cognitive development, cultural change, and its transformation of the Earth's environment have been massive to behold (Clark, 1998). Perhaps humans advanced the technology, diplomacy, and rituals of their ancestor species before learning to communicate in words and sentences (Donald, 1991; Mithen, 1996). But before the invention of the kinds of language humans now speak, there was no way to discriminate between subtly different thoughts, no critical evaluation of their contents, no covenants, treaties, or currencies; no oral histories, lyrics, or poems; no mathematical proofs or algorithms, no formal languages, no computer language, and no computer technology. No

---

[43] D. Dennett (1978) adopts the anti-intellectualist route and derides our efforts to articulate and accept true claims as a fetishistic hobby: the "collection of true sentences." I applaud Dennett for granting other animals beliefs in the "full and proper" sense of the term, but arguments for the truth of this claim gain nothing from the derogation of intellectual discourse and science. I have a similar aversion to Dennett's proposal to use "opinions" to denote all of our articulate beliefs, as this term is associated with high degrees of subjectivity that do not mark the better results of scientific collaboration. Belief in global warming isn't mere opinion.

planes, trains, or automobiles. No motel rooms. No buttocks mistaken for pillows.[44] And yet, we can acknowledge the power of sentential language, and do justice to its role in erecting the critical practices through which we define and refine our thinking, without deriding the relatively inarticulate beliefs of other animals as "impoverished." We have firmly seized control of the globe. Must we also belittle the minds of those we've marginalized?

We must learn to identify with animals, to see ourselves in them and them in ourselves, in order to appreciate their plight and their prospects in a world that has been dominated by human beings simply because human beings can dominate the world—not because we have a right to do so.   (Steiner, 2008, 137)

'You shall have dominion over the fish of the sea, and the birds of the air, and over the cattle, and over all the earth, and over every creeping thing that creeps upon the earth,' we're assured. Taken on its own, as it has been, this is a catastrophic formulation. You can go straight from Genesis 1 to the Monsanto boardroom, pausing for sightseeing picnics at the annihilation of the world's herd game, at some select dust bowls full of cucumbers grown in nitrate powder, at the *Torrey Canyon* wreck, at factory farms, at the edge of a retreating glacier, and at many other uplifting destinations. And you could take in, while on the road, the sport hunting of native peoples everywhere, since they're not made in the image of God, are they?   (Foster, 2016, 25–6).

We obviously attach immense importance to abstract thought and language (a penchant I am not about to mock while writing a book!), but in the larger scheme of things this is only one way to face the problem of survival. In sheer numbers and biomass, ants and termites may have done a better job than we have, focusing on tight coordination among colony members rather than individual thought. Each society operates like a self-organized mind, albeit one pitter-pattering around on thousands of tiny feet. There are many ways to process, organize and spread information, and it is only recently that science has become open-minded enough to treat all these different methods with wonder and amazement rather than dismissal and denial.   (de Waal, 2016, 5).

One might argue that these considerations have nothing to do with science, and that the nature of belief is a scientific question. One might question whether the moral consequences of adopting various taxonomies of the mind are in any way relevant to our choice among them. But this is a decidedly scientistic attitude that runs contrary to the pragmatic picture I am painting here (cf. Stich, 1978, 27–8 and Bortolotti, 2012,

---

[44] RIP John Candy.

45–6). The pragmatist and intellectualist taxonomies are both scientifically "workable." So why not expand the scope of our inquiry in search of
a principled ground for choice?

My own sense, as a reader, is that the intellectualists are unduly
impressed by their admittedly prodigious expressive and critical prowess.
Enthralled by the elegance and clarity of his words, Williams indulges his
disdain for anything less exact. But instead of lauding the beliefs of
sentence-wielding humans as beliefs in the "true and proper" sense,
and referring to animal expectations and memories as beliefs in name
alone, it would seem more natural (and kind) to include inarticulate
beliefs within the general category and then frame hypotheses about the
effect that human language has on the various states of mind that fall
within this class. As O'Connor opines,

> The vast majority of our beliefs neither merit nor require formulation in lan-
> guage. Indeed, one of the commonest ways in which we are brought to recognize
> that we have held a particular belief is our surprise when experience fails to bear it
> out. The majority of our beliefs are implicit unformulated expectations. More-
> over, we commonly attribute—and with good reason—beliefs to animals and
> infants and other creatures without linguistic skills.   (O'Connor, 1968–9, 4)

And let us again hear from Bain.

> The primordial form of belief is expectation of some contingent future about to
> follow on our action ... The humblest insect that has a fixed home, or a known
> resort for the supply of its wants, is gifted with the faculty of believing. Every new
> coincidence introduced into the routine of an animal's existence, and proceeded
> on in the accomplishment of its ends, is a new article of belief.
> (Bain, 1859/1865, 525–6)[45]

Though pragmatists deny that beliefs are essentially discursive, this
doesn't prevent them from theorizing about the dynamic interplay that
exists between those of our beliefs that are poised for expression with

---

[45] Cf. Carruthers (2004, 216). We might compare Bain's ecumenical attitude with Marx's
famous comments on the "operations" conducted by spiders. "A spider conducts operations
that resemble those of a weaver, and a bee puts to shame many an architect in the
construction of her cells. But what distinguishes the worst architect from the best of bees
is this, that the architect raises his structure in imagination before he erects it in reality. And
this subordination is no mere momentary act. Besides the exertion of bodily organs, the
process demands that, during the whole operation, the workman's will be steadily in
consonance with his purpose" (Marx, 1867/1967, 178). I have suggested above that many
animals (e.g. wolves) have the "intentions in action" that Marx here reserves for human labor.

assertion and their less well-defined brethren. Sentential language is something; it just isn't everything.

It is now widely accepted that, even though language assists human thinking by providing categories and concepts, it is not the stuff of thought. We don't actually need language in order to think. (de Waal, 2016, 102)

If language isn't necessary for thought, it isn't necessary for belief in thought's conclusions. Since reasoning is (arguably) a series of thoughts culminating in a belief, language isn't necessary for reasoning, as Hume emphasized so long ago. Nor is language sufficient for thought. Importantly, reflection on racism and similar forms of socially unacceptable bias suggests that spontaneous assertion of a proposition is insufficient for belief, even when the subject feels sincere when saying what she does. The test, again, is action, not just words and feelings.[46]

Even when it is briefly reviewed from a distance, the understanding of animal life emerging from contemporary ethology undermines the intellectualist's emphasis on sentences, utterances, inscriptions, or propositions. We shouldn't limit our focus to discursive cognition or even its supposed analogs in the language of thought hypothesized by J. Fodor (1975).[47] A wolf's belief that she is sending a message to a group of coyotes by devouring their young isn't a "relation" to an inner symbol that means "I am sending a message to the coyotes by devouring their young." I mean, we might imagine a deranged human confederate of O-six killing the coyotes on the she-wolf's behalf. This human coyote-eater might mutter "I am sending a message to those coyotes by devouring

---

[46] See chapter 5 for further discussion. This is another reason to reject the de Sousa-Dennett-Frankish distinction between two types of belief. From a pragmatic perspective, assertions and dispositions to assert are not different kinds of belief, but defeasible evidence of the kind of belief humans share with other animals, however vague and partial it may be.

[47] For views of animal cognition that emphasize differences between the linguistic or proto-linguistic modes of thought employed by humans when reasoning from their beliefs in contrast with the graphic, iconic, pictorial, or otherwise distinct modes of cognition employed by other animals see Bermudez (2003), Camp (2007), Carruthers (2008), and Rescorla (2009). Camp provides a particularly effective response to Fodor's (1975) attempt to shop his Language of Thought hypothesis as the "only game in town." As she concludes, "Ultimately, any plausible cognitive system, including especially our own, is likely to be highly multi-modal: storing and manipulating information in the formats of multiple sensory modalities, and centralizing information in cartographic, diagrammatic, and sentential formats" (2007, 175). For a Fodorian reply see Blumson (September 2012). Cf. the "pragmatic" language of thought defended by Schneider (2011).

their young" as she executes this shocking act. And there are some similarities between the self-understanding guiding O-six in the case Safina describes and the mindset of this psychotic character. But these similarities are not well described by saying they both stand in the "belief relation" to one or more of the propositions we would use to describe what these two characters take themselves to be doing. We (author and reader) conceptualize their acts in similar ways. So it makes sense to say that we're gossiping about a single claim or proposition when we go on about the lady who ate those baby coyotes. But O-six's frame of mind lacks this determinacy. She does not grasp the claims we're circulating. Still, she knows what she's doing. So she's guided by belief.

Even the broader category of communicative acts—and the states of mind responsible for them—looks too narrow to capture those self-determined, creative behaviors that animals plan and execute in largely non-communicative contexts (Bermudez, 2003; van Schaik et al. 2013). Perception, memory, feeling, and emotion all conspire to guide an animal's purposive actions. It is reasonable to conjecture that these seemingly non-propositional states of mind actually *constitute* that animal's beliefs unless she takes steps to suppress them or ignore their promptings in an effort to assimilate information with which they conflict (cf. Glock, 2010). The wild diversity in the contents of those beliefs you attributed to yourself when answering the questions posed in this book's preface is testament to this. You have beliefs about who is funny and who depressing, where you're located and where you've been, how to win friends and why you should look both ways before crossing the street. There is little evidence that these beliefs are stored in a common neural structure or "belief box," much less one associated with your comprehension of those sentences you would use to report or express your opinions to others. Belief is not limited to non-sensory, phenomenologically anemic, "amodal" representation. Instead, information is stored where it is formed (Martin, 2009; Carruthers, 2015; Edmiston and Lupyan, 2017).[48]

---

[48] "The information about salient object properties—such as how they look, move, and are used, along with our affective associations to them—is stored in the neural systems that support perceiving, acting, and feeling. It is in this sense that conceptual knowledge is... grounded and embodied" Martin (2009, 1041). For another instance we have, "Long term memory of what things look like depends on perceptual mechanisms"; Edmiston and Lupyan (2017, 281). The general case is argued by Carruthers (2015).

It would seem, for these reasons, that Fodor's language of thought is an unstable halfway house between Descartes' intellectualism and the pragmatic approach to belief that emerged from philosophical reflection on Darwin's theory of evolution. While Bain's research program was rejected by the behaviorists, and ignored by those machine functionalists who took their zeal for artificial intelligence so far as to claim biology irrelevant to mentality, careful, relatively unbiased ethological observation is finally regaining its proper place within the study of the mind. And it strongly suggests that animal belief is much wider in scope and much more diverse in structure than even the Fodorians allow.

The Newtonian system is no longer the sole paradigm of natural science. Man need not be degraded to a machine by being denied to be a ghost in a machine. He might, after all, be a sort of animal, namely a higher [sic] mammal. There has yet to be ventured the hazardous leap to the hypothesis that perhaps he is a man.

(Ryle, 1949, 328)

But just how deep and diverse is animal belief? A mammal—say a piglet—will begin life "rehearsing nursing" in utero (Keven and Akins, 2016; cf. Dominici, 2011). As she begins to suck, swallow, and prepare for rooting, our prenatal piglet will initiate efforts that depend for their success on an environment appropriately fitted to their execution. Can we then say that the piglet expects to find, upon delivery, a proper target for her prenatal behavior, however instinctual her initial interactions with her mother (or bottle) turn out to be? Does the instinct in question itself constitute, entrain, or arise from her belief that she will find something to suck and swallow upon delivery?

Some theorists say "yes." For example, Dennett (1995) has argued that phototropism is best explained by saying that plants believe that sunlight is coming from the direction toward which they grow (cf. van Duijn, Keijzer, and Franken, 2006). Plants don't just react to the sun. "Leaf laminas reorient during the night toward sunrise, and are able to retain such anticipatory behavior for a number of days in the absence of solar tracking" (Garzón and Keijzer, 2011, 165). And this is not the only plant behavior to pique the interest of evolutionary psychologists. Darwin was sufficiently impressed by the intelligent growth of a plant's roots to compare them to an animal's brain.

It is hardly an exaggeration to say that the tip of the radicle thus endowed, and having the power of directing the movements of the adjoining parts, acts like the brain of one of the lower animals; the brain being seated within the anterior end of the body, receiving impressions from the sense-organs, and directing the several movements.   (Darwin, 1880, 574; cf. Garzón and Keijzer, 2011, 161)

The plant's roots navigate obstacles as they tunnel for water, and its branches stretch themselves out in search of the sun. The plant's biochemistry orchestrates its endeavors in these directions. Mightn't this biochemistry support an alien from of consciousness? The hypothesis excites the imagination.

Consider, on this score, recent research done at the University of Missouri showing how the Arabidopsis plant discriminates the precise pattern of vibrations that caterpillars make when eating its leaves. In response to these tickling marauders, the Arabidopsis produces mustard oil to defend its leafy integrity. The headlines announcing this discovery are great. The *Farm Journal* reads, "Plants Can Hear Pests Attack." *Business Week* concludes, "Researchers Have Found that Plants Know When They're Being Eaten."[49] Nor are agents of the popular press the only purveyors of provocative promiscuous attributions of cognitive capacity. Several of our leading philosophers of mind—Thomas Nagel, Galen Strawson, and David Chalmers—take seriously the possibility that inorganic matter has sentience of some kind.[50]

One guiding idea here, embraced by Dennett in a great deal of his writing on this subject, is that "belief" is an instrumentalist or "interpretationist" concept. Roughly speaking, an organism or "system" believes something just in case it can be fruitfully interpreted as believing that thing, where the system's internal structure places no independent constraints on our efforts to determine which interpretations are fruitful and which are not. There is a sense in which the neural structure that realizes the piglet's rooting instinct can be fruitfully interpreted as the belief that she will find an udder or nipple or what I have been calling an "appropriate target" for her behavior upon delivery. The piglet therein has this belief,

---

[49] See http://www.businessinsider.com/plants-know-they-are-being-eaten-2014-10, http://modernfarmer.com/2014/10/plants-can-tell-theyre-eaten/, http://www.agweb.com/article/plants-can-hear-pests-attack/, and http://www.newyorker.com/magazine/2013/12/23/the-intelligent-plant.

[50] Dennett (1981), Nagel (1979, 181–95), Strawson (2009), and Chalmers (2015). Cf. Bruntrup and Jaskolla (2016). Contemporary panpsychism is summarily dismissed by Kornblith (2012, 50–1).

however greatly it differs in biological and experiential terms from a mature adult's conviction that the earth revolves around the sun.[51]

In contrast, the pragmatic definition I proposed above issues a negative answer. "Belief" is appropriately limited in its application to the information that guides relatively attentive, controlled action, and the prenatal piglet has not yet acquired the agency requisite for this form of activity. She must first interact with her mother (or bottle) and use perceptual feedback gleaned from her initial endeavors to gain control over her feeding before we can say that she is bringing beliefs to bear on the task.[52] After she has gained some level of mastery over the process, she can then "outsource" it to some extent—dividing her attention—as she would were she to continue to nurse while fending off siblings competing for the relevant resource.

The act of Sucking is generally said to be purely reflex in the newborn infant. The act of swallowing remains reflex to the last. But . . . the giving over sucking, when there is no longer relish, is volition in the germ . . . whatever be the exact moment when a present feeling first influences a present action, that is the moment of the birth of volition. We reach this point by inward growth. Having reached it, the education of the will is thenceforth a process actually begun, and ready for improvement.   (Bain, 1859/1865, 320–1)

There are, of course, other options beyond intellectualism, pragmatism, and panpsychism. For instance, though behaviorism has long lost its grip on social science, some contemporary philosophers follow Gilbert Ryle (1949/2012) in equating belief with a "multi-track" disposition to move and feel certain ways given certain stimuli (e.g., Schwitzgebel, 2001a).

---

[51] Where does this stop? Though bacteria lack nervous systems, they contain a two-component signal transduction system mediating between the chemical stimuli to which they are exposed and their motor responses to these stimuli: e.g. swimming or tumbling (Taylor, 2004). We might then consider the idea that the five hundred (or more) species of bacteria said to be living in our guts interact with one another on the basis of their beliefs in much the way that we interact with one another on the basis of ours (van Dujin, Keijzer, and Franken, 2006). Are we responsible for the denizens of our inner bacterial ecosystems? Is inessential use of antibiotics immoral? Is it comparable to killing animals for sport? Can you entertain the possibility of these tiny intestinal agents without wondering, with Spinoza, whether the universe is itself an organism whose "gut" we modify?

[52] It has long been known that human infants copy mouth movements within the first hour of birth. See Metzoff and Moore (1997). But researchers continue to debate whether this is intentional, controlled activity, or the kind of resonance behavior displayed by flocks of birds and schools of fish, which coordinate their movements in what is supposed to be a relatively automatic fashion. See Jeannerod (2006, 122–4).

These are just *quasi*-behaviorists: they assure us they believe in the existence and explanatory importance of sensations, feelings, and other "phenomenally conscious" states. They do not limit their theorizing to an animal's movements through space and its dispositions to such. But those who have embraced the neo-behaviorist label view beliefs and intentions as "theoretical posits," and they deny the need to include concepts of attention and self-control in their analyses. And in this they depart from Bain and the pragmatists he inspired, who all insisted that controlled action must be distinguished from automatic reaction in the analysis of belief.

[Readiness] to act in a certain way under given circumstances and when actuated by a given motive is a habit; and a deliberate, or self-controlled, habit is precisely a belief.   (Peirce, 1931–5, 5.480, 330)

The pragmatists would also quarrel with the neo-behaviorist focus on sensory, affective, and motor *dispositions*, which passively await some triggering stimulus. As Bain emphasized, we are born doing things of our own accord. Unless you're a teenager (or depressed) you don't *need* an argument to get you out of bed in the morning. You awake in action, opening your eyes or deliberately keeping them shut. "We are active beings from the start" (Dewey, 1896, 239). Indeed, even if you are a languishing teen, you're probably doing *something* while you wile away the morning hours in the sack. (Snicker, snicker.) As Oscar Wilde noted with characteristic aplomb, "Doing nothing at all is the most difficult thing in the world, the most difficult and the most intellectual" (1891/2007, 174). As those skilled in meditation can attest, we must work hard to refrain from moving and thinking. We are not limited to responses, much less rigid reactions to stimuli arriving from without (Hampshire, 1959, 47–8). Our beliefs can be gleaned from our impact on history, not its impact on us.

Happily, after its long, cold behaviorist winter, the academy is gradually recovering this pragmatic understanding of "cognition."

Behaviorism...presented animals as passive, whereas I view them as seeking, wanting and striving. True, their behavior changes based on its consequences, but they never act randomly or accidentally to begin with. Let's take the dog and her ball. Throw a ball at a puppy, and she will go after it like an eager predator. The more she learns about prey and their escape tactics—or about you and your fake throws—the better a hunter or fetcher she will become. But still, at the root of everything is her immense enthusiasm for the pursuit, which takes her through shrubs, into water, and sometimes through glass doors.   (de Waal, 2016, 30–1)

Bain was way ahead of this emphasis on our "enthusiasm for the pursuit." Our initial actions are not responses at all, but the results of our "spontaneous passing through the usual stages into the voluntary" (1859/1865, 325).

Movement precedes sensation, and is at the outset independent of any stimulus from without; and that action is a more intimate and inseparable property of our constitution than any of our sensations ... the facts of the case are so strong as not to be easily gainsaid. Perhaps the most striking are those furnished by the initial movements of infancy, and the restless activity of early years generally, and of the young and active members of the brute creation. The bustling and bounding spirit of exercise, in these instances, is out of all proportion to any outward stimulants, and can be accounted for only by a central fire that needs no stirring from without ... We see this well illustrated in the daily experience of children, whose exuberance is manifested at their first awakening in the morning, after meals, and on release from lessons. On all such occasions, we see evidently nothing else than the discharge of an accumulated store of inward energy. It is not any particular incitement from without that is the cause of all this vehemence. The effect is explosive, like a shot, or the bursting of a floodgate. It would not be difficult at those moments, indeed it would be the natural course of events, to perform some great feat. The boy let out from school, incontinently leaps over ditches, breaks down barriers, and displaces heavy bodies, and should these operations be required at the moment, no special or extraordinary stimulus would be needed to bring the requisite power into play.   (Bain, 1859/1865, 297–305; cf. 12)

Bain defines belief in terms of the paths we blaze with this "central fire." In favorable conditions, our initial movements are rewarded with pleasure and nourishment and comfort and love. We strive to sustain these goods, improve upon them, and guard against the pain, hunger, and illness that invariably threaten whatever happiness we've secured. What we believe is whatever information we bring to bear in these endeavors. "What we believe, we act upon" (Bain, 1868/1884, 372).[53]

---

[53] "In the primitive aspect of volition, which also continues to be exemplified through the whole of life, an action once begun by spontaneous accident is maintained, when it sensibly alleviates a pain, or nurses a pleasure. Here there is no place for belief, any more than for plot-interest, deliberation, resolution, or desire. The feeling, that is, the end, prompts at once the suitable exercise of the voluntary organs, and that is all. In this primitive and elementary fact, we have the foundation of the most complicated forms of voluntary procedure, but as yet we have no indication of those subsequent developments. The process in that rudimentary stage might be termed reflex, although differing in almost vital consideration from the reflex actions commonly recognized, namely the presence of consciousness as an essential link of the sequence. There is an instantaneous response to the state of pleasure or pain, in the shape of some voluntary movement modifying, or sustaining that state, according as the case may be. Circumstances arise, however, to prevent this immediateness of response, or to interpose delay between the occurrence of the feeling that

But then how is belief to be distinguished from desire? According to the pragmatic analysis, we first form beliefs by paying attention to our mothers or caregivers and doing what we can to control or guide our rather clumsy attempts to nurse from them or the bottles of formula they supply. The information that guides us in these most basic actions is the very first information we believe. And the same is indeed true of our first desires: the needs we feel for nourishment, comfort, and the like. The attribution to the infant of a "desire to nurse" grows in propriety as she begins to train her attention on her caregivers and channels her energies towards securing a satisfying engagement with them. So doesn't Bain's definition classify these desires as "beliefs"? To avoid this paradoxical conclusion, must we join the intellectualists in augmenting Bain's definition with some reference to truth?[54]

is the motive and the movements that answer to it . . . the very same condition of suspense is necessary to the manifestation of Belief. If every pain could be met by an appropriate movement for relieving it on the instant, and the same with pleasure, we might still talk of doing or action, but there would be no place for believing" (Bain, 1859/1865, 524–5; cf. Bain, 1859/1865, 507 and Bain, 1888, 505–6). Note that the ability to generate activity endogenously is part of some contemporary definitions of "nervous system." See, e.g., Lichtneckert and Reichert (2007).

[54] I thank an anonymous referee for Oxford University Press for pressing this objection, but I must comment here on the inaccuracy inherent in the common practice of labeling this concern "Humean" in orientation. According to Hume, beliefs are "forceful and vivacious" ideas. His paradigms are memories and expectations: ideas that have a characteristic experiential quality (vivacity) and a heavy influence on subsequent thought, experience, and behavior (force). Hume also countenances "perfect ideas" which lack force and vivacity, and are what psychologists would now call semantic or declarative memories: mere acceptance of some claim separable from any accompanying imagery and direct behavioral potential beyond assertion and affirmation. And Hume's category of "impressions" is meant to include sensations (in all the sensory modalities) and composites of sensations and ideas, which composites Hume called "impressions of reflection": desires, emotions, plans, and passions of various other sorts. In contrast with Hume, the analytic philosophers who cleanly distinguish beliefs from desires treat desires (or preferences) as "propositional attitudes." You can believe that you have a cold glass of milk or desire that you have one, and since the "propositional content" of these states of mind is the same, analytic philosophers of mind typically posit differing "attitudes"—marked by "belief" and "desire"—to label their functional or causal differences, this being comparable to the "force" of which Hume spoke. (Most analytic philosophers deem inessential the phenomenological differences Hume marked with "vivacity.") The most popular proposal is to liken a difference in attitude to two different "boxes" which both feature a single language of thought sentence: e.g. "I have a glass of milk" (Fodor, 1975). When "I have a glass of milk" is written in a being's belief box, she is "satisfied" in some non-phenomenological sense of this term; when it is instead written in her desire box, she initiates a search for the stuff. Note that this way of thinking makes it seem as though desires *are* representations—i.e. language of thought sentences—albeit with "satisfaction conditions" rather than conditions of truth or accuracy.

No, the retreat to intellectualism is not forced upon us, as the equation of certain kinds of desire with certain kinds of belief has an illustrious past and substantial current following. As the medieval philosophers emphasized, we typically desire under the "guise of the good" (McCann, 2001). When it seems appropriate to describe the infant as "wanting to nurse" it would seem equally appropriate to describe her as representing this activity as pleasurable or nourishing or *good* for her in some way (cf. Proust, 2015a).[55] And when it seems right to say that she has developed an aversion to her siblings' interruptions, it will consequently seem right to describe her as representing these rude breaks from her meals as annoying, or detrimental, or as "bad" in some shape or form. Desire is no more a "mere" behavioral disposition than is belief (Quinn, 1993). Desire is as much a frame of mind—as much a representation of the world and one's place in it—as any thing we discriminate in folk psychological discourse.

Is the desire to nurse, then, a "confused" representation of value, as Plato's Socrates once proposed? Does its perfection await the child's mastery of language or the tools she needs to conceptualize the object of her affections? Hardly. The positive correlation between obtaining nourishment and surviving to reproduce provides no small basis on which to grant these distinctively mammalian conative representations a positive review. In desiring to nurse, the piglet or infant child believes to be good for her what is in fact good for her in a biological sense of that term. In developing an aversion to the interruptions of her siblings, the little beast comes to believe to be bad for her what is in fact bad for her in this same biological sense. And though we come to want much of what is biologically detrimental or "bad" for us in the varying (non-biological) senses people come to attach to this term, our mature, more fully

And this marks a substantive departure from Hume's taxonomy, which instead treats desires as impressions "annexed" to ideas: the idea being a representation of the desired state of affairs (e.g. my having milk) and the impression being the forceful and vivacious attraction that has become associated with this idea. Hume doesn't similarly treat belief as an impression—e.g. a feeling of conviction—that is "annexed" to an idea representing what is believed, though he famously agonized over this decision in his Treatise's first appendix. As far as the history goes, I join the pragmatists in thinking Bain's definition an improvement over Hume's, but I break with many in the analytic tradition (e.g. Brandom, 2009) in thinking reductive functionalism a backward step.

[55] Though Proust provides an attractive account of the content of the feelings she characterizes as "affordance representations," she assumes the traditional propositional attitude analysis of belief.

articulated desires can still be described as roughly accurate representations of the varying species of value we learn to differentiate.

> Questions of ultimate ends do not admit of proof, in the ordinary acceptation of the term . . . the sole evidence it is possible to produce that anything is desirable, is that people do actually desire it.   (Mill, 1863/2002, 269–70)

In this way, the pragmatic scheme nicely captures the kind of conflict we experience when we struggle to act prudently. The desire for late night ice cream represents to be good for you what you know to be bad. This is why you feel pressure to rationalize taking another scoop, if you are not prepared to pass on the carton. In wanting it, you construe it as delicious, and it's hard to fully discount this consideration as the evening wears on.

When a person pursues some end while acting in a controlled, attentive way, we can conclude that she desires that state of affairs in a certain distinctive sense: we mark this by saying that she believes it to be good in some respect or other. But if we suppose that she instinctively responds to the activity or object in a positive fashion—that she is immediately attracted to it to some degree—but that she avoids it when in full possession of her faculties, we will then say she desires it in a sense that does not obviously entail evaluative belief. She will have a mere appetite for it, or a "passion" she must control in service of her "reason." The examples of this most commonly cited by the philosophical and religious authorities are lust, a taste for sugar, overindulgence in drugs and alcohol, and a similar thirst for money, prestige, and power over others. Not that you can buy a shot of tequila, open a package of donuts or dominate a conversation without controlling your words and deeds. But the mind of a conflicted profligate fluctuates between habitual use, events that bring to mind a vivid understanding of its costs to health and family, resolutions to reform, and a strongly felt attraction (or "craving") for the object of experience. Pragmatism endorses this entirely commonplace description of our entirely commonplace struggles to be good or prudent. Beliefs are the representations that guide our deliberate movements in body and mind. Some desires are beliefs of this sort. Some are not.[56]

---

[56] The critical reader might compare and contrast this traditional distinction between evaluative beliefs and "mere" desires with H. Frankfurt's (1971) distinction between first- and second-order volitions, G. Watson's (1975) distinction between desires and values, T. Nagel's (1979) distinction between motivated and unmotivated desires, and a number of other proposals.

4

Belief and Pretense

Nothing can be set forth as belief that does not implicate in some
way or other the order, arrangements, or sequences of the universe.
Not merely the sober and certain realities of every man's experience, but also superstitions, dreams, vagaries, that have found
admittance among the most ignorant and misled of human beings,
are conversant with the same field. When we people the air with
supernatural beings, and fill the void of nature with demons, ghosts,
and spirits; when we practice incantations, auguries, charms, and
sacrificial rites, we are victims of a faith as decided and strong as our
confidence in the most familiar occurrences of our daily life. In all
such cases, the genuineness of the state of belief is tested by the
control of the actions, while the subject-matter of it is some supposed fact, or occurrence, of nature ... we must not depart from
their reference to action, and the attainment of ends, otherwise they
lose their fundamental character as things credited, and pass into
mere fancies, and the sport of thinking.

(Bain, 1859/1865, 526–7)

If belief is a disposition to use information to guide our actions, the
explanation of why we cannot just believe whatever we want to believe
cannot be extracted from belief's definition. But this failure is compatible
with the existence of irresistible beliefs. According to most psychologists
and philosophers, we begin life with relatively innate behavioral and
cognitive instincts, which give rise to relatively innate expectations that
we ineluctably extend upon observing regularities in our environments
(Spelke, 1994; Spelke and Kinzler, 2007). You can't stop believing in the
Earth beneath your feet, acknowledging the air you've breathed into your
lungs, and anticipating the downward trajectory of an object dropped
from above. As Hume noted,

We may well ask, "What causes induce us to believe in the existence of body?" but 'tis in vain to ask, "Whether there be body or not?" That is a point, which we must take for granted in all our reasonings.   (Hume, 1740/2000, 1.4.2.1)

Admittedly, skeptical epistemologists might be thought to provide an exception to Hume's observation. Can't I doubt the reality of those physical bodies I seemingly observe around me by telling myself I could be dreaming right now? Descartes claimed to pull this off, at least while staring into his fire in contemplation. Mightn't I be a brain in a vat stimulated by a supercomputer to have the sensory experiences I am now enjoying? We still ask such questions in our epistemology classes as a way of drawing attention to the fallibility of even our most reliable sources of belief and knowledge. But from a pragmatic perspective, the doubts in question are only psychologically real if they eventuate in madness.

A person may, it is true, in the course of his studies, find reason to doubt what he began by believing; but in that case he doubts because he has a positive reason for it, and not on account of the Cartesian maxim. Let us not pretend to doubt in philosophy what we do not doubt in our hearts.   (Peirce, 1868, 141)

To resist belief in the external world I would have to quash the assumptions that guide my deliberate movements through space. To maintain this state overtime would spell certain death. Reflex, instinct, and habit might serve other organisms just fine. But humans cannot survive and reproduce without exhibiting complex forms of agency, which in turn depend on our belief in each other and the environment in which we interact.[1]

The pragmatist insists, however, that the kind of irresistibility that attends our belief in physical bodies is not a feature of the class as a whole. Some beliefs are predictions you make from your hunches or informal assessments of the relative "strength" of the evidence available to you at the time. For example, many of us predict, and so believe with a significant degree of conviction, that the Earth's temperature will continue to rise for the foreseeable future; but many still do not (Borick and Rabe, 2010). And these beliefs seem to allow us more wiggle room or space for discretion. They invite talk of the "burdens of judgment" and the decision you made to either believe what seemed fairly well supported by the

---

[1] Descartes seems to have agreed, as in the Synopsis prefixed to his *Meditations* he writes, "No sane person has ever seriously doubted that there really is a world or that human beings have bodies." See Cottingham (1997, 36).

evidence, or to instead suspend conviction while you waited for more information to arrive. Since we often form beliefs we needn't have formed, and regularly fail to believe much of what we can believe, irresistibility has no place in the concept's definition.[2]

In things of experimental, inductive, or deductive certainty—the rise of tomorrow's sun, the flow of the tides, the mortality of living beings—there is no room for the influence of fluctuating states of feeling. Under the highest elation, and the deepest gloom, we count alike on these events. But, in the many cases where exact knowledge of the future cannot be had, we are at the mercy, not merely of conflicting appearances, but of our own changing moods. The prospective tranquility of Europe, the coming harvest, the issue of a great trading speculation, the behavior of some individual or body in matters affecting us, the recovery of a patient from critical illness—being unascertainable by any process with certainty, are termed cases of probable evidence, and we decide them differently at different times according to the aspect that turns up.

(Bain, 1859/1865, 544–5)

The man of much knowledge and experience, inured to reflection and to the handling of evidence, with habits of submission to proof, carries his tone of rational conviction a considerable way into the region of probability, reclaiming a larger track from the domain where the feelings of the moment give the cue; but in this, as in other things, there is only an approximation to the absolutely perfect. The soldier in a campaign, cherishing and enjoying life, is unmoved by the probability of being soon cut off. If, in spite of the perils of the field, he still continues to act in every respect as if destined to a good old age, his conviction is purely a quality of his temperament, and will be much less strong at those moments when hunger and fatigue have depressed his frame, or when the sight of dying and dead men has made him tremble with awe. I formerly quoted a happy expression of Arthur Helps, "where you know nothing, place terrors;" but, given the sanguine, buoyant, and courageous temperament; given youth, spirits, and intoxication; given a career of prosperity and success,—and where you know nothing, you will place high hopes. Under this hypothesis of no positive evidence, elevation of tone and belief of good to come, are the same fact.

(Bain, 1888, 523–4)

Of course, logicians, philosophers, rabid atheists, skeptics, and other epistemic scolds are free to insist that our evidence-transcendent beliefs are irrational. Perhaps we can allow the more rigorous among their

---

[2] It is compatible with this that no one can believe something while simultaneously believing that she is sustained in her belief by factors *entirely* unconnected to the truth of what she believes. For defense of this more limited thesis see Winters (1979) and Hoyer (1983); cf. van Fraassen (1984).

number a sense of "should" according to which we should limit ourselves to those degrees of credence we cannot resist and those we can derive from this basic class by reasoning in accordance with Bayes's theorem or some similarly vetted "credence update rule." But this is a normative claim that needs to be defended on normative (or value-laden) grounds. As against it, we might side with James's observation that, "The most interesting and valuable things about a man are his ideals and over-beliefs...the agnostic 'thou shalt not believe without coercive sensible evidence' is simply an expression (free to any one to make) of private personal appetite for evidence of a certain peculiar kind" (1896/1912, xiii–56). The skeptics overreach when they bake their normative views about which beliefs we ought to hold into the nature of belief itself.[3]

Now some distinction must be drawn between belief and pretense. Merely saying that you believe in God and heaven doesn't make it so. Nor is acting as though you believe something the same as believing it. But the difference between acting as though you believe something and *really* believing it can be characterized in many different ways. And those characterizations that do focus on a difference in control needn't go "all in." Perhaps we have less control over our beliefs than we do over most if not all of our acts and assertions, but we can nevertheless exercise some discretion over the former in favorable cases.

I say that our beliefs are less malleable than "most" of our physical actions because there exist a range of mechanically possible behaviors that we cannot intentionally execute. More precisely, there are actions we are prevented from performing by obstacles that are just as "internal" to our minds as those doxastic scruples which prevent us from forming beliefs we judge to be contravened by the evidence in our possession. I can't kill myself by holding my breath. Indeed, I can't intentionally kill

---

[3] Davidson was perhaps the most egregious "essentializer" of the normative. He claimed, for instance, that, "it does not make sense to ask, concerning a creature with propositional attitudes, whether that creature is in general rational, whether its attitudes and intentional actions are in accord with the basic standards of rationality. Rationality, in this primitive sense, is a condition of having any thoughts at all" (2004, 196). But Velleman (2000) is a close second. For a related criticism of the instrumental norms codified by formal decision theory—namely, that they are inappropriately interpreted by their purveyors as simultaneously descriptive and normative—see Korsgaard (1986), though Korsgaard makes a similar move when treating Kant's categorical imperatives as both norms and conceptual constraints on the classification of behavior as action. For an empirically motivated rejection of normative essentialism with regard to belief see Bortolotti (2009).

myself at all except by "losing" my mind: by becoming profoundly depressed, self-loathing, or psychotic. So while it's true that I can't come to believe in the presence of a giant pink elephant without the aid of drugs and torture, this does not reflect a distinction in kind between belief and action. And this confirms the conceptual link between belief and behavior that pragmatists emphasize: I can't rid myself of my most basic expectations without therein killing myself. My inability to kill myself with a knife without first willing myself to become deranged is of a piece with my inability to adopt a skeptical or solipsistic mindset without first signing off on an end to it all. We know that the Samurai employed ritual suicide—seppuku—in response to shame. And terrorists have been blowing themselves up at a depressing rate. But are these behaviors supposed to be more rational or more easily understood than belief in the healing power of crystals or the fortune-telling abilities of Miss Cleo? They aren't from a biological perspective.

So pragmatists can allow that some or even most of our beliefs are involuntarily adopted and involuntarily revised or "updated" in light of new experience, testimony, and other forms of evidence. The qualified thesis the pragmatist embraces is just that "One may [also] obtain *some* beliefs by directly willing to have them": a thesis labeled "voluntarism" by L. Pojman (1985, 38) and attributed to such philosophical luminaries as St. Thomas Aquinas, John Locke, Søren Kierkegaard, Cardinal Newman, William James, Josef Pieper, Roderick Chisholm, and Jack Meiland. A. Chignell (2011) adds Immanuel Kant to the list (cf. Montmarquet, 1986; Ginet, 2001 and Ryan, 2003). The pragmatic definition I introduced above articulates a conception of belief that is only "voluntarist" in this same limited sense. It is only when you have it within you to be consistently and stably guided by a piece of information in both your actions and deliberations that you have it within you to believe this information "at will."[4]

Of course, belief is not itself an action. We are driven by the expression's grammatical role to think of belief as a *state* of mind, not a transition in thought or movement. So understood, belief can't be performed; and if it can't be performed, it can't be performed voluntarily or "at will." There is

---

[4] For Bain's reflections on the legislation of belief and the degree of doxastic control this implies, see his note on "Responsibility for Belief" (Bain, 1859/1865, 522–3).

therefore a trivial sense in which belief is non-voluntary.[5] But our folk psychology recognizes various acts of belief-formation, entrenchment, retention, resurrection, and the like. At least from time to time, we draw conclusions, renew convictions, recall what we've learned, and change our opinions. And these acts are not invariably involuntary. The state of mind that results from such an act is not a passive assumption or unavoidable expectation. Nor is it the inevitable result of exposure to overwhelming evidence. Sometimes, a judge exercises her discretion. And in non-scientific contexts, she can often defend her act of believing beyond or beneath what the evidence seemed to strongly suggest.

The pragmatist can offer a similar response to the supposed "category mistake" inherent in the equation of beliefs with dispositions. There is, as Williams notes, something odd in describing a disposition as true or false.

> If somebody just has a habit of a certain kind, it is not appropriate to ask whether this habit of his is true or false, nor does that habit or disposition relate to something which can be called true or false.   (1973, 139)

But does this show, as Williams maintains, that beliefs are not dispositions and so not standing dispositions to utilize information in thought and action? No. It only shows that the word "belief" is not equivalent in usage to the word "disposition" and the other terms pragmatists employ when framing their definitions. The inequivalence of belief-talk and disposition-talk is what makes the analysis of belief in terms of dispositions of one or the other variety substantive or potentially enlightening in the way a litany of synonyms would not be. Belief is conviction, confidence, or credence. True enough. But we can improve upon the understanding of belief afforded to us by even the best thesaurus, so long as we are willing to engage in the necessary reflection.

Play involves belief. If an actor loses track of her movements through space or fails to draw on her knowledge of word meaning—if she suspends *all* perceptual judgment and lexical memory—she cannot

---

[5] This is not to be confused with Aristotle's notion of the "non-volunatry" which was meant to denote Oedipus' inadvertent incest. That intercourse involved a series of more or less controlled movements, which were thus "voluntary" in the dominant sense of the term. But since Oedipus did not suspect that Jocasta was his mother, the acts were not performed "as" acts of incest. They are therefore labeled "involuntary" in a derived sense better suited to assessing the propriety of various forms of punishment.

successfully engage in pretense. The same might be said of her beliefs about any "rules of play" she might articulate in advance, or the constraints on such she might extract from the improvisation as it unfolds over time. If you object when I stop your "bullets" with my wristbands, it's likely that you've forgotten that I'm playing Wonder Woman.[6]

Controversy only enters when we consider the body of information the actor is treating as true for the purposes of the game on hand. Is an actor fully immersed in her role as a murderer guided by the "information" that she's killed people? Intuitively speaking, she doesn't believe she has cause to repent, and our definition would be grossly deficient if it implied otherwise. But this is where its dispositional language—its talk of believers being "primed" to utilize information to guide their behavior—really comes into play. In the words of one of pragmatism's founding fathers, C.S. Peirce (1839–1914), "Belief does not make us act at once, but puts us into such a condition that we shall behave in some certain way, when the occasion arises" (1877, 5).[7] An actor has beliefs about the person she's pretending to be, beliefs about how her character would walk, talk, scheme, and respond to others were that character to walk, talk, scheme, and respond at all. These beliefs characterize at least some of the information that "guides" her movement and speech when she succeeds in pretending to be the person she has imagined. The same might be said of her beliefs about the world she has conjured, insofar as she is pretending to be somewhere or "somewhen" other than she is. But to define an actor's *beliefs* in terms of her occurrent thinking and action we need to evaluate what that actor would think and do in contexts in

---

[6] For a classical discussion of these and related phenomena see Walton (1990).

[7] "The difference between mere conceiving or imagining... and belief, is acting or being prepared to act when the occasion arises," Bain (1884, 372). "The readiness to act is thus what makes something more than fancy. We may act upon imperfect knowledge, but that knowledge must be believed by us. We may have perfect knowledge without acting on it; much of our highest theoretic knowledge is seldom reduced to practice. The reason is, not want of faith, but want of opportunity. The preparedness to act is still the only test of this highest kind of knowledge" (1888, 507). Bain connects this to Aristotle's distinction between potentiality and actuality (cf. Fisch 1954, 419). See too Ramsey's criticism of Bertrand Russell's analysis of mind: "[Russell] argues that in the course of trains of thought we believe many things which do not lead to action. This objection is however beside the mark, because it is not asserted that a belief is an idea which does actually lead to action, but one which would lead to action in suitable circumstances; just as a lump of arsenic is called poisonous not because it actually has killed or will kill anyone, but because it would kill anyone if he ate it" (1931, 169–70).

which she is not deliberately pretending. The actor doesn't believe she is a murderer insofar as she doesn't worry about revenge or incarceration for her pretended homicide when she isn't putting on a show. Indeed, if she did slip into these concerns, we would begin to question her sanity.

Consider, for instance, the method actor Daniel Day Lewis, who recently played the former U.S. President Abraham Lincoln in a major motion picture film and stayed in character throughout the shoot, insisting on being called "Mr. President" by the cast and crew, even when the cameras were off. What does it mean to say that Mr. Lewis "stayed in character"? He didn't ask about the smartphones on the set the way Lincoln would have were he to have found himself in Lewis's circumstances. Nor did Lewis sit with the film's director—Steven Spielberg—and sincerely inquire into the events that unfolded after "his" death. Who shot me? Was it really Booth? Acting alone? What happened to Mary and my surviving boy, young Thomas?

According to the pragmatic account proposed, these missing *dispositions* to inference and overt action are what distinguish Lewis's pretense, however "deep" it was, from genuine belief. When someone starts off pretending to be someone, and ends up employing the information that she is that person in a stable manner, in all or almost all of the voluntary actions and deliberations she engages in throughout the day, then pretense really has given way to belief. When such pretense is psychologically debilitating or too obviously false to be borne by her friends and acquaintances, the pretender is labeled "delusional."

An idea of the imagination may acquire such force and vivacity, as to pass for an idea of the memory, and counterfeit its effects on the belief and judgment. This is noted in the case of liars; who by frequent repetition of their lies, come at last to believe and remember them, as realities; custom and habit having in this case, as in many others, the same influence on the mind as nature, and infixing the idea with equal force and vigour.   (Hume, 1740/2000, 1.3.5.6)

Hume's observations are confirmed by contemporary findings. For example, researchers have found that statements read several times are more likely to be judged true than statements read just once even when all such statements are labeled fictions (Brainerd and Reyna, 2005). Repeating a message drums it home. A part repeatedly enacted tends to worm its way into an actor's self-conception.

If our novels are to be trusted, the Russian spy pretends to be an ordinary American by studying our suburban rituals and then enacting them to perfection. And if she hasn't gone rogue, the spy immediately does what's instructed when her handler makes contact. She is all along "primed" to act on his directions. But if she loses this mindset, if she becomes so disposed that she would respond to the Kremlin's call with exasperation or confusion, she has come to believe what she previously just pretended. Agents who lose themselves in this way perfectly illustrate Hume's contention that pretense can evolve into belief. A good mole blends in without losing those beliefs that supply her identity and mission. But a person can forget who she is. We are all vulnerable to delusion.[8]

The confounding of ideas of Imagination with ideas of Memory [is] one great cause of illusion and delusion. Occasions arise when the ideas of Imagination take on something of the vivacity and circumstantiality of ideas of the Memory, and a mind disqualified by emotion for fine distinctions is led to confound the two. In a less excited state of mind, the difference would be felt.   (Bain, 1888, 522)

Of course, there are many different kinds of delusion, and some have relatively clear neurological causes and correlates. T. Stone and A.W. Young (1997) review a number of species, but focus on Capgras syndrome, a pathological failure of recognition. More precisely, a patient is diagnosed with Capgras when brain lesions induce aberrant emotional reactions to her visual perception of someone familiar to her, and a patently irrational cognitive response to these aberrant experiences. When the Capgras patient looks at a familiar person, that person is seen as unfamiliar and on this incredibly weak evidence judged an imposter (cf. Langdon and Coltheart, 2000). (I harp on the "visual experience" part of this because the sound of a loved one's voice doesn't have the same effect.) Does the typical Capgras patient really believe that her husband or brother has been replaced with a qualitatively similar duplicate? Well, she will assert this claim in seeming sincerity and defend her assertion when pressed.[9] Some patients even grow violent. In a subsequent review, Young (2000) describes the horrifying consequences.

One of Christodoulou's (1977) patients reported to the police that her husband had died and been replaced by an identical-looking man; she put on black

---

[8] See the continuity thesis defended by Bortolotti (2009).

[9] Rose, Buckwalter, and Turri (2014) argue that "the folk" are willing to attribute belief on this basis.

mourning clothes, refused to sleep with the double and angrily ordered him out of the house, shouting "go to your own wife." In other reported incidents, a man who believed that his family had been replaced by clones used a toy gun to force a television newscaster to read out a statement about the substitution, and a man who believed wicked people had moved into the bodies of his family shot his father and his nephew, killing one and seriously wounding the other (Silva, Leong, Weinstock and Boyer, 1989). De Pauw and Szulecka (1988) noted a particularly chilling incident in which a patient accused his stepfather of being a robot and decapitated him to look for batteries and microfilm in his head.

If actions reflect the strength of one's convictions, there can be no doubting the sincerity of these patients. A review of 260 cases of delusional misidentification by Förstl et al. (1991) found that physical violence had been noted in 46 cases (18%).

But what about the other 82 percent? It seems that Capgras rarely leads to murder. Most patients don't even search for the loved ones they claim to miss. And why not? Are they prevented from doing so by their knowledge that everyone thinks they are crazy to believe what they do? That sort of disapprobation wouldn't lead me to give up the search for my wife. Nor would it stop me from looking into the plot that eventuated in the bizarre placement of her doppelgänger in our home. In consequence, many cases of Capgras seem to invite a "three-factor" analysis. Brain lesions induce: (i) an irregular affective response to seeing a familiar person, (ii) distortions in reasoning that lead subjects to conclude from this that the familiar person has been replaced or duplicated, (iii) and a more or less firm dissociation between their verbal defense of these claims on the one hand, and the non-verbal actions that would otherwise accompany them.

Does Capgras then provide reasons for distinguishing in kind between articulate opinions and behaviorally efficacious beliefs? Does it support the intellectualist's distinction between human states of acceptance and non-human degrees of credence?[10] No. There is a spectrum of Capgras cases and they intermingle discursive and non-discursive symptoms in a manner that tells against the proposal. In some cases, the brain lesions that lead to aberrant affect—and the consequent feeling of unreality surrounding a familiar face—fail to induce a delusional judgment of any kind, and those suffering from these phenomenological irregularities

---

[10] See Dub (2015). As noted above, this distinction is drawn by de Sousa (1971), Dennett (1978/1981), and Frankish (2004) among others.

tend not to be diagnosed with Capgras.[11] In cases that are so diagnosed, lesions induce the two factors identified by Stone and Young: affective distortion and some proclivity toward interpreting it in bizarre ways: "He looks like my husband, but it doesn't feel right. He must be an impostor." In these cases the patient's best attempt to explain what she's feeling leads her to embrace a patent falsehood, despite the disapproval and social sanctions this provokes (Coltheart, Menzies, and Sutton, 2010). In some cases the patient acknowledges that her story sounds crazy and that she wouldn't believe it if she didn't have the intuitive evidence made manifest to her when she looks at the purported imposter, but in other cases, the patient lacks this kind of self-awareness. In the vast majority of cases in which a patient reveals in speech that she is fully convinced of the plot, this doesn't lead her into a full-blown meltdown. But as Young's report makes clear, this does in fact happen in a non-trivial percentage of cases. So the cases span the spectrum. From a pragmatic perspective, we should therefore conclude that Capgras typically induces "partial belief," where, again, this expression is used in a non-classical sense that must be distinguished from whatever quantity is measured by assessments of how much subjects are willing to bet on the truth of a given claim. The belief is partial when its content guides a substantive but restricted set of those actions to which it is relevant, so long as this restriction is not intentional in the way it is when we merely accept a claim for the sake of argument, inference, or investigation.[12]

Do (non-delusional) children at play constitute a counterexample to the pragmatic analysis of belief? S. Nichols and S. Stich (2000) convincingly argue that children lost in their imaginations are directly guided by states of the same.[13] Pretending is itself a more or less direct expression of a child's fantasies; it is not exclusively guided by the child's beliefs about the pretense and the actual environment in which she enacts it, nor by her desire to be playing a game with the features she bestows

---

[11] See Turner and Coltheart (2010). It has been suggested that "déjà vu" is a non-pathological experience of duplication from which "healthy" people do not infer that they're really repeating a past event. See Connor and Moulin (2010).

[12] For a complementary diagnosis, which employs a neurological analysis to transcend the debate between doxastic and non-doxastic accounts of delusions, see Gerrans (2013). Cf. Bayne and Pacherie (2005), Egan (2009), and Bortolotti (2012).

[13] See too Nichols (2006a), Nichols (2006b), Schroeder and Matheson (2006), and Weinberg and Meskin (2006). For alternative accounts see Friedman et al. (2010) and Langland-Hassan (2012).

upon it.[14] Must we then invoke some further—non-action-guiding—property to distinguish beliefs from states of imagination?

It should be clear to all of those debating this question that we needn't choose between an explanation of child's play couched entirely in terms of belief and another couched entirely in terms of imagination (Nichols and Stich, 2003, 51–2). Children at play simultaneously act from their imaginations and modify their beliefs about the pretense in which these imaginations figure. The same is true of the other animals, whose behavior makes clear the origins of pretense in practice. To play is to learn in relative safety; to prepare for adulthood, when the real game begins.

In pretense play, two realities are held concurrently in mind: the log is both a newborn in need of care and a mere piece of wood to be abandoned when the game is over. Similarly, a kitten stalking and chasing a feather is not going to eat it as it would prey.   (de Waal, 1999, 263–4)[15]

Of course not all preparatory play involves imagination to the same extent. De Waal's kitten is learning to hunt with a feather, his ape rehearsing childcare with a log. The juvenile cat imagines her toy as prey, just as the young primate endows her prop with the character of offspring. In contrast, pups and rowdy children often learn to fight and hunt by wrestling and sparring and chasing each other down. Often, the youngsters imagine they're engaging in a real fight between superheroes

---

[14] Cf. Velleman (2000, 257–60) and Walton (1990). Though Nichols and Stich are right in viewing a non-doxastic representation as the proximate source or guide of pretense, I am not convinced that anything is gained by positing a "Possible Worlds Box" alongside a "Belief Box" to explain imaginative play. The pragmatic account posits one "box" here: the brain or nervous system. All of the accessible information stored within it *can* constitute an animal's beliefs or her pretenses. The difference between the two is entirely constituted by the range of attentive thoughts and controlled actions a given body of information is "primed" to influence.

[15] The fact that animals play at being grown up answers those questions about the function of pretense raised by Nichols and Stich (2003, 38). There is real biological value to practicing childcare and hunting without worry of losing out on real prey or killing one's actual offspring. See too Currie (1995). Animal play also raises at least prima facie doubts about the utility of the Fodorian approach. Surely, pretense begins with imagination, and imagination begins with imagery, not words. As the authors acknowledge, "If it turns out that some of the mental representations subserving belief and pretense are not quasi-linguistic, the notion of logical form might need to supplemented by some notion which plays a role in explaining how such representations are manipulated by the inference mechanism" (Nichols and Stich, 2003, 33–4, fn. 8).

or army men or cowboys and Indians or colonists and colonized. But they needn't. They can instead just wrestle for the fun of it, without engaging in fantasy. It is the absence of props that opens up this possibility. But it would be wrong to think that meta-level beliefs about the pretense are then rendered inactive. Each participant must remember that she is only playing; otherwise the kids risk fighting in earnest. When one party loses confidence that the other is play fighting, the game ends, the gloves come off, and a real brawl ensues.

Pretense typically involves this kind of reflective awareness of the game and its boundaries (Leslie, 1987). A kid pretending to be an elephant has no problem incorporating you into her drama by assigning you a role or function within the story. And if the child is at all bossy she will act out her part while simultaneously directing the actions of those with whom she is playing. "No," she corrects a friend, "We agreed you're the zookeeper, not a monkey. That's not supposed to be a banana, you're feeding me peanuts." Of course, the constraints imposed by an implicit script are "soft" or open for debate (Nichols and Stich, 2003, 35). I mean, why can't this particular zoo have a monkey manager? And mightn't a monkey zookeeper mistakenly feed the elephants bananas? In my experience, some children (most children?) actually prefer setting, stretching, and updating the rules of play—or adding "backstory"—to physically enacting the plot. (Future writers or directors to be sure.) Setting the rules of play with a receptive audience is the most effective way for everyone involved to coordinate their beliefs about who is playing whom and to what purpose. These beliefs provide the "frame" within which states of imagination are then permitted to run their course. The distinction between belief and pretense is secured by the "causal" (i.e. functional or behavioral) limits set by each player's acceptance of an implicit script of this sort. Our beliefs are typically unconstrained in their effects on our deliberate thoughts and actions. Our states of imagination are not. A desire for accurate representation needn't play a part in this.

The implicit script is but one element of the overall sense of reality limiting the efficaciousness of those states of imagination that fall short of belief (Abelson, 1981; Harris, 1993). A more or less well-developed child won't just snort and shake her "trunk" if you ask her in a serious tone whether she just hit one of her playmates. She'll avoid the question, avert her eyes, protest her innocence, or reluctantly apologize and agree to "hug it out." Thus, the information the child is using to guide her game—her imaginative representation of herself as an elephant—is not "poised" to direct her responses to those stimuli she knows are coming from outside the field of play. Most children, even those little Walter Mittys who most fully lose themselves in glorious afternoons of idle fantasy, distinguish pretense from reality in these modestly sophisticated ways. And those children who cannot—those who cannot step out of character, even when serious consequences attend their failure to do so— really have fallen prey to a delusional belief, even if the delusion is relatively momentary, and the fantasy is clearly distinguished as such before threats of punishment are brought to bear. This is an intuitive consequence that needn't embarrass the pragmatist.

Something similar is true of simpler, more solitary forms of play. If a two-year-old playing elephant breaks a vase, she won't just incorporate this into the game without some distinctively non-elephantine recognition that she's done something to which her caregivers are averse. Again, there may be some "delay" if she is reluctant to disengage from the pretense and confront reality, but a disposition to experience this distinctively non-elephantine reaction distinguishes her from both the toddler who just blunders about without engaging in anything as sophisticated as pretense and the genuinely delusional youngster who must be reminded of her humanity. Correlatively, even a very young child playing elephant won't intentionally crush everything in the room, even if she believes that's what an elephant would do. However deep the pretense, the non-delusional child remains somewhat cognizant of what's permissible in the context at hand.

And the same might be said of assumptions we (adults) make for the sake of argument or the premises we accept only to see where they lead. The information these sentences encode guides a limited range of our attentive, self-controlled deliberations: a class that is more or less clearly delineated in the minds of those who know what they are doing when reasoning in these ways.

But might a state of acceptance guide *precisely* those behaviors we have identified as manifestations of partial belief? Consider the partial beliefs of the Capgras patient described above who reasons and acts on the hypothesis that her loved one has been exchanged with an impostor, but only does so in a limited number of relevant contexts. Suppose, for instance, that she insists the switch has taken place but that she doesn't look for her spouse. Now imagine a hypothetical detective who adopts the patient's story as a theory—jotting down "loved one replaced with an impostor"—but just for the sake of investigating the story more fully. Mightn't the detective be "poised" to utilize the hypothesis in precisely the same contexts in which the deluded subject does? What, then, would distinguish the two characters? Since the detective doesn't even partially believe what she has merely supposed for the sake of investigation, must we add something to the Capgras patient's delusion to account for its doxastic character? Is the Capgras patient trying to figure out the truth of what's happened to her spouse, as the intellectualist insists she must if she is to be credited with belief?

Now it is hard to imagine a detective acting and reasoning from the assumption of an impostor in *precisely* the way our delusive subject does; and this difficulty remains no matter how partial our patient's belief is supposed to be. Again, the typical Capgras sufferer is willing to *argue* that her loved one has been replaced with a doppelgänger even if she doesn't instigate a search, and a detective who has merely assumed a body snatch for the sake of investigation won't do that. Of course, we can stipulate that the detective defends the idea for a stretch; but then she's going to have to signal the pretense to her increasingly vexed superiors. "Look," she'll say, "I don't really believe the spouse was swapped with a doppel-gänger, I'm just trying this out. Humor me." For if she doesn't distin-guish herself from the Capgras patient in this behaviorally manifest way, our detective is facing mandatory medical leave.

So I'm not sure whether we can imagine a complete behavioral match between delusion and mere assumption. But perhaps we can come close if we change the context from inquiry to empathy. We might imagine a therapist who wants to know what it's like to experience her patient's delusion without suffering the malady herself. How well might she pull this off? Surely, a difference would still mark her intentions in contrast with those of her patient. The therapist is *intentionally* limiting her use of the impostor hypothesis to precisely that set of contexts in which the Capgras patient organically deploys it as a basis for thought and action. The therapist is just pretending for the sake of empathy. The Capgras patient lacks this cognitive set. We can admit this without saying that the Capgras patient is trying or intending to represent the truth in believing what she does about her loved one.

Must there also be some difference in the phenomenologies and forward-looking cognitive dispositions of the pair? There may be some sense in which the Capgras patient feels she *should* be doing more to find her mate. A patient often enough acknowledges that looking for her loved one is the rational thing to do given the position she's defending. A patient of this sort will feel some pressure to explain why she isn't doing what her beliefs dictate. And this is a cognitive set—or disposition in thought—that her counselor will almost certainly lack. A partially deluded subject has a glimmer of her own malady; an embarrassed sense of cognitive dissonance that even the most empathetic therapist would be hard pressed to simulate.

So the pragmatist can insist that there can be no difference in belief without some such difference in will. These differences typically manifest themselves in both mental action and bodily movement. But it may be possible to willfully adopt the behavioral dispositions of a partial believer without adopting her correlative mental dispositions. And if this is possible, you might approximate a state of partial belief without quite sharing it. This might even be done from intentions more noble than the pragmatist's notorious taste for self-deception. Like C. Foster (2016), you might want to know what it's like to be a badger. More bizarrely, you might want to know what it's like to be C. Foster without therein coming to know what C. Foster wants to know: viz. what it's like to be a badger. After all, people are strange, and you're a person.

But beware, empathetic identification with the delusional is a dangerous game. Were our therapist to forget the (meta-level) fact that she has premised her reasoning on a supposition she does not yet believe, she might then use the consequences she has derived from it more widely than she thinks warranted. (Imagine her contacting the police to lobby for a manhunt on behalf of her patient. There goes the medical license!) When we lose track of having made an assumption, we risk believing something on grounds we ourselves regard as insufficient. Sadly, this happens.

A full belief is poised to guide any attentive, well-regulated action or deliberation to which it might prove relevant. States of acceptance, assumption, and pretense are more circumscribed in their effects.

5

The Authority to Define "Belief"

A scientific definition is not to be controlled by unscientific usage; but at the same time we must, for the sake of being intelligible, keep as closely as we can to the meanings that have obtained currency.

(Bain, 1859/1865, 555)

In the choice of these man-made formulas we can not be capricious with impunity any more than we can be capricious on the common-sense practical level. We must find a theory that will *work*; and that means something extremely difficult; for our theory must mediate between all previous truths and certain new experiences. It must derange common sense and previous belief as little as possible, and it must lead to some sensible terminus or other that can be verified exactly. To "work" means both these things; and the squeeze is so tight that there is little loose play for any hypothesis. Our theories are wedged and controlled as nothing is. Yet sometimes alternative theoretic formulas are equally compatible with all the truths we know, and then we choose between them for subjective reasons.

(James, 1907/1921, 216–17)

While the pragmatic definition of "belief" advanced above is not without consequence for our thinking about actors and other animals, it would be unduly hyperbolic to describe it as a "theory" of belief. Instead, the attempt to succinctly characterize belief in terms of action is best conceived as a placeholder for a family of theories of belief: theories that might diverge from one another by providing differing accounts of the functional roles and neurological realizations of attention, self-control, and the "guidance by information" they enable. Following Hilary Putnam (1982), we might say that the equation of our beliefs with representations that guide our relatively attentive and self-controlled actions is a philosophical "picture" of belief rather than a theory.

Let me lower the account's pretensions still further: I won't make believe that the definition I have provided is the only way to reasonably think about belief. That belief is information guidance of the sort described isn't a "true" equation. At best, the proposed equivalence is true or valid relative to a "concept-constituting" decision to think of belief in one of the alternative ways theorists have proposed. This is itself an abstract and exceedingly controversial claim. And my attempts to argue for it considerably expand the scope of the inquiry beyond its already unmanageable boundaries.

This book, then, has two main theses. Both are pragmatic and both concern belief and our conception of it. The first thesis is what we might call a "ground-level" analysis of belief: Belief is canonically manifested in controlled, attentive information-guidance and can be distinguished from other mental/neural phenomena on this basis. The second claim is a "meta-level" thesis: The nature of belief cannot be determined by scientific theorizing alone, but must be relativized to a set of theoretically underdetermined taxonomic choices.

To assess this meta-level claim we need to reflect on the various conceptions of belief we might adopt and consider whether the decision to adopt one of these varying conceptions is irreducibly "philosophical" in some sense. When science, math, and logic are conjoined with one another, do they determine a uniquely correct answer to our target question "What is belief?" My answer is "no." But assessing this answer means discussing the evolution and current shape of those folk psychological capacities we bring to bear in figuring each other out—i.e. the nature of our folk psychology—and it means saying something about the current state of academic psychology, and it means saying something further about the relation between these two bodies of knowledge. Since I cannot pretend to have a detailed understanding of the history of psychological theorizing and its relation to various forms of social interaction, my discussion of these issues is, again, provisional, biased, and partial. I therefore ask that you examine it critically, with a grain of salt in hand and a heap of the stuff ready in your shaker.

The meta-level view I defend is pragmatic insofar as it asks each one of us to play a role in "fixing the concept" of belief for ourselves. Resolving the matter of how to think about belief is "up to you" to some degree.

You needn't defer to scientists or other academics on the issue. Nor need you defer to an expert's assignment of particular beliefs and intentions to you, even if she is your therapist and you can tell she's put some real thought into her analysis. A good therapist can help you decide how to interpret your fantasies, thoughts, assertions, emotions, and actions, but it is reasonable for you to exercise your own agency when arriving at a considered judgment about what you believe. You have final say on this matter, because it is your mind and your self that's at issue.

But why should this be? If our beliefs are states of our minds, and our minds are more or less our nervous systems, shouldn't we defer on the nature of belief to those who devote their time to studying our nervous systems and the way these systems respond to controlled stimuli in controlled environments? Shouldn't we adopt whatever theoretical conception of belief these experts develop within the lab, so as to best inform our understanding of one another outside of it? You wouldn't trust your intuitions, best guesses, or considered judgments on the operations of your circulatory system, or your endocrine system, or your digestive system were these intuitions to conflict with textbook accounts. Chest pain or breathing trouble might convince you that *something* must be wrong, but you're willing to defer on the rest. And this is because you know the textbook accounts of these internal states and processes are written by those with knowledge of what is going on inside of you or the "best beliefs" that can be formed on the matter. You don't exercise final judgment on the state of your heart, glands, and intestine. You defer to a description formulated by those who have "looked under the hood" and thought long and hard about what they have there observed. Why should states of your mind/brain be any different?

No doubt knowledge of academic psychology improves one's understanding of oneself and others, and medical doctors and licensed therapists are right to offer a range of therapies premised in academic research. These include different forms of neurosurgery, the prescription of psychotropic medication, behavioral modification, hypnotherapy, and the avowedly non-judgmental advice of someone trained (and paid) to ask you the "right questions" and listen carefully to your answers. Researchers continue to employ these therapies in various permutations, assess their efficacy with various measures, and revise recommended practices in directions suggested by their findings. And surely, if you have to go under the knife, you want a team of neurosurgeons who have done their best to carefully study all there is to know about the human nervous system. We might even suppose that academic psychologists on the whole—a diverse group to be sure—and those who have the time and access to benefit from the lessons of academic psychologists—an even more diverse clan—in some sense "lead better lives" than the rest of humanity—even after we've adjusted for confounding factors: by adopting, for example, the reasonable conjecture that those who read academic psychology or consult with psychiatrists and other academic psychologists are more often suffering from psychological problems than those who neither seek nor are mandated to accept such support.[1]

The issue is a subtle one. We all need to listen to other people, and the more insightful our advisors the better. All things being equal, knowledge of the details of your "case"—i.e. knowledge of your particular thoughts, experiences, behavior, biochemistry, and neurology—makes for better advice. More general knowledge—knowledge of the results of controlled behavioral experiments, knowledge of brain chemistry, knowledge of the purportedly universal taxonomies of the mind advanced by cognitive neuropsychologists, and knowledge of other general theories informed by these various bodies of data—can augment someone's insight into your mind. But does this body of knowledge inevitably improve diagnoses? Don't you assess each potential advisor before trusting her, where knowledge of academic psychology is but one factor among many you bring to these assessments?

At any rate, we are here concerned with a more extreme possibility. No matter how insightful academic psychologists turn out to be in comparison to their folk psychological cohorts, and no matter how effective various therapeutic interventions become, there's a large gap between privileging the advice of academically trained therapists and allowing this community to establish a definition of "belief" in the way that members of the International Astronomical Union did when deciding in 2006 that "neighborhood clearance" is necessary for planethood, and

---

[1] There are a diverse range of therapies and interventions that might be assessed: surgical, pharmacological, behavioral, and talk therapies are all commonly employed and combined with one another. This makes the sociology of psychiatry and psychology both interesting and intractable. For an evaluation of recent attempts to utilize the lessons of social psychology and behavioral economics to improve the lives of non-pathological (i.e. relatively "flourishing") people see Kahn (January 17, 2016). These "lessons" are further discussed in what follows.

that, in consequence, Pluto is not a planet.[2] And that's the first taxonomic question we need to tackle: Should we allow scientists to define "belief"? Would this be the first step toward allowing them to *tell us* what we do and don't believe?

Adoption of the pragmatic definition of "belief" is incompatible with such blind deference. If you believe whatever information guides your more controlled thoughts and actions, you have a kind of control over your beliefs that resembles, in some ways, your control over these actions. To believe a piece of information you just need to consistently and stably act, plan, and deliberate on its basis. If the information is not directly contradicted by what you can observe and remember—and is not directly in conflict with the more obvious implications of what you can observe or remember—this is often something you can pull off.

But perhaps you are not drawn to the above definition of belief. If you are not, and you do not have a preferred alternative in hand, you might consider deferring to the relevant community of experts on belief, just as you probably do on "planet," "photon", and the rest.[3] It is useful, then, to consider the kind of taxonomic issue that would arise were you to take this stance, and the stakes that attend your decision on the matter.

Suppose, to indulge in a grossly simplified example,[4] that those implicit biases that lead an avowed white liberal to remain more wary of black men than white, are realized in some neural structure—A—that is anatomically distinct from the structure—B—that is operative when we say what is on our minds without prior calculation and so speak "sincerely," in one sense of that term.[5] To aid the imagination, let "A" name the association cortex, let "B" name declarative memory stores, and let

[2] The vote was 237–157 and the other 9,500 members of the IAU's General Assembly were not present. Which raises the possibility that this vote will be reversed and Pluto restored to full planet status.

[3] For classical discussions of semantic deference see Putnam (1975b), Burge (1979) and (1986), and Loar (1988). Cf. Lessig (1995).

[4] For more nuanced discussions of these phenomena see Anderson (2010), Steele (2010), and Haslanger (2015).

[5] As Williams says, "Sincerity at the most basic level is simply openness, a lack of inhibition" (2002, 75). The literature on implicit bias is vast and growing daily. For overviews see Crosby, Bromley, and Saxe (1980), Cunningham, Preacher, and Banaji (2001), and Ito et al. (2015). For criticism see Fiedler, Messner, and Bluemke (2006).

these structures be surgically dissociable.[6] And suppose, moreover, that we have very good evidence that our self-described liberal's B structure is indeed "liberal" insofar as it is configured in a way independently correlated with paradigmatically sincere expressions of racial equality, but that we have equally good evidence that our patient's A structure is "illiberal" insofar as it is configured in ways independently correlated with paradigmatic behavioral expressions of xenophobia. We could interpret this revelation as showing that the avowed liberal doesn't really believe what she says because structure A "houses" our beliefs (or is essential to their neural realization). Or we could say that the liberal does believe what she says because our beliefs are realized in B structures whereas A structures realize some discrete type of mental state: associations, "construals," or somatic reactions of some kind (Zimmerman, 2007a).

This last proposal is the consequence of adopting what I am here calling a pragmatist definition of "belief" which restricts its application to the information guiding the person you're assessing when she's controlling herself and paying attention to the task at hand (cf. Zimmerman, 2007a). But I'm here emphasizing that this consequence is not forced on us by the data or evidence accumulated to date. We *could* say that there are two kinds of belief under review, and that the liberal is right in thinking she has a B-belief in the equal level of risk posed by black and white men but wrong in thinking she has rid herself of prejudicial belief altogether, as that would require a revision of those A-beliefs or "aliefs" realized in her A structures (Gendler, 2008a, 2008b).[7] And there are a host of further taxonomies that might be proposed.[8] If we are already

---

[6] Note that causal influence is compatible with dissociability. For evidence that negative racial associations influence more or less explicit judgments see Maner et al. (2005), Navarette, Fessler, and Eng (2007), and Shapiro et al. (2009).

[7] T. Gendler (2008a) and (2008b) doesn't think aliefs are a kind of belief, but utilizing the concept requires ascribing aliefs to oneself with an associated content. In this it resembles psychoanalytic application of "unconscious belief." The liberal white says to her black friend "I believe that you're fine, but I alieve that you're a threat." We might compare this with Kahneman's more thoroughly distancing self-attribution: "My system 1 believes that you're a threat, but my system 2 thinks you're all right." Gendler's account is similar to my own, and though I am not convinced that "alief" will prove socially indispensible, it may prove helpful in academic conversations about racism, sexism, and other pernicious forms of bias.

[8] See, e.g., Schwitzgebel (2001), Frankish (2004), (2009), and (2012), and Buckwalter, Rose, and Turri (2015) for views that posit ambiguity or semantic indeterminacy, though these theorists differ with one another over the various concepts that usage of "believes" and "thinks" is supposed to express. Mandelbaum (2016) argues that implicit bias is the

clear on folk usage of "belief" and allied terms, and already clear on the neural structures or—to speak in full generality—the "biological phenomena" that correspond with these folk psychological descriptions, there doesn't seem to be further experimentation that will help us decide which if any of these interpretations is superior to the others.

And yet, though our alternative interpretations are in this sense "empirically equivalent," the choice between them may still be a substantial one, given the different ramifications each will have for the subsequent understanding of one another we bring to our interactions outside the lab and seminar room: It is one thing to admit to being implicitly biased against races different from your own and quite another to admit that despite your best efforts you still believe "deep down" that black men are more violent than white. Correlatively, it is one thing to think of people as reacting to you with fear because of your appearance despite their knowledge of your relative harmlessness, and quite another to conceptualize them as believing "deep down" that you intend them harm.

A self-described "white person" who says that she believes in racial equality, but who regularly discriminates against the members of other racial groups, is typically accused of insincerity or of failing to know what "racial equality" really means. If the proposition in question is further fixed—as, say, the claim that, holding all else equal, black Americans are no more dangerous than white Americans—and the subject in question is not lying or just saying what she thinks her audience wants to hear, we expect that she will do her best to "act on" the claim that black people are no more violent than whites. If she does this in her hiring decisions, in her selection of friends, in her support for political representatives and choice of neighborhood—if her speech (or "what she gives"), and her

---

expression of propositionally structured "unconscious" beliefs, and Levy (2015) argues for a view that in some sense "splits the difference" between Mandelbaum's view and my own. The dialectic is complicated by Mandelbaum's naïve characterization of associations—rebutted by Dacey (2016b)—and the assumption common to Mandelbaum, Levy, and most analytic philosophers that beliefs invariably have "propositional structure." These assumptions were rejected by both the Humeans and the Pragmatists, and are now questioned by a growing number of cognitive scientists. Cf. Papineau and Heyes, "Much contemporary psychology assumes a fundamental distinction between associative explanations of animal behavior, in terms of unthinking 'conditioned response' and rational explanations, which credit animals with relevant 'knowledge' or 'understanding' or 'concepts'…this dichotomy is both unclear and methodologically unhelpful, serving only to distract attention from serious questions about which genitive abilities are present in which animals" (2006, 187).

deliberate manner (or "what she gives off") don't irk or alarm the population in question—we are tempted to say that she *does* believe in racial equality (in the relevant sense), even if her startle reflex is more acute when triggered by black faces than by white, or a differential amygdala response to these populations is detected by functional magnetic resonance imaging (fMRI), or she adopts a subtly different bodily posture when interacting with other races.[9]

Clearly, there is a range of such cases, which are distinguished from one another by the automaticity, frequency, and obviously inegalitarian nature of the subject's responses. But though we can't extract a sorting algorithm from our definition, it does gesture towards a recipe for dealing with each such case. If the startle reflex isn't an action, it's irrelevant to what the subject believes, so long as that concept is limited to action guidance in the manner proposed.[10] The first task, then, for any pragmatist, is to identify or "chunk" the agent's actions by describing their more manifest properties. The self-described liberal white, who hasn't fully assimilated her ideology, still *adopts* a more wary visage when looking at black faces than white, finds it harder to *pair* the word "black" with happy or friendly faces than angry or menacing ones, *assumes* a more guarded posture when in black company than white, and so on. Next, after identifying each target action, we must make some assessment of its automaticity: looking wary is perhaps more automatic than a defensive posture, which is in turn more automatic than quickly pairing words with faces, etc.[11] The next step is to assess the degree to

[9] For the "give" v. "give off" distinction see Goffman (1959) as discussed by Moran (2005, 334). For the relatively automatic manifestations of racial bias referenced in the text see, e.g., Amodio, Harmon-Jones, and Devine (2003), Lieberman et al. (2005), and Vanman et al. (2013). For an overview see Kubota, Banaji, and Phelps (2012).

[10] Those instrumentalists, like Dennett, who think reflex actions are guided by belief (if not opinion), exit the bus at this stop.

[11] D. Velleman might describe these as mere activities, a category which includes absentmindedly drumming one's fingers, scratching one's head while focused on what one is reading, and uttering various "Freudian slips"; a category he categorically distinguishes from "genuine actions." See Velleman (2000, 1–31; 2000, 123–44). But, from the perspective on belief advocated in this book, Velleman's distinction between actions and activities is another artificial dichotomy imposed on the spectrum of attentiveness and control, a dichotomy introduced by Velleman to distinguish "full blooded or fully human" behavior from the activities of other animals (2000, 2 fn. 3, and 2000, 123–44). Velleman fails to provide a compelling rationale for introducing a distinction in kind here, and when he subsequently denies that other animals can act, his taxonomy proves itself unacceptable. The likely consequences of adopting an action–activity dichotomy are at least as insidious

which the person who performed the target action was attending to her facial gestures, comportment, or her choice of words, and attending, too, to the effects these were having on the people with whom she was interacting. If attention was paid, and control exerted, and the response was nevertheless identifiably inegalitarian, the subject under review has racist beliefs, no matter what she has to say on the matter. But to the degree that attention and control are either absent or diverted to other components of the agent's overall cognitive-cum-behavioral output, things will be less clear. When divergence is discovered, we know the agent's mind is conflicted. According to our definition, this conflict is often best described as the agent's *believing* in racial equality while *construing* the members of other races in a manner that belies her beliefs.

Admittedly, there is a sense in which measures of one's automatic physiological and emotional reactions are more reliable indicators of one's overall attitude toward the members of (what one takes to be) other races. One can always lie when answering questions about one's attitude toward different races, but very few of us can fake an egalitarian startle response or affective association. As Anthony Greenwald and colleagues write, implicit association tests are, "Relatively resistant to impression management."[12] But lying is not equivalent to self-deception, even if the two phenomena sometimes shade into one another, as when we are tempted to say that a person is "lying to herself."

Now this might be questioned. The alternative view is that any case in which a person's reactions are guided by information that she won't assert must involve some kind of self-deception (Huddleston, 2012; cf. Mellor, 1977–8 and Moran, 2005). But I think this stance radically contradicts our standard conceptions. At the very least, those embracing

---

as those that attend the distinction between beliefs in the "true and proper sense" which are unique to humans and their "impoverished" animal cousins. Note too that by limiting belief's paradigmatic expression to the guidance of relatively controlled behavior we can agree with Velleman (2000, 270–3) that striking a wall in rage or shouting at the TV to protest a referee's call needn't be an expression of belief, and we can do this without accepting Velleman's thesis that truth is belief's "constitutive aim."

[12] See Greenwald et al. (2009), quote at p. 20. For these reasons, Fazio and colleagues (1995) describe their implicit measure as a "bona fide pipeline" into a person's attitudes. Greenwald and his associates found that implicit attitude toward race had greater predicative validity than self-report, but that self-report had greater predictive validity on less "socially sensitive" issues, supporting the hypothesis that people lie to look respectable. Cf. Ekman (1988), Banse, Seise, and Zerbes (2001), and Kim (2003).

so expansive a definition of self-deception must then draw a distinction between people and their sub-personal psychological systems. Otherwise, you'd count as deceiving yourself about what you believe because incapable of articulating, asserting, or self-ascribing belief in the information that guides your vision, proprioception, and motor control as you walk, run, and then snag a ball out of the air. You are aware of the sound of the bat striking the ball, the movement of the ball through the air, and the clump, clump, clump of your cleats in the sod as you track it down. You want to catch the ball. You are trying to catch it. You know that this is what you are doing and why. But those of us trained to catch fly balls cannot describe our movements in any but the grossest terms, and our attempts to explain exactly how we adjust the depth of a run to make a catch are typically erroneous (Fourneret and Jeannerod, 1998; Moore and Haggard, 2008; Reed, McLeod, and Dienes, 2010). If knowledge requires conceptualized or articulate awareness, you are ignorant of the information that guides the execution of your deliberate movements in service of this aim. Still, we needn't *deceive* ourselves as to the existence and nature of these motor representations and the micro-behaviors they guide, because neither these structures nor the information they encode are available to us in the first place. We "outsourced" reaching and then grasping and grabbing. We "delegated" walking and then trotting and sprinting. And we can visually track an object's movement through space while focusing much of our attention on other things. Does the information that guides these "sub-components" of a fielder's efforts to snatch a pop-up really figure among her beliefs?

The same question might be asked of at least some of those implicit biases identified above: those we can only discern with the aid of third-person evaluation of our brains, bodies, and behaviors. As many social psychologists and epistemologists have emphasized, this is part of the reason racial bias, gender bias, and other forms of pernicious oppression cannot be corrected in full by autonomous agents working by themselves to improve themselves.[13] As James Weldon Johnson remarks, "Colored people of this country know and understand white people better than the white people know and understand them" (Roediger, 1998).

---

[13] E. Pronin, D. Lin, and L. Ross (2002) and Pronin (2008). For dissent see Hahn et al. (2014).

Given the economic, political, historical, and nonreciprocal necessity for non-white people to work in and understand the world of white people, nonwhite people often have had to be very familiar with the lives and manners of white people in ways that white people have not had to be with nonwhites. Both globally and locally, nonwhite slaves, migrant workers, and domestic help (just to name a few) have had to travel to the world of the white masters, bosses, and homes, and this world-traveling has been and largely still is optional for white people.

(Sullivan, 2004, 198, citing Lugones, 1987, 19; cf. Mills, 2007)

W.E.B. Du Bois provided what is perhaps the most famous expression of this knowledge of white Americans, when he spoke of the painful "double-consciousness" that results from internalizing a white suprema-cist perspective he could not avoid.

After the Egyptian and Indian, the Greek and Roman, the Teuton and Mongo-lian, the Negro is a sort of seventh son, born with a veil, and gifted with second-sight in this American world—a world which yields him no true self-consciousness, but only lets him see himself through the revelation of the other world. It is a peculiar sensation, this double-consciousness, this sense of always looking at one's self through the eyes of others, of measuring one's soul by the tape of a world that looks on in amused contempt and pity. One ever feels his two-ness—an American, a Negro; two souls, two thoughts, two unreconciled strivings; two warring ideals in one dark body, whose dogged strength alone keeps it from being torn asunder.   (1903/1997, 38)[14]

Socially powerful white Americans lack this kind of forced knowledge of the "other's" sense of them, and many also lack an awareness of the diminishing mode or belittling manner with which they gaze at their black and brown brothers and sisters. Of course, someone who professes egalitarian ideals might still know when she is made to feel uncomfort-able by an individual from another race. But to uncover our implicit biases in full, we must interact responsively with those against whom we are biased.[15]

---

[14] The photographs Du Bois presented at the Paris Exposition of 1900 represent this double-consciousness by featuring the sweet faces of black and mixed-race Americans displayed in a mugshot format (Smith, 2003). For the influence of James and Santayana (Harvard's pragmatists) on Du Bois see West (1989, 138–50) and Harris (2003, 221).

[15] For evidence that people are reliable judges of their implicit biases see Hahn et al. (2014). For a normative framework see Medina (2013). I agree, too, that we also need laws and policies that will enable people of good faith to hammer out more egalitarian arrange-ments: racially sensitive educational policies, gender sensitive parental leave, equal pay for equal work, and effective public transportation among other social or structural improve-ments. See Haslanger (2015) for defense of these proposals.

The question of whether implicit bias inevitably incorporates prejudicial belief is complicated by a certain looseness in our use of "self-deception" and a consequent diversity in the phenomena it can be taken to denote. In the least paradoxical sense—the sense deployed most commonly by academic scientists—"self-deception" denotes garden-variety irrationality or epistemic irresponsibility. A person holds onto a false belief (say in her innocence or superiority) that she wouldn't have were she to assess the evidence available to her in a neutral or fair-minded way, where her inability to attain the requisite neutrality can be traced to her aversion to the experience she would have were she to revise the belief in question. Thus, according to W. von Hippel and R. Trivers, who have conducted an extensive review of the literature on the subject, "What marks all ... varieties of self-deception is that people favor welcome over unwelcome information in a manner that reflects their goals or motivations" (von Hippel and Trivers, 2011, 1; cf. Mele, 2001).

So understood, self-deception is as commonplace as biased searches for evidence. When someone favors a hypothesis, she will keep acquiring evidence relevant to the matter so long as it confirms what she wants to say, but cut off the search when data proves recalcitrant (Ditto and Lopez, 1992).[16] Greater neutrality is possible, especially when we regularly bust one another for "cherry-picking" the data. But the "default" mode we deploy when formulating our views in concert with one another is justification or argumentation, not a dispassionate evaluation of all the seemingly relevant facts (Hart et al. 2009).

When anything strongly excites our feelings, making us long for the full possession of it, the mind is so much under the sway of the emotion as to suffer the blinding effect peculiar to such a situation. We then refuse to entertain the obstacles in the way of our desire, and eagerly embrace every view and appearance favourable to our wishes. Such is the tendency of any intense longing, and such is the result in a mind not strongly disciplined to hunt out all sides of a question, in spite of the feelings.   (Bain, 1859/1865, 549)

No better example can be given of the power of the Will, as representing our likings and dislikings, to shape our creeds, than our being ready to believe in the

---

[16] Cf. Mills: "Rather than continually challenging the conceptual adequacy by the test of disconfirming empirical data, we tend to do the opposite—to interpret the data through the grid of the concepts in such a way that seemingly disconcerting, or at least problematic, perceptions are filtered out or marginalized" (2007, 25).

healthiness of the particular regimen that we are inclined to. Equally strong is the tendency to believe that what is for our own interest is also for the interest of others, and fulfills our duties towards others. The cool pursuit of self-interest amounts to perhaps one-third of the force of an ordinary man's conviction of what is right. The Free-trader and the Protectionist may not merely affect to believe, but believe really, that their own interest is fully coincident with the interest of the entire nation. The class bias makes men sincere believers, and not necessarily hypocrites. (Bain, 1888, 525)

But in what sense does cherry-picking evidence involve *deceiving* one-self? Can you reason in a biased way without thinking about whether you are doing this? If you don't think about whether you're just arguing your side, there may be no *call* to deceive yourself into thinking you're being objective. As Bain observes above, self-interest can distort our thinking without entraining hypocrisy. In the contemporary idiom of psychologists T. Wilson and E. Dunn,

Modern research on unconscious processes paints a simpler picture than models of repression and suppression. There is no need to demonstrate people's motives for repression or suppression; the assumption is that a great deal of mental processing is simply inaccessible to conscious scrutiny.

(Wilson and Dunn, 2004, 499)

In either event, we must distinguish: (a) someone's engaging in biased reasoning about people of other races to confirm her antecedent views on these matters (Uhlmann, Brescoll, and Machery, 2010), (b) a person's lying so as to hide her bigoted or unsavory opinions on race (lots-of-people, now), and (c) a person's implicitly associating other races with dangerousness or ignorance or some other stereotyped quality (ibid.).

In the most paradoxical and hard to explain cases of self-deception, the subject literally refuses to talk about the issue, or literally turns her eyes from the evidence that would undermine a belief on which her happiness or sanity depends. For example, a mother's refusing to listen to a police officer's testimony would seem to constitute good evidence that she knows that he is there to report the death of her only son. (If it were anything else, the police would have called her instead, and she knows this.) But if she already knows that the police officer is there to inform her of her son's death, how can her refusing to listen to his report aid her efforts to remain ignorant of the truth? There is a temptation to say that since she already believes her son is dead she *can't* hide this information from herself.

If we are not going to destroy all the evidence—all consciousness of the evidence—we have to have a project for steering ourselves through the world so as to avoid the embarrassing evidence. That sort of project is the project of the man who is deceiving himself, and he must really know what is true; for if he did not really know what was true, he would not be able to steer around the contrary and conflicting evidence. (Williams, 1973, 151)

Perhaps, then, our anguished mother only suspects that the officer is there to report her son's death, and she knows she won't *really* believe it if she doesn't have to hear the cop's speech. If she's right about this, is she really deceiving herself? If I choose not to learn my weight or my IQ, that's self-deception in a sense. I'm hiding my weight from myself by looking away from the scale. But I still know that this is what I am doing. And though my weight and IQ are facts about me, they are not beliefs of mine. They are not information I use when reasoning and acting. Can I use the information while hiding this from myself? This is only possible if I *don't* know what I am doing, under the relevant representation.

The question, again, is a taxonomic one, and there is no reason to treat an expansive definition of "self-deception" as sacrosanct when evaluating its more plausible answers. The first question for you is whether you want to draw a distinction between (b) and (c) above. Is there a genuine difference between someone's hiding her racist beliefs from others with lies by asserting what she doesn't believe on the relevant range of issues and someone's failing to bring her genuinely egalitarian beliefs to bear on her more automatic or less controlled behaviors?[17] If you do want to draw that distinction—whether on the basis of personal experience or laboratory studies—you must then address the question of how we ought to capture it in the language we employ with one another in the workplace, church, theater, and barroom in light of the deliverances of cognitive neuroscience. And while I'm only officially selling one definition in this book, I think the "explicit/implicit" distinction is ideally suited to the purpose. We might say that explicit racism essentially involves racist belief (as the pragmatist defines it), but that a "purely"

---

[17] The distinction between these phenomena would be entirely lost were we to adopt Schwitzgebel's (2001) proposal, which instructs us to characterize a paradigmatic egalitarian, contrast this with a paradigmatic racist, and make do with the unitary spectrum we can fan out between the pair. Can we equate the degree to which you believe in racial equality with your position on such a scale? From a pragmatic perspective, the measure is too coarse.

implicit racism wouldn't involve racist belief at all.[18] Purely implicit racism would be restricted to differential reflexive responses or reactions like those measured above, dispositions that can be masked or quashed by an implicit-but-not-explicit racist out of a belief in racial equality and a desire to more fully assimilate this conviction.

Is there a potential danger in adopting this taxonomy? If people of good faith adopt this conceptualization are they less likely to aim at further assimilation of their egalitarian beliefs?

The great thing, then, in all education, is to *make our nervous system our ally instead of our enemy.* It is to fund and capitalize our acquisitions, and live at ease upon the interest of the fund. *For this we must make automatic and habitual, as early as possible, as many useful actions as we can,* and guard against the growing into ways that are likely to be disadvantageous to us, as we should guard against the plague. The more of the details of our daily life we can hand over to the effortless custody of automatism, the more our higher powers of mind will be set free for their own proper work.   (James, 1890/1950, 122, emphasis in original)

Is laziness or indifference to the project of assimilating an egalitarian ideology more likely than it would be were the parties in question to adopt an alternative conceptualization of belief and belief's relation to implicit prejudice?

The truly dedicated egalitarian who uses a third-person measure to discover that she responds differently to members of different races will inaugurate a process of self-examination and a project of inner reform in service of her egalitarian beliefs. It is compatible with this that she has not completed this project and perhaps cannot successfully do so in full. (This is an "empirical" question still being actively debated.) The pragmatist will say that a person's belief in the superficiality of racial categories or the moral, political, and psychological equality of diverse peoples explains why she is upset at her own reactions and does what she can to alter them. Her beliefs explain why she takes up this project. Her implicit associations explain why it is necessary.

---

[18] Of course, a person may explicitly hold a racist belief without thinking that it is racist. Mills provides a compelling example: the false belief that blacks generally had opportunities equal to whites in the United States following the abolition of slavery. According to Mills, that belief often arises "because of suppression of the pertinent knowledge" without prejudice on the part of the believer (Mills, 2007, 21).

The force of the will is set in array against a power of a different sort, the power of the intellectual associations. Contiguous adhesion, and similarity, call up foregone states with a certain amount of energy. Against this we place the voluntary detention of the inward view upon some one object, and the result shows which is the stronger.   (Bain, 1859/1865, 375)

However one thinks of such attempts at self-improvement in general, they reveal themselves to be absolutely essential when we consider the ramifications of implicit prejudice for our criminal justice system (Correll, Park, Judd, and Wittenbrink, 2002). Judges, jurists, prosecutors, and police are now obligated to think of themselves as dedicated egalitarians in the intended sense. As representatives of the state, they must act from its avowed ethos while on duty. To date, this has been an ethos of verbalized equality before the law and institutionalized racism, sexism, and homophobia. But there is a growing sense that this is not okay. For example, there is a growing sense that judges, jurists, prosecutors, and police should not only act on the assumption that blacks are no more dangerous than whites, but should do what they can to better assimilate this dictum into their minds. Of course, pragmatism about the nature of belief isn't essential to this stance. The claim, instead, is that pragmatism provides the best way to explain what it entails, and the most useful package in which to sell it to the parties who need it most.[19]

The proposal, then, is to stop speaking of "implicit beliefs" or "unconscious beliefs" and to instead join the social psychologists in talking of implicit racial *attitudes*, a concept we construct by describing a white person's differential construal of other races, her differential reactions to their faces or speech, the different associations she draws from recognizably

---

[19] I wrote all this before more than 62 million U.S. citizens voted for U.S. President D.J. Trump, who advocated the deportation of millions of undocumented immigrants, a nationwide policy of racial profiling and harassment ("stop and frisk"), and an outright ban on Muslim immigration, while shrugging off criticisms from women, Muslims, Mexican-Americans, black Americans, and liberal white men who found many of Trump's assertions and behaviors sexist, racist, and xenophobic. Trump's success must renew doubts about the growth of an egalitarian ideology in America, even among the most optimistic pragmatists. Though pragmatism is a philosophy of tolerance and compromise (Menand, 2001), its adherents needn't blindly tolerate this entrenched form of intolerance, especially when they recognize that this would undercut their efforts to spread the pragmatic philosophy they embrace. It is entirely coherent for pragmatists to simultaneously attempt to outmaneuver and educate the agents of intolerance—by, e.g., seeking to abolish the electoral college while inculcating an abhorrence of white nationalism as a "term of communion" among the U.S. electorate.

black names than white, her different micro-behaviors in the presence of members of the two groups, and so on. No doubt, these are real phenomena manifesting relatively automatic responses to what are really perceived as the racial features of those with whom our avowedly liberal (or egalitarian) subject interacts. According to the present proposal, however, these symptoms, however permuted or combined, fail to warrant a diagnosis of illiberal belief.

> A very strong association between "apple" and "sweetness", generated by hearing the words often joined together (as from the "dulce pomum" of the Latin Grammar), would make the one word suggest the other, and the corresponding ideas likewise suggest each other; but the taking action upon them still requires an active bent of the organs, growing out of the causes of our activity—spontaneity and a motive; and, until these are brought into play, there is no action and no active disposition, or belief.   (Bain, 1884, 379–80)

> As regards indissoluble association, there may exist along with this the temper of disbelief. There is an indissoluble association in most minds educated in the New Testament between "Diana of the Ephesians" and the epithet "great" but without attaching any credit to the proposition thus affirmed…I do not know any purely intellectual property that would give to an associated couple the character of an article of belief; but there is that in the volitional prompting which seizes hold of any indication leading to an end, and abides by such instrumentality if it is found to answer.
>
> (Bain, 1859/1865, 536–42; cf. Bain, 1888, 527 and Moran and Bar-Anan, 2013)

The benefits of this way of thinking are to some degree obscured by the metaphysician's tendency to focus on unanalyzed attributions of "moral responsibility" when theorizing about our wills and the extent to which they are "free" in a sense that would justify blame and similarly "reactive attitudes" (Strawson, 1962).[20] The metaphysical moralist I have in mind adopts the perspective of St. Peter deciding who shall enter the pearly gates of the reputational heaven she has imagined for herself and who turned away because of a misshapen soul. And she notes, when she examines the record of evaluations that she has made, that she is picking

---

[20] Strawson's analysis is justly famous for deriding intuitions of the "fittingness" of blame as a "pitiful intellectualist trinket for a philosopher to wear as a charm against the recognition of his own humanity," but it suffers (as Strawson himself acknowledges) from his lumping "childhood" together with those psychological abnormalities widely recognized as exceptions to the propriety of blame and other reactive attitudes. It may be that parenting—and remediation for failed parenting—is the only social context in which reactive attitudes are usefully deployed.

up on things beyond the controlled, attentive behavior of those she is judging. This is in part because we typically assess people for failing to pay attention to the humans and other animals they affect, and because we ask each other to control appetites and inclinations in the service of healthy living, or prudence, or the successful discharge of our more onerous obligations. We judge a person for an inattentive slight, gluttonous binge, or dereliction of duty when we conclude that she could and would have acted rightly had she cared enough about herself or the animal, person, or institution she harmed or neglected when proceeding as she did. But there is also a distinctively non-Kantian, non-voluntarist strain in our judgments of "moral fiber" and the consequent esteem or disdain we have for those who prove strong or weak along this dimension. A person's *character* is thought to consist, at least in part, in her habits and instinctive reactions to trying situations. And there are many moralists who are prepared to judge a person for having a bad character—to assign her to the reputational analog of hell for this shortcoming—even when it is clear that the target of her disdain didn't voluntarily acquire the flaw in question nor willingly ignore opportunities to work on it.

Of course, you can make judgments of character without "moralizing" them. Famously, Hume pointed out that evaluations of our "natural virtues" are often more important to us than judgments of our actions. We'd rather be judged smart but too lazy to realize our potentials than hardworking but too stupid to succeed. This is a characteristically Humean observation, insightful in its measured cynicism. We want to be admired. And it is nice to be admired for statistically rare excellences—to feel *special*—whether or not these excellences have their source in effortful activity. But the desire for admiration of this kind has little if anything to do with moral responsibility. Indeed, in a well functioning community, people are regularly kind and fair in their interactions with one another. If you are fortunate enough to live within a group of this sort, mathematics alone dictates that your admiration for statistically uncommon forms of goodness will be trained on the extra-moral features of those you know. It's great that you're so nice. But what have you done for us lately? Telling each other that we're virtuous has been advised as an effective course of moral coaching, or what M. Alfano (2013) describes as the deployment of "moral technology." And you can get behind that kind of proposal without blaming people for things they can't control.

More problematic practices are encouraged by the idea of a "deep self" that is "revealed" to all in an agent's less controlled reactions. We might consider, in defense of this idea, A. Smith's recent argument that an omission can "express" a tacit value judgment that its bearer disavows (Smith, 2005). To rework one of Smith's examples: my failure to remember my father's birthday might be said by him to "express" my tacit judgment that the happiness I know he would experience upon receiving my call or letter isn't really more important (to me) than the other things I have going on. Isn't my dad right to blame me for this omission, all things being equal? And if he does blame me for failing to remember his birthday, isn't he judging me for something over which I lack all control?

The question is hard for me to answer in a neutral way, as my memory for dates is beyond horrible. Luckily, I've been able to outsource the responsibility: My smartphone tells me of the birthdays I don't remember on my own, and my loved ones seem more or less okay with this. The question posed by the "deep self" theorist is whether the horrible nature of my memory allows me to justly reject Smith's interpretation of my admittedly gross failure to recall the birthdays of those I claim to love.

Of course, I want to say that my failure to remember my father's birthday without the aid of a smartphone doesn't "express" my judgment that his happiness is not as important to me as the rest of what I have going on. But suppose that he also refuses to conceptualize my failure in this way. He doesn't attribute the failure to my "deep self"—an inner me constituted by judgments my memory failures "express." In that case, Smith's arguing that these failures *really do* express the judgment in question would mean adopting an unduly naïve form of realism about the propositional "contents" of my mind/brain.

But suppose, instead, that my father does hold me morally responsible for the failure. In what would this consist? He can't justly ask me to commit his birthday to memory if he knows I am incapable of this. He can justly criticize me for failing to program my phone with his birth date; and he can admonish my callous indifference to his feelings if I refuse; but these requests and admonitions target the kind of action I *can* control. To focus on my memory failures and beat me up about them without describing something I could have done to avoid them would mean abandoning the loving perspective we expect parents to adopt. It would mark a departure from what religious leaders—like M.L. King Jr.—call a "love ethic." It would impair our relationship.[21]

Those ethicists who defend the rationality of non-Kantian blame might acknowledge this. After all, a judge is not supposed to think of herself as friend or family to any of the parties before her. Instead, she acts as proxy for the injured or aggrieved parties in question, seeking a more impartial justice than their revenge would bring. Might defenders of character-targeted blame argue that judges and juries should evaluate the "moral fiber" of a defendant when determining whether or not there is evidence sufficient to prosecute or convict her of a crime?

Admittedly, implicit moral fiber (as measured by the relevant slate of IATs) might provide evidence of a propensity to a certain class of crimes. But this wouldn't distinguish it from psychological conditions like the post-traumatic stress syndrome of returning soldiers, a condition that has been statistically linked to violent behavior. While these syndromes provide evidence of a susceptibility to criminal violence and abuse, they provide almost no evidence of any particular act that might be alleged.[22]

And it makes little sense to blame a soldier for having PTSD, if she is doing everything she can to cope with it. Whether we blame her for the violent acts she performs in its wake will depend, I submit, on an assessment of her capacity for "executive function." She is traumatized

---

[21] The "cognitive process" that my smartphone executes to remind me of the date unfolds outside my senses. On the date in question, I react to an audible chime, see that it's my dad's birthday, and then react to this information in a manner that "expresses" my beliefs and values. Because of this, the initial cognitive process is not attributable to "me" even if we accept the liberal taxonomy of people and their minds advanced by Clark and Chalmers (1998). These authors would say my father and I ought to use "belief," "know-ledge," and "memory" in such a way that I count as maintaining a memory of my dad's birthday so long as I don't lose my phone.

[22] "Suppose that 99% of people from a certain reference class cheat on their taxes. Does this mean that we are justified in charging and sentencing someone in this class with tax evasion, without further evidence? No, of course not; we require more evidence than simply their membership in the reference class in question"; Colyvan, Regan and Ferson (2001, 172). There is considerable debate about the "reference class problem" and, more generally, the role that probabilistic evidence ought to play in both conviction and sentencing. See, e.g., Cohen (1977) and Redmayne (2008). The Supreme Court of the United States of America recently weighed in on this issue when reversing the Unites States Court of Appeals for the Fifth Circuit in the case of *Buck v. Davis* (2017). Buck was sentenced to death on the basis of a psychologist's testimony that his African-American race was statistically significant evidence of his propensity to violence, a decision our highest court found unconstitutional.

and angry. If she lashes out, her victims will justly judge her for this only if they determine that she could have acted differently. The victims of a fully implicit racial bias might adopt a similar attitude to their detractors.

Still, mightn't we encourage the use of implicit assessments of character in sentencing? More determinately: Should we allow or encourage judges and juries to employ the IAT and other measures of a defendant's implicit attitudes when they are deciding how to punish her for a crime? What if it's a crime against a woman or a member of a minority race or ethnicity, and the state suspects that misogyny, racism, or xenophobia played a role in the defendant's choice of victim?

Though the IAT and similar measurements of implicit attitude are still in their infancy, it's difficult to envision their playing this role. Defendants guilty of hate crimes and domestic violence are explicit misogynists or racists almost by definition. The crime in question is a deliberate act guided by a representation of the victim and her group as bad or in some way worthy of destruction. An explicit egalitarian or feminist (as defined above) could only commit such violence were she hypnotized or neurologically manipulated throughout the act. And if the jurists knew she had been manipulated in these ways, her failure on the IAT shouldn't affect their sentence.

Still, the IAT may prove effective as a sort of "racial lie detector test" in establishing the discriminatory purport of supposedly race-neutral policies. As R. Saujani argues,

Despite the growing acceptance by the courts of the existence of "unconscious racism," some proof of legislator's racial animus or their discriminatory intent must be demonstrated for liability under the Equal Protection Clause of the Fourteenth Amendment. The evidentiary requirements to establish the subjective state of mind of legislators are so stringent that they allow governing bodies to adopt numerous measures that harm minorities. While the existing doctrine undercuts the Constitution's prohibition on racial discrimination, it also allows legislators to practice purposeful discrimination quite easily because the doctrine scrutinizes mostly voluntary self-incrimination ... Researchers do not yet know how well the IAT can uncover racial stereotypes; however if the IAT could discern the state of mind of decision-makers, it could enable all acts of race-dependent decision-making to be subject to pre-scrutiny analysis under the Equal Protection Clause. Currently, facially race-neutral statutes are practically impervious to constitutional challenges by aggrieved plaintiffs because discriminatory intent often cannot be "located" by the Court. This barrier has continued to shield legislators from judicial scrutiny. The IAT could "smoke out" illegitimate purposes by demonstrating that the classification does not in fact serve its stated purpose.   (Saujani, 2002–3, 396)

Saujani also suggests that unconsciously biased legislators can use their failures on the IAT to re-examine their support for a "facially" race-neutral policy (2002–3, 411), and she recommends that the IAT be used to screen jurors for bias (2002–3, 413). Clearly, these well-intentioned policies are compatible with a pragmatic attitude toward belief, though they depend for their warrant on continued demonstrations of the validity and reliability of the tests in question.

Though pragmatists are as concerned as anyone to identify their own shortcomings and the shortcomings of those with whom they interact, they have little tolerance for institutionalized judgments of character, and little use too for psychological taxonomies crafted to justify them. Indeed, most self-described pragmatists endorse some version of J. S. Mill's harm principle, according to which "the only purpose for which power can be rightfully exercised over any member of a civilized community, against his will, is to prevent harm to others."[23] And those who are politically motivated by their philosophical pragmatism try to more closely attain the ideal captured by Mill's principle by lobbying against legal penalties for "victimless crimes" (e.g. sexual "deviance" and many forms of drug use) while advocating admittedly intrusive government actions with the expressed aim of protecting vulnerable people—often members of ethnic and racial minorities, women, gay people, differently abled people, transgender people, and the poor—from murder, extortion, enslavement, sexual assault, humiliation, starvation, irremediable ignorance, persistent unemployment, and putative harms of other kinds.[24] When we pragmatists implore other people not to inflict these harms upon us, we are treating them as agents capable of paying attention to our interests and exercising self-control to this end. And

---

[23] Mill (1859/2002, 8). Recall, too, "The individual is not accountable to society for his actions, in so far as these concern the interests of no person but himself. Advice, instruction, persuasion, and avoidance by other people, if thought necessary by them for their own good, are the only measures by which society can justifiably express its dislike or disapprobation of his conduct... that for such actions as are prejudicial to the interests of others, the individual is accountable, and may be subjected either to social or to legal punishments, if society is of opinion that the one or the other is requisite for its protection" (1859/2002, 79).

[24] One might think that belief in an expansive list of "positive" rights is a recent invention, the product of coddled Ivy League intellectuals who accept an expansive list of harms that goes well beyond physical damage. But one would be wrong. Recall that ignorance is one among the harms Mill cites in *On Liberty* to justify requiring parents to either educate their children or allow the state to do so (1859/2002, 89).

when we resolve not to inflict these harms upon others, we adopt the same perspective. The pragmatist asks that judgments of esteem and merit that come apart from these more useful, forward-looking attitudes be left to St. Peter. They should be kept out of the courts. They are not at all helpful when we are trying to interact within a community of persons each one of whom thinks she is due the respect of the others. Hate the game, not the players.

All of us make mistakes. And at times we are lost. And as we get older, we learn we don't always have control of things—not even a president does. But we do have control over how we respond to the world. We do have control over how we treat one another. (Obama, 2016)

As these reflections make clear, the phenomena under consideration considerably transcend the taxonomy of racism. What if someone seems sincere when he praises my intellect, but he also seems to consistently place the most inane gloss on my comments? Mightn't I continue to "strike" him as dumb at some "level" even though he sincerely asserts an entirely flattering assessment of my qualities? Should I say he has contradictory opinions on the matter—that he both believes that I'm smart and believes that I am dumb? Or perhaps he has a univocal view but hasn't fully assimilated this conviction? Must I accuse him of self-deception?

Surely, the answers I formulate to these taxonomic questions are not "academic" in any real sense, as they will directly impact the relationships that constitute our social lives. If the guy thinks I'm smart but reacts to me as if I'm dumb, I need to call his reactions to his attention. After all, if he genuinely *believes* that I'm smart, and he recognizes that he's reacting to me *as though* he thinks I'm dumb, then he will do whatever he can to suppress, quash, and modify his reactions.[25] But if, in contrast, he isn't yet convinced that I'm smart, I'll have to supply him with some evidence. I'll have to say something clever, or solve one of his problems, or just dismiss these efforts as not worth my time.

---

[25] This intuitive distinction is regularly assumed in the social psychology literature. For instance, there is evidence that those who try to suppress prejudicial associations out of egalitarian belief are more successful in these efforts than are those who suppress to appease social expectations. See Devine et al. (2002). Cf. Moskowitz, Gollwitzer, Wasel, and Schaal (1999) and Moskowitz, Salomon, and Taylor (2000). For an overview see Amodio and Devine (2010).

Can I make these assumptions without positing a taxonomic distinction between beliefs and mistaken perceptions, reactions, associations, or construals of various kinds? It's hard to see how. But if I do this, I will be treating science as a "handmaiden" to social life by drawing a distinction between mental (and presumably neural) structures because I need this distinction to separate potential friends from lost causes. Mightn't investigation into our evolved neurology reveal that no such distinction can be maintained? How would I assimilate the envisioned theory into practice?

If we adopt the pragmatic stance I am advocating here, we will not grant scientists the authority to answer these questions for us. Perhaps some non-metaphorical form of Kahneman's "two systems" hypothesis will be vindicated, as beliefs will be seen to be surgically dissociable from the non-doxastic implicit attitudes we posit when coping with one another outside of the laboratory. The pragmatist need only insist that this kind of vindication from below is not a necessary precondition for the reasonable retention of the relatively folkish conceptual scheme pragmatists accept when embracing their definition of "belief."[26]

And the social is the political: for suppose I'm "effeminate" or "country" or "inner city" in my speech and comportment and that the person who I suspect thinks I'm weak or stupid or dangerous—or thinks I'm strong, smart, or peaceful but regularly reacts to me as though I'm weak, stupid, or dangerous—is my teacher. Or suppose I have a visible disability, deformity, burn, or scar, and the person I suspect thinks I'm ugly—or thinks I'm attractive but seemingly perceives me as ugly—is a family member or lover or self-described friend or colleague? Or, again, suppose

---

[26] I have stated this concern counterfactually because I think that the pragmatic conception of belief defined above actually integrates nicely with most existing scientific taxonomies. I am here thinking of distinctively "scientific" taxonomies as those conceptions of belief and related phenomena formulated by those who explicitly eschew pragmatic considerations. (These are usually, but not invariably, "academic" psychologists in a sociological sense of that expression; cf. Rorty (1988).) For examples see Daw, Niv, and Dayan (2005) and Hitchcott, Quinn, and Taylor (2007). Since debates about the concept of modularity and the extent to which our minds/brains are compartmentalized continue unabated, it would be an exaggeration to say that the pragmatic definition already accords with the "best" scientific taxonomies, but see Zimmerman (2007a) for reasons to think that this result is at least as likely as not. For what it is worth, Bain's pragmatic philosophy of mind bets against radical modularity when defending the "cognitive penetration" of sensation by cognition. "When we consider ourselves as performing the most ordinary act of seeing, or hearing, we are bringing into play those very functions of the intellect that mark its development and its glory in its highest manifestation" (Bain, 1859/1865, 582).

I'm African American and the person treating me as though she thinks I'm threatening is a police officer, or lawyer, judge or jurist? I've asked these questions from the perspective of someone being judged. But each can be asked from the perspective of the judge herself. If you are trying to be friends with someone, you don't want her to think that you think badly of her without cause. Speaking for myself, if someone I like thinks that I think he is ugly or stupid or dangerous, I will try to dissuade him of this opinion. For if I can't, and he shares my policy of not being friends with those who think of one as ugly, stupid, or dangerous, the friendship doesn't stand a chance. It might seem obvious to me, from the first-person perspective, that I don't think the person in question is ugly, stupid, or dangerous. Is it compatible with this that I am uneasy at his approach, react with aversion to his appearance, or put uncharitably inane glosses on his comments? If I answer this question affirmatively, have I therein decided to think of belief as something distinct from these reactions and perceptions?

In sum, your choice on how best to conceptualize belief will impact your understanding of what people think about you and what you think about them, where this understanding—in conjunction with your words and deeds—constitutes your social existence. And this fact certainly places into question the wisdom of *blind* deference on the matter to the taxonomic choices of experts. After all, many of us value social understanding more than anything else. My evaluation of myself, and the self-esteem that it either brings or fails to bring in tow, is largely determined by what I believe others believe about me.[27] If that's true of you as well, your self-respect hangs on a certain conception of what others believe about what you believe. Is it reasonable to grant a stranger the authority to determine the answer to a question that will so greatly

---

[27] This is an exaggeration. I have read enough Emerson, Thoreau, Whitman, Nietzsche, etc., and seen enough Westerns and cool loner movies to be ashamed of this need. I am therefore conflicted about the importance of what others think of me. How do I know this about myself? Mightn't I be wrong in judging that my self-esteem hangs on the approval of those whose opinions I periodically despise myself for valuing? Social psychologists measure a person's need for approval, prestige, and power with the Thematic Apperception Test (TAT) and similar devices. Subjects tell stories about characters shown to them in pictures and these stories are then "coded" for the presence of the relevant needs. Several studies show that TAT assessment is not well correlated with the needs subjects attribute to themselves upon reflection, raising the happy possibility that I don't care what you think about me. See, e.g., Spangler (1992) and Brunstein, Schultheiss, and Grassmann (1998).

affect your mental health? Is there a form of "expertise" that would warrant such deference? What kind of expertise might this be? These questions provide the basis for a (meta-theoretic) worry about the authority of academic psychology: We *can* set these limits. Where should we set them?

It can also be seen from these reflections that both first-order inquiry into the nature of belief and meta-level inquiry into the nature of questions about the nature of belief are inextricably bound up with concerns about autonomy. The first source of entanglement can be found in the proposed definition of "belief" itself. I have argued that "belief" should not be equated with just any old form of information guidance, as instincts, habits, associations and emotional reactions involve information guidance that need not rise to the "level" of belief (cf. Zimmerman, 2002 and 2007a). To distinguish belief from other forms of information guidance we must invoke concepts of attention and self-control, concepts we use to describe the most basic forms of autonomy.

But it is equally clear that a concern with autonomy enters in at the meta-theoretic level: Your ideas about what you believe and what others believe about you shape your actions and reactions to the actions of other people. Because of this, *maximizing control* over your actions and reactions means assessing various ways of thinking about belief. If you conduct this kind of philosophical inquiry, you can then self-consciously meddle with your beliefs about what belief is and the beliefs you are willing to attribute to yourself and others on the basis of this general take on belief, and your social interactions will be informed by the results of this relatively sophisticated, relatively autonomous investigation. But if you don't assess the pros and cons of adopting various conceptions of belief, if you refuse to engage in this meta-level investigation, if you outsource the question of what belief is—and the conceptually related question of which beliefs you have—to cognitive neuroscientists or decision theorists or formal epistemologists or cognitive ethologists, you won't avail yourself of a form of autonomy or freedom you might otherwise possess.

Of course, a person who defers to Bain or James on the definition of "belief" will rightly see herself as possessing a large degree of autonomy over what she believes. At any rate, she will experience herself as having more autonomy over her beliefs than she would were she to adopt one of the neo-behaviorist or machine-functionalist alternatives on offer. But if she does not choose this definition for herself on the basis of her appreciation of its advantages, her autonomy will remain incomplete. Contrast her with the reader who reads into cognitive neuroscience and understands the taxonomic choices it leaves open, and who *chooses* the pragmatic definition of "belief" as the best means of integrating this wonderful science with the concepts she uses to evaluate the words and deeds of those with whom she interacts. The latter subject has a kind of meta-level autonomy: an autonomy that is incompatible with blind deference. There is freedom granted by a benevolent master and freedom achieved through revolution. Both are forms of freedom, but the latter is more complete.

And yet, despite the rhetoric of revolution I have here employed, there is nothing particularly radical about this call to place limits on our deference to the taxonomic choices of those scientific communities who study the human mind or nervous system. Indeed, the moral, political, or (more broadly) pragmatic dimension of psychological classification emerges in many different spheres. When physicians and parents worry that pressure from pharmaceutical companies has led to overly lax criteria for diagnoses of attention deficit hyperactivity disorder (ADHD)—and consequent pressure to purchase Ritalin—they are worried about the impurity of psychological taxa. When parents worry that the criteria for autism established by the latest iteration of the Diagnostic and Statistical Manual of Mental Disorders (DSM) are overly restrictive, and would deny them the diagnosis they need to obtain subsidized instruction for their children, they are worried about the pragmatic effects of the same. These concerns shape our assessment of the reliability of psychiatric diagnoses and the "prescriptive authority" of clinical psychologists (Fox et al. 2009; Schwarz, 2016). The differences between ADHD and autism on the one hand, and belief and intention on the other, concern the greater abstractness, familiarity, antiquity, and centrality of the latter pair to our social lives. But these are differences of degree, not kind. No doubt, scientists are legitimate authorities on these matters. We need to understand what they have discovered about the minds and brains of those they have studied. But their authority is not absolute. Diagnostic criteria and taxa invariably require classificatory decisions that are underdetermined by both evidence and explanatory need. We must therefore keep our own ends in mind when we decide how to best employ the language we use to understand one another in our efforts to interpret the discoveries scientists report in their scholarly journals.

Those familiar with Rudolph Carnap's (1950) work will recognize its influence here: The question of what definition of "belief" to adopt is, as Carnap allowed, an "external" question, which cannot be answered on the basis of evidence and "theoretical" reasoning alone.[28] In arguing for these claims, Carnap echoed the great pragmatists—John Dewey (1859–1952) and C.I. Lewis (1883–1964) in particular—who insisted that we are not entirely bound by the definitions, meanings, and conceptions currently in play within our linguistic communities. It is up to us to adopt and utilize concepts that fit our needs. "We have in every respect complete liberty with regard to the forms of language... Before us lies the boundless ocean of unlimited possibilities" (Carnap, 1937, 305).[29] At one point Peirce actually defined "pragmatism" in terms of this liberty of thought and the intellectual decisions it forces upon us.

The word *pragmatism* was invented to express a certain maxim of logic... The method prescribed in the maxim is to trace out in the imagination the conceivable practical consequences,—that is, the consequences for deliberate, self-controlled conduct,—of the affirmation or denial of the concept; and the assertion of the maxim is that herein lies the *whole* of the purport of the word, the *entire* concept.... As to this, it is to be remarked that actions beyond the reach of self-control are not subjects of blame. Thinking is a kind of action, and reasoning is a kind of deliberate action; and to call an argument illogical, or a proposition false, is a special kind of moral judgment, and as such is inapplicable to what we cannot help. (1931–5, 8.190–1, 148–9)

The existentialist element embedded within this pragmatic outlook comes to the fore once we recognize the indeterminacy inherent in all (or nearly all) decision-making. When we decide how to act, we recognize that some options are bad, others are good, but none is clearly best. We typically must exercise our agency beyond the evaluation of possible

---

[28] Carnap credits Moritz Schlick with the general idea and alludes to Ludwig Wittgenstein's influence on Schlick. See Carus (2007) for a more detailed account of the idea's genesis, which included inspiration from the German Youth Movement in which Carnap participated and technical help from Gödel. For the relationship between the pragmatists and Carnap see Richardson (2007).

[29] See Richardson (2007, 305) for analysis of the larger passage from which this quote is taken; cf. Carus (2007, 35 and 38–42).

outcomes and the assessment of their relative likelihoods to choose among more or less incomparable options to which we remain ambivalent, conflicted, or indifferent (Chang, 1997). As Carnap recognized, the same thing is true when the action in question is not itself a bodily motion, but a series of actions and reactions that will result from adopting a new concept, or changing an existing concept, or thinking of things in one way rather than another.[30]

These are pretty "meta" points. The target question "What is belief?" doesn't seem vague or weird in any way. It seems to call for a straightforward scientific investigation into the minds—and therefore brains—of humans and other animals to discover what makes them think, act, and communicate as they do. But I have been suggesting that these appearances are deceiving. The choice of a conceptual scheme for thinking and speaking about your beliefs and the beliefs of those with whom you interact is a "normative" one: it is in part a question of how to live. And normative questions are irreducibly "philosophical" in the sense memorably captured by Dewey.

> There is, I think, another alternative, another way out. Put badly, it is to deny that philosophy is in any sense whatever a form of knowledge. It is to say that we should return to the original and etymological sense of the word, and recognize that philosophy is a form of desire, of effort at action—a love, namely, of wisdom; but with the thorough proviso, not attached to the Platonic use of the word, that wisdom, whatever it is, is not a mode of science or knowledge. A philosophy which was conscious of its own business and province would then perceive it is an intellectualized wish, an aspiration subjected to rational discriminations and tests, a social hope reduced to a working program of action, a prophecy of the future, but one disciplined by serious thought and knowledge.
>
> (Dewey, 1918/1929, 843)

No doubt, we all enter maturity accepting norms we haven't yet evaluated. This is true of the linguistic norms that constitute the more or less stable, more or less determinate meanings of words like "belief" and "intention," but it is also true of norms of conversation, dress, etiquette, comportment, and the like. So the fact, if it is a fact, that norms are implicated in our adoption of a conception of belief does not show that we do (or even can) freely adopt whatever conception we favor. Nor does

---

[30] Famously, T. Kuhn (1962/2012) argued that these decisions mark the history of science in cases of "paradigm shift."

it show that we cannot reasonably defer to academic psychologists or neurologists on the question of how best to define "belief" and how best to understand the psychosocial phenomena so defined. Nevertheless, even if you were raised to maturity in an exceedingly traditional or orthodox community where the pressures to conform were enforced with threats of shame, estrangement, or parental violence, you probably weren't a wholly passive recipient of the norms you currently accept. Instead, you felt the expectations of parents, teachers, and peers to think, talk, dress, speak, and act in the ways they would prefer, and you passively acceded to some of these expectations, accepted others because you agreed to their wisdom, and pressed back against the rest. (Perhaps you are right now, at this very moment, vacillating between different sets of norms and principles, fixing on and revising your rules of thought, speech, and action *while* living the life you subject to their guidance.) Because of this, the rules you now live by, the norms you have internalized and use to judge yourself and others, are "personalized" to some extent. Though they were not "freely chosen" *ex nihilo*, they are *yours*. You don't wholly or purely defer to anyone when settling on your philosophy for life.[31]

When an individual dissents from the notions of duty entertained in the community that he belongs to, either renouncing what they impose, or constituting for himself new obligations, he may be said to have a conscience purely his own. That such consciences are very uncommon, proves in the strongest manner how little this part of our nature is innate. It is generally a superabundance of study and reflection—that is, a more than ordinary exercise of the mature observation and intelligence—that develops the dissenting conscience, when not simply a spirit of rebellion against social restraints.   (Bain, 1859/1865, 486)

In contrast, all of us must defer to others to avoid ignorance on a host of matters on which we lack both knowledge and any (individualistic) route to its acquisition. This is a universal predicament—a need that inevitably arises from diversity in our experiences and a consequent diversity in our knowledge and expertise.

Here in this room, we all of us believe in molecules and the conservation of energy, in democracy and necessary progress, in Protestant Christianity and the

---

[31] I'm not saying this is a good thing. I can predict that you actively shaped the code by which you live, in ignorance of whether or not you would have been better served by more fully deferring to people I judge nicer or fairer or more reasonable than you.

duty of fighting for "the doctrine of the immortal Monroe," all for no reasons worthy of the name. We see into these matters with no more inner clearness, and probably with much less, than any disbeliever in them might possess. His unconventionality would probably have some grounds to show for its conclusions; but for us, not insight, but the prestige of the opinions, is what makes the spark shoot from them and light up our sleeping magazines of faith. Our reason is quite satisfied, in nine hundred and ninety-nine cases out of every thousand of us, if it can find a few arguments that will do to recite in case our credulity is criticized by some one else. Our faith is faith in some one else's faith, and in the greatest matters this is most the case.   (James, 1896/1912, 9; cf. Coady, 1994)

Established usage prevents you from defining "belief" as a miniature horse or an heirloom tomato. If you use the word in these ways, no one will understand you. And an entirely appropriate deference to contemporary neuroscience prevents you from defining "belief" as Descartes did, as whatever state of your immaterial soul is accessed by your pineal gland for the purposes of cognition and communication. Scientists have amassed a strong body of evidence that your mind is nothing over and above your nervous system. And the pineal gland just doesn't work as Descartes once supposed. So I'm not suggesting that you can just believe whatever you want about belief. It's not that science and customary usage fail to constrain our conceptions in any way; it's that the constraints they legitimately place on our thoughts about one another inevitably leave us with some space for discretion.

We think that not only the common sense but also the scientific usage of concepts such as intelligence, memory, behavior, nervous system, brain, and cognition remains to a significant extent based on intuition. We often cannot tell *why* we apply these concepts in specific cases, even when it remains intuitively self-evident without much discussion where to apply them. Of course, we also develop definitions for these notions... but it is intuitive usage that drives the definitions rather than the other way round.   (Garzón and Keijzer, 2011, 166)

In arguing that "What is belief?" is not an entirely scientific question, I am arguing that within the limits set by brain science and communicative need, you needn't defer to others on how "belief" is best defined. As Simone Weil put it, "Liberty is the power of choice within the latitude left between the direct constraint of natural forces and the authority accepted as legitimate" (1943/1981). It is this form of liberty that distinguishes the choice of what to believe about belief from both instinct and science.

6

Pragmatic Self-Deception

The habitual dreamer is not instructed by a thousand failures of pet projects; he enters upon each new attempt as full of confidence as if all the rest had succeeded. We note with surprise, in everyday life, than an individual goes on promising to himself and to others, with sincere conviction, what he has never once been known to execute; the feeling of self-confidence lords it over the experience of a life. He has not stated to himself in a proposition the conflicting experience. He does not know that he never fulfills his purposes. So with the Affections that have others for their objects; love's blindness is the world's oldest proverb.

(Bain, 1859/1865, 26)

Imagine that you're scheduled to compete against nine opponents in a running race, opponents you know to be similar to you in both speed and endurance. Indeed, suppose that you have run exactly one hundred races against these very opponents and that each one of you has won exactly ten of these one hundred events. But here's something else that you know: prior to running the ten races that you managed to win, you were firmly convinced that you would win. A quick survey of your opponents reveals their similarity in this regard: each of them was firmly convinced that she would win on those occasions on which she won. A pattern emerges: when a runner among the ten is convinced she will win, she still more often loses than wins. (It has always been the case that three or more runners were convinced they would win, and who wins among them is for all intents and purposes random.) But no runner wins unless she believes outright that she will prevail. As they used to say when pushing the NY state lottery, "You gotta be in it to win it."[1]

---

[1] See too A. Reisner's (2008, 23) case of the basketball player who knows she will shoot 5 percent worse than whatever free-throw percentage she self-attributes.

What happens next? Can you believe you will win in the face of ample evidence to the contrary? Or does your awareness of the odds preclude conviction? Is this a parable for life in our competitive society? The only citizens who "win" the jobs, money, power, and prestige that they would otherwise lack, are those who believe, against the odds, that they will prevail in their attempts to secure an extraordinary share of these goods. Exuberant confidence is radically insufficient for "success," but for all that, it remains essential to its attainment (Baumeister, 1989; Benabou and Tirole, 2002).

Cases of this kind provide the strongest case for pragmatism in one of its various forms. The propositions believed in these scenarios are not mere curiosities or "ethically neutral propositions" in the sense given that phrase by Ramsey (1931, 177). We *care* whether they are true. But they are not only that. They are propositions that are in part *caused* to be true by the very fact of someone's having them.

> There are, then, cases where a fact cannot come at all unless a preliminary faith exists in its coming. And where faith in a fact can help create the fact, that would be an insane logic which should say that faith running ahead of scientific evidence is the "lowest kind of immorality" into which a thinking being can fall. Yet such is the logic by which our scientific absolutists pretend to regulate our lives!   (James, 1896/1912, 25)

The most extreme examples of this phenomenon are "self-verifying" judgments (Burge, 1988).[2] Consider your belief that you have at least one belief. The belief that you form in believing that you have at least one belief "renders" itself true. After all, it's a belief of yours, and that's exactly what it "says": it's the belief *that you have at least one such belief.* But your believing a proposition can promote the truth of that very belief without insuring it or even making it more likely than not on your evidence. Being semi tongue-in-cheek, we can call the judgments that constitute this latter class "self-promoting." If she manages to believe that she will win, our runner's belief is "self-promoting" in this sense. The runner's believing that she'll win the race increases her chances of victory substantially without raising them anywhere close to 50 percent. The belief promotes its own truth—and the epistemic rationality of holding it—without quite forcing these statuses.

---

[2] Self-verifying beliefs are the corollaries of self-undermining beliefs: e.g. the belief that I don't have any beliefs. For more subtle variations see Conee (1987) and Foley (1993, 27–30).

When you want a proposition to be true, and you know that believing it will promote that goal, and when you nevertheless recognize that the belief you would hold were you to manage this feat will remain "epistemologically irrational," you will feel torn by the normative constraints in play. From the scientific perspective you would adopt were you to remain squarely focused on truth and knowledge, you oughtn't to hold the belief in question. But when you adopt a more practical or pragmatic perspective, you judge you should.

I do not know how often we face these conditions, but they are not radically uncommon. Indeed, R. T. McKay and Dennett (2009) argue that overly optimistic self-assessments—so called "positive illusions"—are biological *adaptations* that remain biologically *adaptive*.[3] In broad strokes, many of us have the ability and proclivity to believe in ourselves against the odds, and we do so because our parents somehow passed these traits on to us with some mix of genetics, training, and enculturation. As J.D. Brown (a pioneer in this area of research) concludes, "For the most part, people believe positive things about themselves because they receive mostly positive feedback from the people they spend most of their lives with" (Brown, 2009, 514; cf. Murray, Holmes, and Griffin, 1996). If McKay and Dennett are right, an extravagant self-image helps those who have it outbreed those who don't, and this has been playing out on a grand scale since humans first evolved. Indeed, it may be one of those relatively fixed points in human nature that constrains the set of workable political or social arrangements (Flangan, 1991). "The power to control belief is no less signal; the mother's faith in the child passes every other form of credulity" (Bain, 1859/1865, 79). If we were as promiscuous as bonobos—and so uniform in appearance and behavior that none of us knew which children were our own—we might stop offering the kind of ridiculously biased evaluations of our offspring and mates that we often do—a cultural practice that sustains a population of overconfident adults. But our family structures—and the extravagant love for mates and offspring they make possible—are among the things most of us most value about our lives. We can experiment with community parenting—as they have on the kibbutzim in Israel—but this arrangement is unlikely to secure widespread adoption anytime soon. If anything,

---

[3] See too Alicke (1985), Brown (1986), Taylor and Brown (1988), Taylor (1989), and Marshall and Brown (2007).

societies are becoming less communitarian over time. The pragmatic analysis better fits this arguably "structural" feature of human psychology than do its more intellectualist alternatives. Our belief-forming mechanisms serve several purposes, and accurate representation is surely among them. But Velleman and Williams overstate things when they posit truth as belief's overarching aim. As Dewey (1938) insisted, the function of intellection is problem solving, not accuracy for its own sake. When accuracy is itself part of the problem, it is no longer part of the end.

> A teacher might set out to find out which of her pupils was responsible for breaking a window, but coming to realize that she would then have to face the unpleasant task of scolding the guilty pupil, she might decide that she is better off not forming the belief at all. This is ... an instance of weighing the aim of belief against practical aims, and deciding in favor of the practical one.
>
> (Steglich-Petersen, 2009, 403)[4]

J.M. Ackerman et al. (2009) add several "negative" beliefs to the class of positive illusions. Married people are helped in their commitments by the belief that their spouses are better than they in fact are, but they are also aided by the sense that "attractive relationship alternatives" are less appealing than they would be were they actually pursued (Ackerman, Shapiro and Maner, 2009; Johnson and Rusbult, 1989; Simpson, Gangstead and Lerma, 1990).

> The strong partialities induced by affection and friendship, the blindness to obvious facts, the incapability of entertaining injurious interpretations, are among the most notorious and irresistible characteristics of human nature. The stronger kinds of affection are able to sustain the wildest hopes, and to convert dreams into convictions. The mind dwells in other worlds with as much certainty as on anything seen or realized around it.   (Bain, 1859/1865, 77)

Still, we cannot ignore the negative consequences that often attend overconfidence.

> You say I'm complicated
> That I must be out of my mind
> But you've had me underrated
> What's wrong with being confident?   (D. Lovato et al. 2015)

---

[4] Note, though, that Steglich-Petersen endorses Velleman's intellectualist claim that the aim of truth is "intrinsic" to belief.

Here's what: men regularly overestimate how sexually or romantically interested women are in them (Abbey, 1982). Some theorists argue that this too is an adaptation, considering the costs to reproductive fitness that attend passing on a legitimate chance at consensual copulation (Haselton and Buss, 2000).[5] Indeed, the belief that women are more interested in you than they in fact are may be one of those beliefs that helps promote its own truth insofar as women are more attracted to those men who come across as romantically interested in them. We all love to feel loved.

> Do you like me or not? . . . Whether you do or not depends, in countless instances, on whether I meet you half-way, am willing to assume that you must like me, and show you trust and expectation. The previous faith on my part in your liking's existence is in such cases what makes your liking come. But if I stand aloof, and refuse to budge an inch until I have objective evidence, until you shall have done something apt, as the absolutists say, *ad extorquendum assensum meum*, ten to one your liking never comes. How many women's hearts are vanquished by the mere sanguine insistence of some man that they must love him! He will not consent to the hypothesis that they cannot. The desire for a certain kind of truth here brings about that special truth's existence; and so it is in innumerable cases of other sorts. Who gains promotions, boons, appointments, but the man in whose life they are seen to play the part of live hypotheses, who discounts them, sacrifices other things for their sake before they have come, and takes risks for them in advance? His faith acts on the powers above him as a claim, and creates its own verification.   (James, 1896/1912, 23–4)

And yet, despite its purported adaptiveness, the anxiety and distress wrought by the bias in question are salient to almost any woman you might care to ask about the issue. Just go to your local bar and see whether a physically attractive woman, who *clearly* wants to be left alone, is able to wait for a friend without interruption.

> My name is no.
> My sign is no.
> My number is no.
> You need to let it go.
> You need to let it go.
> You need to let it go.[6]

---

[5] I say nothing here about rape, which, despite it horrifying regularity, implicates psychological traits beyond species-typical desires for consensual copulation and reproduction.

[6] Traynor and Kasher (2016). Does this illusion happen at the level of belief alone or does it affect experience as well? S. Siegel describes the kind of evidence that would support

Indeed, to help bring home the negative consequences of inflated self-esteem, D. Dunning asks us to, "Answer yes or no to the following thought question: When flying, I prefer my pilot to have an overconfident view of his or her ability to handle rough weather" (2009, 517).[7] And what about the head of state, the nation's pilot? What if he believes every flattering claim that occurs to him; even those contravened by the evidence at his disposal? What if he dismisses criticism from a deep-seated conviction in his flawless perfection? Without a healthy susceptibility to observation, evidence, and testimony to provide our headpiece with an accurate map of our shared reality, where will he lead us?

Carol Dweck and colleagues have identified a more subtle danger: overconfidence can lead people to think they can succeed without trying hard. It can lead us to expect that success will come without obstacles, making us more likely to give up when these expectations are not met. For this reason, children perform better at difficult tasks when praised for their effort rather than the intelligence they bring to the endeavor (Mueller and Dweck, 1998; Kamins and Dweck, 1999; and Cimpian et al. 2007).

How often are our positive self-illusions destructive and how often beneficial to us? Surely, this depends on the context. A characteristically pragmatic attitude would advise you to be overconfident—and to indulge in the self-deception necessary to achieve overconfidence—in precisely those contexts in which it seems, upon reflection, to promote what you value upon reflection: lasting love, affection, and what, by your own lights, counts as an "achievement." Can we think better of our prospects for realizing these noble ends than the evidence warrants without risking aeronautical disaster or an overly "entitled" attitude to those forms of success we know require both time and focused labor? Call me an optimist, but I think we can.

---

the latter hypothesis. "Jack sees Jill, who is wearing a neutral expression. Jack wants her approval, and as a result, has an experience attributing happiness to Jill's face. If her face were nearly happy, he would still experience it as happy, but if it were clearly sad (or clearly angry), Jack would experience it as it is. In a facial morphing task, where a range of faces that differ slightly in their expression are lined up, with sad (or angry) Jill-faces at one end that change gradually and end up with happy Jill-faces at the other end, approval-craving Jack places the line between sad and happy faces closer to the sad end, whereas on a different day, when he's feeling more autonomous, he puts the line farther away from the sad end" (Siegel, Feb 2016, 18). Cf. Bain (1859/65, 545–7).

[7] For reviews see Dunning, Heath, and Suls (2004) and Dunning (2005).

Moreover, despite the nuances that attend the phenomenon, it is important to recall that the pragmatist rests the cogency of her picture of belief on a significantly more modest claim than the adaptionist hypothesis posited by McKay and Dennett. Perhaps Mother Nature has not selected the current population—or will not select subsequent generations—on the basis of their overconfidence.[8] Still, people are not *invariably* forced to believe what they do by their sensory experiences, or their memories, or even by the totality of what they take to be the evidence available to them, so long as "the evidence" is identified with known frequencies and similarly truth-indicative factors. Contemporary academic research on positive illusions is important because it reveals that overly positive self-evaluation is fairly widespread, if more prominent in the individualistic "West" than the collectivist "East."[9] If we accept the experts' analysis of this phenomenon, we will conclude that people often believe against the evidence in full awareness that this is what they are doing. The purported "datum" on which Williams bases his intellectualism—his widely endorsed claim that we cannot believe at will—is no datum at all (cf. Funkhouser, 2003).

Very few of our beliefs are self-verifying. Descartes' famous "cogito ergo sum"—"I think, therefore I am"—probably has this status insofar as one cannot judge that one is thinking unless one exists. And I would argue that your judgments about what you are thinking about right now are probably self-verifying too. You cannot judge that you are considering whether all moons spin without therein considering whether all moons spin (Zimmerman, 2006). But almost every living philosopher I've met or read rejects the case for introspective infallibility that Descartes constructed from the foundation established by his "cogito."

---

[8] "Even with regard to an inflated opinion of one's children, studies have presumably not polled the opinions of the parents (including potential ones) who terminated pregnancies— or who committed infanticide, physical and/or sexual abuse, and the more common acts of neglect. If even such parents, as is possible and even likely, were to have an inflated idea of the merits of their offspring and potential offspring, this would raise interesting questions about the meaningfulness of using the questionnaire—retrospective research approach to probe matters relevant to evolutionary adaptation"; Konecni (2009, 524). Cf. Baumeister et al. (2003) and Kruger, Chan, and Roese (2009), who point out contexts in which people regularly underestimate themselves (and their kin) as well.

[9] "Positive illusions are found to be a feature of Western societies, which focus on individuals and their personal prowess, but these illusions are absent or considerably weaker in Eastern cultures that focus on self-criticism, self-improvement, and adjusting to others"; Dweck (2009, 518). Cf. Heine et al. (1999) and Kitayama et al. (1997).

Most of what we think about ourselves doesn't render itself accurate. And though the class of self-promoting judgments is of course much wider than the class of self-verifying claims, it is limited to our beliefs about our own minds and actions, and our beliefs about the minds and actions of those we parent, coach, teach, and instruct to be better than they currently are. Does control over our beliefs end there? Or can we direct judgment on questions when we know their answers lie *entirely* beyond our control?

A recent experience speaks to the issue: Several months ago, after two prior weeks of undiagnosed headaches, dizziness, and disequilibrium, my wife and I took our four-year-old daughter to the emergency room at Children's Hospital in Los Angeles. A subsequent CT scan showed "something" on her cerebellum. The neurologists scheduled an MRI to investigate the matter further, and my wife and I managed to remain calm, until, that is, we were told that neurosurgery had also been scheduled should it be required. While we waited for the results, my wife began to dwell on the possibility of a tumor. What did the CT scan show?

I love my daughter beyond words and was of course deeply concerned. But it seems to me that my experience was not what it would have been had I not been writing this book at the time. Perhaps because I'd become convinced of the pragmatist line on belief, I thought to myself, "Hey, you can believe everything is going to be okay right up until there is something to gain from suspecting otherwise. You can wait out this day in fear or calm confidence. Which is it going to be?" (Or, more accurately, I thought to myself some jumbled pre-articulate precursor to this channeling of my inner Newt Rockne.) And perhaps because I think of myself as having some significant influence over my own beliefs, I decided (or seemingly decided) to believe surgery would prove unnecessary. I was not under the illusion that I could therein render surgery unnecessary. I didn't delude myself into thinking I could manipulate my child's brain tissue from a distance. No, I *decided to believe* that surgery would be unnecessary, knowing that this would have no impact on my girl's cerebellum.

In what did the decision to believe consist? I understood what it would mean for the MRI results to come back encouraging. I knew what it would mean to hear that no tumor was found. And I used that hypothesis to guide my speech, thought, and behavior. I asserted that everything would be all right. I smiled and thanked the doctors for their efforts to date. I did what I could to comfort those who were expressing their anxieties, and I waited patiently for the results without (conscious) fear. And though my face broke out in some otherwise inexplicable rash, I experienced myself as having the affect one would associate with belief in a positive outcome. But not only that: I did not try to ascertain the truth of the matter. I did not ask the doctors to give me their best estimates of the "evidentially relevant" probabilities. I did not ask them how often CT scans relevantly like my daughter's were indicative of tumors and how often not. Nor did I ask for the applicable base rate: i.e. the incidence of brain tumors among four-year-old girls living in Los Angeles. I had no use for these scientifically essential frequencies. "Detailed statistics are for research halls, not hospital rooms" (Kalanithi, 2016).[10] Indeed, the bald epistemic irrationality of my belief was only made salient to me afterward, when the radiologist congratulated me and my wife on the results, which thankfully showed significant inflammation but no tumor. "We don't see this very often," she said. "You're very lucky." And I was surprised to hear this. But why? Why was I surprised that the odds favored a tumor unless I had succeeded in giving myself the belief that they did not?

I'm not sure whether this is the best description of my experience. As I said, I'm writing this book defending a pragmatic perspective on the nature of belief, an account that I started defending in print more than fifteen years ago. I therefore have what we can join the intellectualists in calling a "doxastic commitment" to pragmatism: the kind of belief that requires sentential language and a linguistic community prepared to criticize the speaker with charges of inconsistency should she abandon her claim or acknowledge truths with which it conflicts (Velleman, 1989; cf. Carruthers, 2009, 127). And that surely colored both my experience and my take on it. (Is my view on the doxastic character of positive illusions itself a positive illusion?) But if things really did go down within

---

[10] In forgoing the evidence I was guilty of "selective" wishful thinking. In believing what I knew to be poorly supported by the evidence I then had, I was guilty of "responsive" wishful thinking. For this distinction see Siegel (Feb 2016); cf. Bain (1888, 523). I think selective wishful thinking is appropriate in many cases: e.g. it plays an important role in rejecting various forms of racial and ethnic "profiling" by law enforcement. In these contexts, we should make the base rates we want, not reinforce those that are often reported in defense of the kind of pernicious bias manifested in "stop and frisk" styles of policing. Since the pragmatist does not fetishize the "alethic perspective"—nor align herself with hegemonic Bayesianism—she is not vexed by the "epistemic costs" of this policy identified by Gendler (2011).

my head as they seemed to, I was able to indulge in a relatively mild form
of self-deception in relatively full awareness of what I was doing. And
I was therein able to make a point. Belief at will is not limited to self-
verification or even self-promotion. The phenomenon is significantly
more widespread (Armor and Taylor, 1998).

Under this hypothesis of no positive evidence, elevation of tone and belief of
good to come, are the same fact. Where the acquired trust in evidence does not
find its way in any degree, belief is no other than happy emotion. Ply the
resources that sustain the bright class of feelings, and you sustain a man's trust
in the favourable view of the unknown; let the system sink down to nervous and
mental depression, and hope passes to despondency. The condition of belief thus
has two great opposite poles. Evidence and Feeling. The nature of the subject, and
the character of the individual mind, determine which is to predominate; but in
this life of ours, neither is the exclusive master.   (Bain, 1859/1865, 587)

But did things really go down in my head as they seemed to? There are
several possible reasons for doubt. First, theorists might invoke Ramsey's
measure of belief in terms of risk to argue that I didn't have sufficient
confidence in the absence of a tumor to "count" as believing it. How
much would I have bet on the prospect of a welcome result? Would
I have bet my life on it? All my money? The answers to these questions
are difficult to ascertain, as I would have rejected the gambles as insult-
ingly crass. But suppose some pushy economist forced me to place a bet,
or suppose someone gifted me a sum on the condition that I use it to
place a bet. In that case, I probably would have consulted the doctors to
determine the relevant frequencies. And I would have placed my bet
accordingly, knowing that I would need the extra cash to deal with the
costs of a protracted medical drama that I would have then known to be
more likely than not.

But what does this show? How does my disposition to acquire the
relevant evidence and bet on its basis in this imagined scenario relate to
my actual frame of mind when waiting for the results of my child's MRI?
Is an assessment of my betting behavior in this hypothetical scenario an
accurate measure of my actual (non-hypothetical) frame of mind during
the interval in question?

I am a philosophy professor, a student, and (great-great-great) grand-
child of the Enlightenment. So when I know the relevant frequencies,
I feel some pressure to alter my beliefs in their light. The philosopher
David Lewis has dubbed the epistemic norm that guides us in such

situations the "Principal Principle": your subjective degrees of belief (as measured by what you are willing to risk) ought to match the "objective" chances whenever the latter are known.[11] But the ideal of "rationality" Lewis invokes in articulating this principle is a distinctively *scientific* one. And the same might be said of the other models of "rational" belief acquisition and revision articulated by statisticians and formal epistemologists. We want the doctors involved in our lives to know the reliability of the measures they're employing, and the relevant base rates, and we want them to use this information in accordance with Bayes's theorem to *assign* probabilities to the possible outcomes of the various courses of treatment open to them. There is a sense, too, in which we want our doctors to apportion their degrees of belief to the probabilities they assign. And when we are asked to interpret or explain the notion of "degrees of belief" as it is employed in our expression of this last desire, we will surely join Ramsey and his heirs in their focus on functional (i.e. causal) measures. I am less concerned with the degree to which the doctors *feel* convinced that a tumor is growing and more concerned with their *acting as if* they feel more-than-50-but-less-than-100 percent convinced of this, when, as we have imagined, Bayesian reasoning from the known frequencies would lead them to assign some probability in this range. And what does acting as if one feels more-than-50-but-less-than-100 percent convinced of a tumor amount to in the context at hand? It means ordering a relatively expensive MRI scan and making space and time for an invasive and costly neurosurgery, but not going through with the surgical procedure until the results of the scan come in. It means *acting on* the credence in question.

We apply these probabilistic norms to our doctors when they are settling upon a recommended course of treatment because they are scientists who are reasoning in a scientific context. Indeed, conformity to "epistemic decision theory" (Briggs, 2014) or a similar formal model of credence calibration is arguably mandatory in such contexts.[12] Indeed,

---

[11] "If a rational believer knows that the chance of decay [of a tritium atom] is 50%, then no matter what else he might or might not know as well, he would believe to degree 50% that decay was going to occur" (1999, 227). See Lewis (1980). The principle is revised in Lewis (1994).

[12] Cf. Maher (1993) and Greaves (2013). I am, however, favorably disposed toward a permissive or pluralistic view of scientifically acceptable epistemic standards like that defended by M. Schoenfield (2014).

it is not unreasonable to propose that the kind of probabilistic coherence that plays a role in contemporary attempts to formally model rational belief is part of the *meaning* of "scientific reasoning" as that expression is now best defined. And all societies contain individuals who employ scientific thinking in this sense (Malinowski, 1948). But it is compatible with this undoubtedly reasonable view of the matter that patients and their families do not apportion their credences to the evidence and even *ought not* do so.

I simply refuse obedience to the scientist's command to imitate his kind of option, in a case where my own stake is important enough to give me the right to choose my own form of risk... No one of us ought to issue vetoes to the other, nor should we bandy words of abuse. We ought, on the contrary, delicately and profoundly to respect one another's mental freedom: then only shall we bring about the intellectual republic; then only shall we have that spirit of inner tolerance without which all our outer tolerance is soulless, and which is empiricism's glory; then only shall we live and let live, in speculative as well as in practical things.   (James, 1896/1912, 30)

If nothing is to be gained by reasoning in scientific ways and much to be lost, insisting that we must nevertheless reason scientifically borders on epistemic fetishism (cf. Reisner, 2009). How much worse, still, when the intellectualist insists that these norms are essential to belief itself and that those who eschew the relevant statistics are incapable of anything beyond fantasy.

The explanation of the mental state of belief must include alike the cases of assurance well-founded, and assurance ill-founded; the mere mental fact being precisely the same in all. The state of confidence in the astronomer's mind, as to the occurrence of a calculated eclipse, is not different from the wildest anticipation of a deluded day-dreamer or fanatic. The real distinction between the two is important in the highest degree, but the full account of it belongs more to the theory of evidence, than to the theory of belief.   (Bain, 1859/1865, 543fn)

No doubt, science and respect for the norms that define discourse, argumentation, and belief as scientific should be taught in our schools and encouraged in our children. We must resist the blatant lies, fabrications, and inconsistencies of those demagogues who have the most to gain from a "post-truth" society. But to effectively answer dismissive attitudes toward evidence and consistency, we must first acknowledge these attitudes and their attractions. People can believe what they want to believe because they want to believe it. (Even presidents and titans of industry fall prey to this tendency.) As the pragmatists have long insisted, respect for truth and evidence is not "built into" the very nature of belief and credulity. To the extent that evidence does constrain our thinking beyond perception, memory, and sensory expectation, this is the consequence of the hard work of our parents and teachers and our teachers' teachers. Many have died in the breech in the battle for Enlightenment, and many more are sure to follow.

Though the results of science and technology are a "mixed bag," the particular bag in question has already been opened, torn up, and its contents too widely dispersed to be retrieved. So, by all means, let us urge the untutored masses to analyze what they read and hear, to demand evidence, and criticize incoherence. But while we do this, let us also insist—without fear or apology—on greater respect for our moral and spiritual beliefs in the equality of humanity and the value of life in all its forms, even as we acknowledge that these beliefs are not the inevitable result of consistency applied to evidence.

> Prophetic pragmatist sensibilities permit (or even encourage) this rejection of the arrogant scientistic self-privileging or haughty secular self-images of many modern philosophers and intellectuals. The point here is not that serious contemporary thinkers should surrender their critical intelligence, but rather that they should not demand that all people mimic their version of critical intelligence, especially if common efforts for social change can be strengthened ... The severing of ties to churches, synagogues, temples, and mosques by the left intelligentsia is tantamount to political suicide; it turns the pessimism of many self-deprecating and self-pitying secular progressive intellectuals into a self-fulfilling prophecy.
> (West, 1989, 232–4)

Let us not overreact to the propaganda that surrounds us today by pretending that social activity is itself a form of science or demanding that we forever enjoy one another's company within a scientific mindset. Let us leave space for play, and hopeful belief, and trust too in its least pernicious varieties.

Cited Sources

Abbey, A., "Sex Differences in Attributions for Friendly Behavior: Do Males Misperceive Females' Friendliness?" *Journal of Personality and Social Psychology*, 42 (1982), pp. 830–8.

Abelson, R., "Psychological Status of the Script Concept," *American Psychologist*, 36 (1981), pp. 715–29.

Ackerman, J.M., J.R. Shapiro, and J.K. Maner, "When is it Good to Believe Bad Things?" *Behavioral and Brain Sciences*, 32, 6 (2009), pp. 510–11.

Adolph, K.E., W.G. Cole, M. Komati, J.S. Garciaguirre, D. Badaly, J.M. Lingeman, G. Chan, and R.B. Sotsky, "How Do You Learn to Walk? Thousands of Steps and Dozens of Falls Per Day," *Psychological Science*, 23, 11 (2012), pp. 1387–94.

Alfano, M., *Character As Moral Fiction*, Cambridge: Cambridge University Press (2013).

Alicke, M.D., "Global Self-Evaluation as Determined by the Desirability and Controllability of Trait Adjectives," *Journal of Personality and Social Psychology*, 49 (1985), pp. 1621–30.

Amodio, D.M., E. Harmon-Jones, and P. G. Devine, "Individual Differences in the Activation and Control of Affective Race Bias as Assessed by Startle Eyeblink Responses and Self-Report," *Journal of Personality and Social Psychology*, 84 (2003), pp. 738–53.

Amodio, D.M., and P.G. Devine, "Control in the Regulation of Intergroup Bias," in R.R. Hassin, K.N. Ochsner, and Y. Trope (eds.), *Self Control in Society, Mind and Brain*, Oxford: Oxford University Press (2010).

Anderson, E.S., *The Imperative of Integration*, Princeton, NJ: Princeton University Press (2010).

Anscombe, G.E.M., *Intention*, Cambridge, MA: Harvard University Press (1957/2000).

Apperly, I.A., and S.A. Butterfill, "Do Humans Have Two Systems to Track Beliefs and Belief-Like States?" *Psychological Review*, 116, 4 (2009), pp. 953–70.

Armor, D.A., and S.E. Taylor, "Situated Optimism: Specific Outcome Expectancies and Self-Regulation," in M. Zanna (ed.), *Advances in Experimental Social Psychology*, Vol. 30, New York: Academic Press (1998), pp. 309–79.

Armstrong, D., *Belief, Truth and Knowledge*, Cambridge: Cambridge University Press (1973).

Arnold, K., and F. Aureli, "Postconflict Reconciliation," in C.J. Campbell, A. Fuentes, K.C. MacKinnon, M. Panger, and S.K. Bearders (eds.), *Primates in Perspective*, New York: Oxford University Press (2006), pp. 592–608.

Ashton, R.L., and C. De Lillo, "Association, Inhibition and Object Permanence in Dogs' (*Canis familiaris*) Spatial Search," *Journal of Comparative Psychology*, 125, 2 (2011), pp. 194–206.

Baddeley, A., "Exploring the Central Executive," *The Quarterly Journal of Experimental Psychology*, 49A (1996), pp. 5–28.

Baddeley, A., and G.J. Hitch, "Working Memory," in G.H. Bower (ed.), *The Psychology of Learning and Motivation*, New York: Academic Press (1974), pp. 47–89.

Baier, A., "Mind and Change of Mind," *Midwest Studies in Philosophy*, 4, 1 (1979), pp. 157–76.

Baillargeon, R., R.M. Scott, and Z. He, "False Belief Understanding in Infants," *Trends in Cognitive Sciences*, 14 (2010), pp. 110–18.

Bain, A., *The Emotions and the Will*, 2nd Edition, London: Longmans, Green (1859/1865).

Bain, A., *Mental and Moral Science*, London: Longmans, Green (1868/1884).

Bain, A., *Mind and Body*, 2nd Edition, London: Henry S. King and Co. (1873).

Bain, A., *The Emotions and the Will*, 3rd Edition, London: Longmans, Green (1888).

Banse, R., J. Seise, and N. Zerbes, "Implicit Attitudes towards Homosexuality: Reliability, Validity, and Controllability of the IAT," *Zeitschrift für Experimentelle Psychologie*, 48 (2001), pp. 145–60.

Barrett, L.F., K.N. Ochsner, and J.J. Gross, "On the Automaticity of Emotion," in J.A. Bargh (ed.), *Social Psychology and the Unconscious: The Automaticity of Higher Mental Processes*, New York: Psychology Press (2007), pp. 173–219.

Barrett-Lennard, L.G., *Population Structure and Mating Patterns of Killer Whales (Orcinus orca) as Revealed by DNA Analysis*, Ph.D. dissertation, University of British Columbia (2000).

Bauer, G., F. Gerstenbrand, and E. Rumpl, "Varieties of Locked-in Syndrome," *Journal of Neurology*, 221, 2 (1979), pp. 77–91.

Bauby, J-D, *The Diving Bell and the Butterfly*, New York: Alfred A. Knopf (1997).

Baumeister, R.F., "The Optimal Margin of Illusion," *Journal of Social and Clinical Psychology*, 8 (1989), pp. 176–89.

Baumeister, R.F., J.D. Campbell, J.I. Krueger, and K.D. Vohs, "Does High Self-Esteem Cause Better Performance, Interpersonal Success, Happiness or Healthier Life Styles?" *Psychological Science in the Public Interest*, 4 (2003), pp. 1–44.

Bayne, T.J., and N. Levy, "The Feeling of Doing: Deconstructing the Phenomenology of Agency," in N. Sebanz and W. Prinz (eds.), *Disorders of Volition*, Cambridge, MA: MIT Press (2006), pp. 49–68.

Bayne, T.J., and E. Pacherie, "In Defense of the Doxastic Conception of Delusions," *Mind and Language*, 20, 2 (2005), pp. 163–88.

Bechara, A., A.R. Damasio, H. Damasio, and S.W. Anderson, "Insensitivity to Future Consequences Following Damage to Human Prefrontal Cortex," *Cognition*, 50, 1–3 (1994), pp. 7–15.

Bechara, A., H. Damasio, D. Tranel, and A.R. Damasio, "Deciding Advantageously Before Knowing the Advantageous Strategy," *Science*, 275, 5304 (1997), pp. 1293–5.

Bechara, A., H. Damasio, D. Tranel, and A.R. Damasio, "The Iowa Gambling Task and the Somatic Marker Hypothesis: Some Questions and Answers," *Trends in Cognitive Sciences*, 9, 4 (2005), pp. 159–62.

Bechara, A., D. Tranel, H. Damasio, and A.R. Damasio, "Failure to Respond Autonomically to Anticipated Future Outcomes Following Damage to Prefrontal Cortex," *Cerebral Cortex*, 6, 2 (1996), pp. 215–25.

Beilock, S., *Choke: What the Secrets of the Brain Reveal about Getting it Right When You Have To*, New York: Free Press (2010).

Bekoff, M., and P.W. Sherman, "Reflections on Animal Selves," *Trends in Ecology and Evolution*, 19 (2003), pp. 176–80.

Benabou, R., and J. Tirole, "Self-Confidence and Personal Motivation," *The Quarterly Journal of Economics*, 117, 3 (2002), pp. 817–915.

Bennett, J., *Linguistic Behavior*, Cambridge: Cambridge University Press (1976).

Bennett, J., "Why is Belief Involuntary?" *Analysis*, 50 (1990), pp. 87–107.

Beran, M.J., "Maintenance of Self-Imposed Delay of Gratification by Four Chimpanzees (*Pan Troglodytes*) and an Orangutan (*Pongo Pygmaeus*)," *Journal of General Psychology*, 129 (2002), pp. 49–66.

Bermudez, J., *Thinking Without Words*, Cambridge, MA: MIT Press (2003).

Bernstein, R., *Praxis and Action: Contemporary Philosophies of Human Activity*, Philadelphia: University of Pennsylvania Press (1971).

Bernstein, S., and J. Wilson, "Free Will and Mental Quausation," *Journal of the American Philosophical Association*, (May 2016), pp. 1–22; doi: 10.1017/apa.2016.7.

Berry, D.C., and D.E. Broadbent, "On the Relationship between Task Performance and Associated Verbalizable Knowledge," *The Quarterly Journal of Experimental Psychology*, 36A (1984), pp. 209–31.

Blakemore, S-J., and C. Frith, "Self-Awareness and Action," *Current Opinion in Neurobiology*, 13 (2003), pp. 219–24.

Blakemore, S-J., D.M. Wolpert, and C. Frith, "Abnormalities in the Awareness of Action," *Trends in Cognitive Science*, 6, 1 (2002), pp. 237–42.

Blakeslee, N., *American Wolf*, New York: Crown (2017).

Blumson, B., "Mental Maps," *Philosophy and Phenomenological Research*, LXXXV, 2 (September 2012), pp. 413–34.

Bodenhausen, G.V., and J. A. Richeson, "Prejudice, Stereotyping and Discrimination," in R. F. Baumeister and E. J. Finkel (eds.), *Advanced Social Psychology: The State of the Science*, Oxford: Oxford University Press (2010), pp. 341–69.

Boesch, C., and H. Boesche-Achermann, *The Chimpanzees of the Taï Forest: Behavioral Ecology and Evolution*, Oxford: Oxford University Press (2000).

Borick, C.P., and B.G. Rabe, "A Reason to Believe: Examining Factors that Determine Individual Views on Global Warming," *Social Science Quarterly*, 91, 3 (2010), pp. 777–800.

Bortolotti, L., *Delusions and Other Irrational Beliefs*, Oxford: Oxford University Press (2009).

Bortolotti, L., "In Defense of Modest Doxasticism about Delusions," *Neuroethics*, 5, 1 (2012), pp. 39–53.

Bosbach, S., J. Cole, W. Prinz, and G. Knoblich, "Inferring Another's Expectation from Action: The Role of Peripheral Sensation," *Nature Neuroscience*, 8 (2005), pp. 1295–7.

Brainerd, C.J., and V.F. Reyna, *The Science of False Memory*, Oxford: Oxford University Press (2005).

Brandom, R., "When Philosophy Paints Its Blue on Gray: Irony and the Pragmatist Enlightenment," in C. Kautzer and E. Mendenieta (eds.), *Pragmatism, Nation and Race: Community in the Age of Empire*, Bloomington, IN: Indiana University Press (2009), pp. 19–45.

Bratman, M., "Practical Reasoning and Acceptance in a Context," *Mind*, 101 (1992), pp. 1–14, reprinted in M. Bratman, *Faces of Intention: Selected Essays on Intention and Agency*, Cambridge: Cambridge University Press (1999), pp. 15–34.

Briggs, R., "Normative Theories of Rational Choice: Expected Utility," *Stanford Encyclopedia of Philosophy* (2014).

Brown, J.D., "Evaluations of Self and Others: Self-Enhancement Biases in Social Judgments," *Social Cognition*, 4 (1986), pp. 353–76.

Brown, J.D., "Positive Illusions and Positive Collusions: How Social Life Abets Self-Enhancing Beliefs," *Behavioral and Brain Sciences*, 32, 6 (2009), pp. 514–15.

Bruer, J., "Mapping Cognitive Neuroscience: Two-Dimensional Perspectives on Twenty Years of Cognitive Neuroscience Research," in M. Gazzaniga (ed.), *The Cognitive Neurosciences*, 4th Edition, Cambridge, MA: MIT Press/Bradford (2009), pp. 1121–34.

Brunstein, J.C., O.C. Schultheiss, and R. Grassmann, "Personal Goals and Emotional Wellbeing: The Moderating Role of Motive Dispositions," *Journal of Personality and Social Psychology*, 75 (1998), pp. 494–508.

Bruntrup, G., and L. Jaskolla (eds.), *Pansychism: Contemporary Perspectives*, Oxford: Oxford University Press (2016).

Bshary, R., A. Hohner, K. Ait-El-Djoudi, and H. Fricke, "Interspecific Communicative and Coordinated Hunting between Groupers and Giant Moray Eels in the Red Sea," *PLoS Biology*, 4, 12 (2006), p. e431.

Buck v. Davis, 580 United States Supreme Court 15-8049 (2017).

Buckwalter, W., D. Rose, and J. Turri, "Belief through Thick and Thin," *Noûs*, 49, 4 (2015), pp. 748–75.

Burge, T., "Belief De Re," *The Journal of Philosophy*, 74 (1977), pp. 338–62; reprinted in T. Burge, *Foundations of Mind, Philosophical Essays Volume 2*, Oxford: Clarendon (2007), pp. 44–64.

Burge, T., "Individualism and the Mental," in P.A. French, T.E. Uehling, and H. Wettstein (eds.), *Midwest Studies in Philosophy IV*, Minneapolis, Minnesota: University of Minnesota Press (1979), pp. 73–121.

Burge, T., "Sinning against Frege," *The Philosophical Review*, 88, 3 (1979), pp. 398–432.

Burge, T., "Individualism and Psychology," *The Philosophical Review*, 95 (1986), pp. 3–45.

Burge, T., "Individualism and Self-Knowledge," *Journal of Philosophy*, 85, 11 (1988), pp. 649–63.

Burge, T., *Truth, Thought and Reason: Essays on Frege*, Oxford: Clarendon Press (2005).

Burge, T., *Foundations of Mind*, Oxford: Clarendon Press (2007).

Byrne, R.W., and A. Whiten, "Tactical Deception in Primates: The 1990 Database," *Primate Report*, 27 (1990), pp. 1–101.

Byrne, R.W., and A. Whiten, "Cognitive Evolution in Primates: Evidence from Tactical Deception," *Man*, 27 (1992), pp. 609–27.

Call, J., "Inferences about the Location of Food in the Great Apes," *Journal of Comparative Psychology*, 118 (2004), pp. 232–41.

Call, J., and M. Tomasello, "Does the Chimpanzee Have a Theory of Mind? 30 Years Later," *Trends in Cognitive Science*, 12, 5 (2009), pp. 187–92.

Calvin, W., *A Brief History of the Human Mind*, Oxford: Oxford University Press (2004).

Camp, E., "Thinking with Maps," *Philosophical Perspectives*, 21 (2007), pp. 145–82.

Camp, E., "Putting Thoughts to Work: Concepts, Systematicity and Stimulus-Independence," *Philosophy and Phenomenological Research*, 78, 2 (2009), pp. 275–311.

Campbell, J., *Reference and Consciousness*, Oxford: Oxford University Press (2002).

Campbell, J., "The Roots of Diversity in Pragmatic Thought," in J.M. Green, S. Neubert, and K. Reich (eds.), *Pragmatism and Diversity: Dewey in the Context of Late Twentieth Century Debates*, New York: Palgrave Macmillan (2011), pp. 11–24.

Carnap, R., *The Logical Syntax of Language*, trans. A. Smeaton, Countess von Zeppelin, London: Kegan Paul (1937).

Carnap, R., "Empiricism, Semantics and Ontology," *Revue Internationale de Philosophie*, 4 (1950), pp. 20–40.

Carnap, R., *Meaning and Necessity*, Chicago: University of Chicago Press (1956).

Carruthers, P., "On Being Simple Minded," *American Philosophical Quarterly*, 41 (2004), pp. 205–22.

Carruthers, P., "Meta-cognition in Animals: A Skeptical Look," *Mind and Language*, 23, 1 (2008), pp. 58–89.

Carruthers, P., "How We Know Our Own Minds: The Relationship between Mindreading and Metacognition," *Behavioral and Brain Sciences*, 32, 2 (2009), pp. 121–82.

Carruthers, P., *The Centered Mind: What the Science of Working Memory Shows Us about the Nature of Human Thought*, Oxford: Oxford University Press (2015).

Carus, A.W., "Carnap's Intellectual Development," in M. Friedman and R. Creath (eds.), *The Cambridge Companion to Carnap*, Cambridge: Cambridge University Press (2007), pp. 19–43.

Cavalieri, P., and P. Singer, *The Great Ape Project: Equality Beyond Humanity*, London: Fourth Estate (1993).

Chalmers, D., "Panpsychism and Panprotopsychism," in T. Alter and Y. Nagasawa (eds.), *Consciousness in the Physical World: Essays on Russellian Monism*, Oxford: Oxford University Press (2015).

Chambers, W., and R. Chambers, *What is Philosophy? Chambers's Papers for the People*, No. 92, Philadelphia, PA: Lippincott, Grambo & Co (1854).

Chang, R. (ed.), *Incommensurability, Incomparability and Practical Reason*, Cambridge, MA: Harvard University Press (1997).

Chemero, A., *Radical Embodied Cognitive Science*, Cambridge, MA: MIT Press (2009).

Cheney, D.L., and R.M. Seyfarth, *Baboon Metaphysics: The Evolution of a Social Mind*, Chicago: University of Chicago Press (2007).

Chignell, A., "Belief in Kant," *The Philosophical Review*, 116, 3 (July 2011), pp. 323–60.

Christensen, W., J. Sutton, and D.J.F. McIlwain, "Cognition in Skilled Action: Meshed Control and the Varieties of Skill Experience," *Mind and Language*, 31, 1 (Feb 2016), pp. 37–66.

Christodoulou, G.N., "The Syndrome of Capgras," *British Journal of Psychiatry*, 130 (1977), pp. 556–64.

Chua, E.F., and E. Bliss-Moreau, "Knowing Your Heart and Your Mind: The Relationship between Metamemory and Interoception," *Consciousness and Cognition*, 45 (2016), pp. 146–58.

Cimpian, A., H. Arce, E.M. Markman, and C.S. Dweck, "Subtle Linguistic Cues Impact Children's Motivation," *Psychological Science*, 18 (2007), pp. 314–16.

Clark, A., "Magic Words: How Language Augments Human Cognition," in P. Carruthers and J. Boucher (eds.), *Language and Thought: Interdisciplinary Themes*, Cambridge: Cambridge University Press (1998), pp. 162–83.

Clark, A., and D. Chalmers, "The Extended Mind," *Analysis*, 58 (1998), pp. 10–23.

Clayton, N.S., and A. Dickinson, "Episodic-Like Memory during Cache Recovery by Scrub Jays," *Nature*, 395 (1998), pp. 272–4.

Clayton, N.S., J.M. Daly, and N.J. Emery, "Social Cognition by Food-Catching Corvids: The Western Scrub-Jay as a Natural Psychologist," *Philosophical Transactions of the Royal Society B*, 362, 1480 (2007), pp. 507–22.

Clayton, N.S., N. Emery, and A. Dickinson, "The Rationality of Animal Memory: Complex Caching Strategies of Western Scrub Jays," in S. Hurley and M. Nudds (eds.), *Rational Animals?* Oxford: Oxford University Press (2006), pp. 197–216.

Coady, C.A.J., *Testimony: A Philosophical Study*, Oxford: Clarendon (1994).

Code, L., *Rhetorical Spaces: Essays on Gendered Locations*, New York: Routledge (1995).

Cohen, J.R., and M.D. Lieberman, "The Common Neural Basis of Exerting Self-Control in Multiple Domains," in R.R. Hassin, K.N. Ochsner, and Y. Trope (eds.), *Self Control in Society, Mind and Brain*, New York: Oxford University Press (2010), pp. 141–60.

Cohen, L.J., *The Probable and the Provable*, Oxford: Oxford University Press (1977).

Cohen, L.J., *An Essay on Belief and Acceptance*, Oxford: Clarendon (1992).

Colyvan, M., H.M. Regan, and S. Ferson, "Is it a Crime to Belong to a Reference Class?" *The Journal of Political Philosophy*, 9, 2 (2001), pp. 168–81.

Coltheart, M., P. Menzies, and J. Sutton, "Abductive Inference and Delusional Belief," *Cognitive Neuropsychiatry*, 15 (2010), pp. 261–87.

Conee, E., "Evident but Rationally Unacceptable," *Australasian Journal of Philosophy*, 65 (1987), pp. 316–26.

Conway, E.M., and N. Oreskes, *Merchants of Doubt*, New York: Bloomsbury (2010).

Cormier, H., "William James on Nation and Race," in C. Kautzer and E. Mendenieta (eds.), *Pragmatism, Nation and Race: Community in the Age of Empire*, Bloomington, IN: Indiana University Press (2009), pp. 142–62.

Correll, J., B. Park, C.M. Judd, and B. Wittenbrink, "The Police Officer's Dilemma: Using Ethnicity to Disambiguate Potentially Threatening Individuals," *Journal of Personality and Social Psychology*, 83 (2002), pp. 1314–29.

Cottingham, J., "'The only sure sign...': Thought and Language in Descartes," in J. Preston (ed.), *Thought and Language: Royal Institute of Philosophy Supplement 42*, Cambridge: Cambridge University Press (1997), pp. 29–50.

Crosby, E., S. Bromley, and L. Saxe, "Recent Unobtrusive Studies of Black and White Discrimination and Prejudice: A Literature Review," *Psychological Bulletin*, 87, 3 (1980), pp. 546–63.

Cunningham, W.A., K.J. Preacher, and M.R. Banaji, "Implicit Attitude Measures: Consistency, Stability, and Convergent Validity," *Psychological Science*, 12, 2 (2001), pp. 163–70.

Currie, G., "Imagination and Simulation: Aesthetics Meets Cognitive Science," in A. Stone and M. Davies (eds.), *Mental Simulation: Evaluations and Applications*, Oxford: Basil Blackwell (1995), pp. 99–127.

Dacey, M., "The Varieties of Parsimony in Psychology," *Mind and Language*, 31, 4 (2016a), pp. 414–37.

Dacey, M., "Rethinking Associations in Psychology," *Synthese*, online publication (2016b), DOI 10.1007/s11229-016-1167-0.

Dally, J.M., "Food-Caching Western Scrub-Jays Keep Track of Who Was Watching When," *Science*, 312 (2006), pp. 1662–5.

Darwin, C., *The Descent of Man and Selection in Relation to Sex*, Princeton, NJ: Princeton University Press (1871/1982).

Darwin, C., *The Power of Movement in Plants*, London: John Murray (1880).

Davidson, D., *Essays on Actions and Events*, Oxford: Clarendon Press (1980).

Davidson, D., *Inquiries Intro Truth and Interpretation*, Oxford: Clarendon Press (1984).

Davidson, D., "Rational Animals," in E. LePore and B. McLaughlin (eds.), *Actions and Events*, Oxford: Blackwell (1985), pp. 473–80.

Davidson, D., *Problems of Rationality*, Oxford: Clarendon Press (2004).

Daw, N.D., Y. Niv, and P. Dayan, "Uncertainty-Based Competition between Prefrontal and Dorsolateral Striatal Systems for Behavioral Control," *Nature Neuroscience*, 8, 12 (2005), pp. 1704–11.

Della Rocca, M., "The Power of An Idea: Spinoza's Critique of Pure Will," *Noûs*, 37, 2 (2003), pp. 200–31.

Della Sala, S., C. Marchetti, and H. Spinnler, "Right-sided Anarchic (Alien) Hand: A Longitudinal Study," *Neuropsychologia*, 29 (1991), pp. 1113–27.

Dennett, D.C., "How to Change Your Mind," in D. Dennett, *Brainstorms: Philosophical Essays on Mind and Psychology*, Cambridge, MA: Bradford/ MIT (1978/1981), pp. 300–9.

Dennett, D.C., "True Believers: The Intentional Strategy and Why it Works," in A. F. Heath (ed.), *Scientific Explanation*, Oxford: Oxford University Press (1981), pp. 53–75, reprinted in D.C. Dennett, *The Intentional Stance*, Cambridge, MA: MIT Bradford (1987), pp. 13–36.

Dennett, D.C., "Do Animals Have Beliefs?" in H. Roitblat and Jean-Arcady Meyer (eds.), *Comparative Approaches to Cognitive Science*, Cambridge, MA: MIT Press (1995), pp. 111–18.

Descartes, R., *Discourse on Method*, I, D.A. Cress (trans.) Indianapolis, IN: Hackett (1637/1998).

de Pauw, K.W., and T.K. Szulecka, "Dangerous Delusions: Violence and the Misidentification Syndromes," *British Journal of Psychiatry*, 152 (1988), pp. 91–7.

de Sousa, R., "How to Give a Piece of Your Mind (or the Logic of Belief and Assent)," *Review of Metaphysics*, XXV (1971), pp. 55–71.

Devine, P.G., E.A. Plant, D.M. Amodio, E. Harmon-Jones, and S.L. Vance, "The Regulation of Explicit and Implicit Race Bias: The Role of Motivations to Respond without Prejudice," *Journal of Personality and Social Psychology*, 82 (2002), pp. 835–48.

de Waal, F.B.M., *Chimpanzee Politics: Power and Sex Among Apes*, Baltimore, MD: Johns Hopkins Press (1982/2007).

de Waal, F.B.M., "Are We in Anthropodenial?" *Discover*, 18, 7 (1997), pp. 50–3.

de Waal, F.B.M., "Anthropomorphism and Anthropodenial: Consistency in Our Thinking about Humans and Other Animals," *Philosophical Topics*, 27 (1999), pp. 255–80.

de Waal, F.B.M., "Primates—A Natural Heritage of Conflict Resolution," *Science*, 289 (July 2000), pp. 586–90.

de Waal, F.B.M., *Are We Smart Enough to Know How Smart Animals Are?*, New York: W.W. Norton (2016), pp. 221–9.

de Waal, F.B.M., and A. van Roosmalen, "Reconciliation and Consolation among Chimpanzees," *Behavioral Ecology and Sociobiology*, 5, 1 (1979), pp. 55–66.

Dewey, J., "The Reflex Arc Concept in Psychology," *Psychological Review*, 3 (1896), pp. 357–70.

Dewey, J., "Philosophy and Democracy," in J. Ratner (ed.), *Characters and Events*, 2, New York: Henry Holt (1918/1929), pp. 841–55; reprinted in D. Morris and I Shapiro (eds.), *John Dewey: The Political Writings*, Indianapolis, IN: Hackett (1993), pp. 38–47.

Dewey, J., *Logic: The Theory of Inquiry*, New York: Henry Holt (1938).

Dickinson, A., "Action and Habits: The Development of Behavioral Autonomy," *Philosophical Transactions of the Royal Society B*, 308 (1985), pp. 67–78.

Dickinson, A., "Expectancy Theory in Animal Conditioning," in S.B. Klein and R.R. Mowerer (eds.), *Contemporary Learning Theories: Pavlovian Conditioning and the Status of Traditional Learning Theories*, Hillsdale, NJ: Lawrence Earlbaum Associates (1989), pp. 279–308.

Ditto, P.H., and D.F. Lopez, "Motivated Skepticism: Use of Differential Decision Criteria for Preferred and Nonpreferred Conclusions," *Journal of Personality and Social Psychology*, 63 (1992), pp. 568–84.

Dominici, N., Y.P. Ivanenko, G. Cappellini, A. d'Avella, V. Mondi, M. Cicchese, A. Fabiano, T. Silei, A. Di Paolo, C. Giannini, R.E. Poppele, and F. Lacquaniti, "Locomotor Primitives in Newborn Babies and Their Development," *Science*, 334 (2011), pp. 997–9.

Donald, M., *Origins of the Modern Mind*, Cambridge, MA: Harvard University Press (1991).

Douglass, F., "The Meaning of July 4th for the Negro," speech to the citizens of Rochester, July 5, 1852; reprinted in *Selected Addresses of Frederick Douglas*, USA: Wilder Publications (2014).

Douglass, F., and H. Jacobs, *Narrative of the Life of Frederick Douglass, an American Slave and Incidents in the Life of a Slave Girl*, K.A. Appiah (ed.), New York: Modern Library (2004).

Dreyfus, H., "Intelligence without Representation: Merleau Ponty's Critique of Representation," *Phenomenology and the Cognitive Sciences*, 1 (2002), pp. 367–83.

Dub, R., "Delusions, Acceptances and Cognitive Feelings," *Philosophy and Phenomenological Research*, (2015), pp. 1–34; doi: 10.1111/phpr.12220.

Du Bois, W.E.B., *The Souls of Black Folk*, D.W. Blight and R. Gooding-Williams (eds.), Boston: Bedford Books (1903/1997).

Dummett, M., *Origins of Analytical Philosophy*, London: Duckworth (1993).

Dunn, B.D., T. Dalgleish, and A.D. Lawrence, "The Somatic Marker Hypothesis: A Critical Evaluation," *Neuroscience Biobehavioral Review*, 30, 2 (2006), pp. 239–71.

Dunning, D., *Self-Insight: Roadblocks on the Path to Knowing Thyself*, New York: Psychology Press (2005).

Dunning, D., "Misbelief and the Neglect of Environmental Context," *Behavioral and Brain Sciences*, 32, 6 (2009), pp. 517–18.

Dunning, D., C. Heath, and J.M. Suls, "Flawed Self-Assessment: Implications for Health, Education and the Workplace," *Psychological Science in the Public Interest*, 5 (2004), pp. 69–106.

Durkheim, E., *The Elementary Forms of Religious Life*, New York: Free Press (1912/1995).

Dweck, C.S., "Why We Don't Need Built-In Disbeliefs," *Behavioral and Brain Sciences*, 32, 6 (2009), pp. 518–19.

Edmiston, E., and G. Lupyan, "Visual Interference Disrupts Visual Knowledge," *Journal of Memory and Language*, 92 (2017), pp. 281–92.

Egan, A., "Imagination, Delusion and Self-deception," in T. Bayne and J. Fernandez (eds.), *Delusion and Self-deception: Affective and Motivational Influences on Belief Formation*, Hove: Psychology Press (2009).

Ekman, P., "Lying and Nonverbal Behavior: Theoretical Issues and New Findings," *Journal of Nonverbal Behavior*, 12, 3 (1988), pp. 163–75.

Eldridge, M., "Dewey on Race and Social Change," in B.E. Lawson and D.F. Koch (eds.), *Pragmatism and the Problem of Race*, Bloomington, IN: Indiana University Press (2004), pp. 11–21.

Engel, A.K., A. Maye, M. Kurthen, and P. König, "Where's the Action?" *Trends in Cognitive Science*, 17, 5 (May 2013), pp. 202–9.

Evans, J.L., "Error and the Will," *Philosophy*, 38 (1963), p. 136.

Evans, J. St. B.T., "How Many Dual-Process Theories Do We Need? One, Two or Many?" in Evans and Frankish (eds.), *In Two Minds: Dual Processes and Beyond*, Oxford: Oxford University Press (2009), pp. 33–54.

Evans, J. St. B.T., and K. Frankish, "The Duality of Mind: An Historical Perspective," in J. Evans and K. Frankish (eds.), *In Two Minds: Dual Processes and Beyond*, Oxford: Oxford University Press (2009), pp. 1–29.

Evans, J. St. B.T., and K.E. Stanovich, "Dual Process Theories of Cognition: Advancing the Debate," *Perspectives on Psychological Science*, 8, 3 (2013), pp. 223–41.

Evans, T.A., and M.J. Beran, "Chimpanzees Use Self-Distraction to Cope with Impulsivity," *Biology Letters*, 3 (2007), pp. 599–602.

Fazio, R.H., J.R. Jackson, B.C. Dunton, and C.J. Williams, "Variability in Automatic Activation as an Unobtrusive Measure of Racial Attitudes: A Bona Fide Pipeline?" *Journal of Personality and Social Psychology*, 69 (1995), pp. 1013–27.

Fiedler, K., C. Messner, and M. Bluemke, "Unresolved Problems with the 'I,' the 'A,' and the 'T': A Logical and Psychometric Critique of the Implicit Association Test," *European Review of Social Psychology*, 17 (2006), pp. 74–147.

Field, H., "Theory Change and the Indeterminacy of Reference," *Journal of Philosophy*, 70, 14 (1973), pp. 462–81.

Finkleman, P., "Coming to Terms with Dred Scott: A Response to Daniel A. Farber," *Pepperdine Law Review*, 39, 1 (2013), pp. 49–74.

Fisch, M.H., "Evolution in American Philosophy," *The Philosophical Review*, 56, 4 (July 1947), pp. 357–73.

Fisch, M.H., *Classic American Philosophers*, New York: Appleton-Century-Crofts (1951).

Fisch, M.H., "Alexander Bain and the Genealogy of Pragmatism," *Journal of the History of Ideas*, 15, 5 (June 1954), pp. 413–44.

Fisch, M.H., "Was There a Metaphysical Club in Cambridge?" in E.C. Moore and R.S. Robin (eds.), *Studies in the Philosophy of Charles S. Peirce*, Amherst, MA: The University of Massachusetts Press (1964), pp. 3–32.

Fiske, S.T., M. Lin, and S.L. Neuberg, "The Continuum Model," in S. Chaiken and Y. Trope (eds.), *Dual-Process Theories in Social Psychology*, New York: Guilford Press (1999), pp. 231–54.

Flanagan, O., *Varieties of Moral Personality: Ethics and Psychological Realism*, Cambridge, MA: Harvard University Press (1991).

Fodor, J., *The Language of Thought*, Cambridge, MA: Harvard University Press (1975).

Foley, R., *Working without a Net*, Oxford: Oxford University Press (1993).

Ford, J.K.B., "Killer Whale *Orcinus orca*," in W.F. Perrin, B. Wursig, and H.G.M. Thewissen (eds.), *The Encyclopedia of Marine Mammals*, New York: Academic Press (2002), pp. 669–76.

Förstl, H., O.P. Almeida, A.M. Owen, A. Burns, and R. Howard, "Psychiatric, Neurological and Medical Aspects of Misidentification Syndromes: A Review of 260 Cases," *Psychological Medicine*, 21 (1991), pp. 905–10.

Foster, C., *Being a Beast: Adventures across the Species Divide*, New York: Profile Books (2016).

Fourneret, P., and M. Jeannerod, "Limited Conscious Monitoring of Motor Performance in Normal Subjects," *Neuropsychologia*, 36 (1998), pp. 1113–40.

Fourneret, P., J. Paillard, Y. Lamarre, J. Cole, and M. Jeannerod, "Lack of Conscious Recognition of One's Own Actions in a Haptically Deafferented Patient," *Neuroreport*, 13 (2002), pp. 541–7.

Fox, R., and C. McDaniel, "The Perception of Biological Motion by Human Infants," *Science*, 218 (1982), pp. 468–78.

Fox, R.E., P.H. De Leon, R. Newman, M.T. Sammons, D.L. Dunivin, and D.C. Baker, "Prescriptive Authority and Psychology: A Status Report," *American Psychologist*, 64, 4 (2009), pp. 257–68.

Francione, G. L., *Animals as Persons: Essays on the Abolition of Animal Exploitation*, New York: Columbia University Press (2007).

Frankfurt, H., "Freedom of the Will and the Concept of a Person," *The Journal of Philosophy*, 68, 1 (1971), pp. 5–20.

Frankish, K., *Mind and Supermind*, Cambridge: Cambridge University Press (2004).

Frankish, K., "Systems and Levels: Dual-Systems Theories and the Personal—Sub-personal Distinction," in Evans and Frankish (eds.), *In Two Minds: Dual Processes and Beyond*, Oxford: Oxford University Press (2009), pp. 89–107.

Frankish, K., "Dual Systems and Dual Attitudes," *Mind and Society*, 11, 1 (2012), pp. 41–51.

Frege, G., *Conceptual Notation and Related Articles*, T.W. Bynum (ed.), Oxford: Oxford University Press (1972).

Fricker, M., *Epistemic Injustice: Power and the Ethics of Knowing*, Oxford: Oxford University Press (2007).

Fridland, E., "They've Lost Control: Reflections on Skill," *Synthese*, 191 (2014), pp. 2729–50.

Friedman, O., K.R. Neary, C.L. Bumstein, and A. Leslie, "Is Young Children's Recognition of Pretense Metarepresentational or Merely Behavioral? Evidence From 2- and 3-year-olds' Understanding of Pretend Sounds and Speech," *Cognition*, 115 (2010), pp. 314–19.

Frith, C.D., "Acting, Agency and Responsibility," *Neuropsychologia*, 55 (2014), pp. 137–42.

Funkhouser, E., "Willing Belief and the Norm of Truth," *Philosophical Studies*, 115, 2 (2003), pp. 179–95.

Garzón, P.C., and F. Keijzer, "Plants: Adaptive Behavior, Root-Brains and Minimal Cognition," *Adaptive Behavior*, 19, 3 (2011), pp. 155–71.

Gates Jr., H.L., *The Trials of Phillis Wheatley*, New York: Basic Civitas Books (2003).

Gawronski, B., and L.A. Creighton, "Dual Process Theories," in D.E. Carlston (ed.), *The Oxford Handbook of Social Cognition*, New York: Oxford University Press (2013), pp. 282–312.

Gazzaniga, M., "Consciousness and the Cerebral Hemispheres," in M. Gazzaniga (ed.), *The Cognitive Neurosciences*, Cambridge, MA: MIT Press (1995), pp. 1391–1400.

Gazzaniga, M., *The Cognitive Neurosciences*, 5th Edition, Cambridge, MA: MIT Press (2009).

Gendler, T.S., "Alief and Belief," *Journal of Philosophy*, 105 (2008a), pp. 634–63.

Gendler, T.S., "Alief in Action (and Reaction)," *Mind & Language*, 23 (2008b), pp. 552–85.

Gendler, T.S., "On the Epistemic Costs of Implicit Bias," *Philosophical Studies*, 156 (2011), pp. 33–63.

George, R., and P. Lee, *Body-Self Dualism in Contemporary Ethics and Politics*, Cambridge: Cambridge University Press (2008).

Gerrans, P., "Delusional Attitudes and Default Thinking," *Mind and Language*, 28, 1 (2013), pp. 83–102.

Gigerenzer, G., and T. Reiger, "How Do We Tell an Association from a Rule?" *Psychological Bulletin*, 119 (1996), pp. 23–36.

Gilbert, D., "How Mental Systems Believe," *The American Psychologist*, 46, 2 (1991), pp. 107–19.

Ginet, C., "Deciding to Believe," in M. Steup (ed.), *Knowledge, Truth and Duty*, Oxford: Oxford University Press (2001), pp. 63–76.

Glock, H.J., "Animals, Thoughts and Concepts," *Synthese*, 123 (2000), pp. 35–64.

Glock, H.J., "Concepts: Where Subjectivism Goes Wrong," *Philosophy*, 84 (2009), pp. 5–29.

Glock, H.J., "Can Animals Judge?" *Dialectica*, 64 (2010), pp. 11–33.

Goffman, E., *The Presentation of the Self in Everyday Life*, New York: Doubleday (1959).

Goodale, M.A., D. Pelisson, and C. Prablanc, "Large Adjustments in Visually Guided Reaching Do Not Depend on Vision of the Hand or Perception of Object Displacement," *Nature*, 320 (1986), pp. 748–50.

Goodale, M.A., and G.K. Humphrey, "The Objects of Action and Perception," *Cognition*, 67 (1998), pp. 181–207.

Goodall, J., *In the Shadow of Man*, London: Collins (1971).

Goodman, R.B., *American Philosophy before Pragmatism*, Oxford: Oxford University Press (2015).

Greaves, H., "Epistemic Decision Theory," *Mind*, 122, 488 (2013), pp. 915–52.

Greenwald, A.G., D.E. McGhee, and J.L.K. Schwartz, "Measuring Individual Differences in Implicit Cognition: The Implicit Association Test," *Journal of Personality and Social Psychology*, 74 (1998), pp. 1464–80.

Greenwald, A.G., T.A. Poehlman, E. Uhlmann, and M.R. Banaji, "Understanding and Using the Implicit Association Test: III. Meta-Analysis of Predictive Validity," *Journal of Personality and Social Psychology*, 97 (2009), pp. 17–41.

Hahn, A., C.M. Judd, H.K. Hirsh, and I.V. Blair, "Awareness of Implicit Attitudes," *Journal of Experimental Psychology: General*, 143, 3 (2014), pp. 1369–92.

Haidt, J., "The Emotional Dog and its Rational Tail: A Social Intuitionist Approach to Moral Judgment," *Psychological Review*, 108 (2001), pp. 814–34.

Haidt, J., *The Happiness Hypothesis*, New York: Basic Books (2006).

Halpern, J., *Reasoning about Uncertainty*, Cambridge, MA: MIT Press (2000).

Hampshire, S., *Thought and Action*, London: Chatto and Windus (1959).

Harcourt, H., and F.B.M. de Waal, *Coalitions and Alliances in Humans and Other Animals*, Oxford: Oxford University Press (1992).

Hare, B., J. Call, and M. Tomasello, "Do Chimapnzees Know What Conspecifics Know?" *Animal Behaviour*, 61 (2001), pp. 139–51.

Hare, B., V. Wobber, and R. Wrangham, "The Self-Domestication Hypothesis: Evolution of Bonobo Psychology is Due to Selection against Aggression," *Animal Behavior*, 83, 3 (2012), pp. 573–85.

Harris, P., "Pretending and Planning," in S. Baron-Cohen, H. Tager-Flusberg, and D. Cohen (eds.), *Understanding Other Minds: Perspectives from Autism*, Oxford: Oxford University Press (1993), pp. 228–46.

Harris, S.M., "Constructing a Psychological Perspective: The Observer and the Observed in The Souls of Black Folk," in D. Hubbard (ed.), *The Souls of Black Folk: One Hundred Years Later*, Columbia: University of Missouri Press (2003), pp. 218–50.

Hart, W., D. Albarracin, A. Eagly, I. Brechan, M. Lindberg, and L. Merrill, "Feeling Validated versus Being Correct: A Meta-Analysis of Selective Exposure to Information," *Psychological Bulletin*, 135 (2009), pp. 555–88.

Haselton, M.G., and D.M. Buss, "Error Management Theory: A New Perspective on Biases in Cross-Sex Mind Reading," *Journal of Personality and Social Psychology*, 78, 1 (2000), pp. 81–91.

Haslanger, S., "Distinguished Lecture: Social Structure, Narrative and Explanation," *Canadian Journal of Philosophy*, 45, 1 (2015), pp. 1–15.

Hassabis, D., and E.A. Maguire, "The Construction System of the Brain," *Philosophical Transactions of the Royal Society B: Biological Sciences*, 364 (2009), pp. 1263–71.

Heine, S.J., D.R. Lehman, H.R. Marcus, and S. Kitayama, "Is There a Universal Need for Positive Self-Regard?" *Psychological Review*, 106, 4 (1999), pp. 766–94.

Helming, K.A., B. Strickland, and P. Jacob, "Making Sense of Early False-Belief Understanding," *Trends in Cognitive Sciences*, 18, 4 (2014), pp. 167–70.

Hieronymi, P., "Controlling Attitudes," *Pacific Philosophical Quarterly*, 87 (2006), pp. 163–96.

Hillemann, F., T. Bugnyar, K. Kotrschal, and C.A.F. Wascher, "Waiting for Better, Not for More: Corvids Respond to Quality in Two Delay Maintenance Tasks," *Animal Behavior*, 90 (2014), pp. 1–10.

Hitchcott, P.K., J.J. Quinn, and J.R. Taylor, "Bidirectional Modulation of Goal Directed Actions by Prefrontal Cortical Dopamine," *Cerebral Cortex*, 17, 12 (2007), pp. 2820–7.

Hodos W., and C.B. Campbell, "Scala Naturae: Why There Is No Theory in Comparative Psychology," *Psychological Review*, 76 (1969), pp. 337–50.

Holton, G.A., "Defining Risk," *Financial Analysts Journal*, 60, 6 (2004), pp. 19–25.

Holmes Jr., O.W., *The Common Law*, Boston, MA: Little Brown and Co. (1881).

Horne, G., *Negro Comrades of the Crown: African Americans and the British Empire Fight the U.S. before Emancipation*, New York: New York University Press (2012).

Hoyer, R., "Belief and Will Revisited," *Dialogue*, XXII, 2 (1983), pp. 273–90.

Huddleston, A., "Naughty Beliefs," *Philosophical Studies*, 160 (2012), pp. 209–22.

Huijding J., and P. J. de Jong, "Specific Predictive Power of Automatic Spider-Related Affective Associations for Controllable and Uncontrollable Fear Responses toward Spiders," *Behavior Research and Therapy*, 44 (2006), pp. 161–76.

Hume, D., *A Treatise of Human Nature*, D.F. Norton and M.J. Norton (eds.), Oxford: Oxford University Press (1740/2000).

Humphrey, N., "Bugs and Beasts Before the Law," in N. Humphrey, *The Mind Made Flesh: Essays from the Frontiers of Psychology and Evolution*, Oxford: Oxford University Press (2002), pp. 235–54.

Humphreys, G.W., and M.J. Riddoch, "Fractioning the Intentional Control of Behavior: A Neuropsychological Analysis," in J. Roessler and N. Eilan (eds.), *Agency and Self-Awareness*, Oxford: Clarendon (2003), pp. 201–17.

Hutchison, K.A., "Is Semantic Priming Due to Association Strength or Feature Overlap? A Microanalytic Review," *Psychonomic Bulletin and Review*, 10, 4 (2003), pp. 785–813.

Iacoboni, M., I. Molnar-Skakacs, V. Gallese, G. Buccino, J.C. Mazziotta, and G. Rizzolatti, "Grasping the Intentions of Others with One's Mirror System," *PLoS Biology*, 3 (2004), pp. 529–35.

Imanishi, K., *Man*, Tokyo: Mainichi-Shinbunsha (1952).

Inoue-Nakamura, N., and T. Matsuzawa, "Development of Stone Tool Use by Wild Chimpanzees," *Journal of Comparative Psychology*, 111 (1997), pp. 159–73.

Ito, T.A., N.P. Friedman, B.D. Bartholow, J. Correll, C. Loersch, L.J. Altamirano, and A. Miyake, "Toward a Comprehensive Understanding of Executive Cognitive Function in Racial Bias," *Journal of Personality and Social Psychology*, 108, 2 (2015), pp. 187–218.

James, W., *Principles of Psychology*, New York: Dover (1890/1950).

James, W., *The Will to Believe: And Other Essays in Popular Philosophy*, New York: Longmans, Green (1896/1912).

James, W., *Pragmatism: A New Name for Some Old Ways of Thinking*, New York: Longmans, Green (1907/1921).

Jeannerod, M., *Motor Cognition: What Actions Tell the Self*, Oxford: Oxford University Press (2006).

Jeffrey, R., "Dracula Meets Wolfman: Acceptance vs. Partial Belief," in M. Swain (ed.), *Induction, Acceptance, and Rational Belief*, Dordrecht: Reidel (1970), pp. 157–85.

Jeon, H., and A. D. Friederici, "Degree of Automaticity and the Prefrontal Cortex," *Trends in Cognitive Science*, 19, 5 (2015), pp. 244–50.

Johnson, D.J., and C.E. Rusbult, "Resisting Temptation: Devaluation of Alternative Partners as a Means of Maintaining Commitment in Close Relationships," *Journal of Personality and Social Psychology*, 57 (1989), pp. 967–80.

Jonides, J., M. Naveh-Benjamin, and J. Palmer, "Assessing Automaticity," *Acta Psychologica*, 60, 2–3 (1985), pp. 157–71.

Joyce, J.M., "A Nonpragmatic Vindication of Probabilism," *Philosophy of Science*, 65, 4 (Dec. 1998), pp. 575–603.

Kagan, J., "Human Morality is Distinctive," *Journal of Consciousness Studies*, 7 (2004), pp. 46–8.

Kahn, J., "The Happiness Code," *The New York Times Magazine*, (January 17, 2016), pp. 38–45, 55.

Kahneman, D., "A Perspective on Judgment and Choice: Mapping Bounded Rationality," *American Psychologist*, 58 (2003), pp. 697–720.

Kahneman, D., *Thinking, Fast and Slow*, New York: Farrar, Straus and Giroux (2011).

Kahneman, D., and S. Frederick, "Representativeness Revisited: Attribute Substitution in Intuitive Judgment," in T. Gilovich, D. Griffin, and D. Kahneman (eds.), *Heuristics and Biases: The Psychology of Intuitive Judgments*, New York: Cambridge University Press (2002), pp. 49–81.

Kahneman, D., and S. Fredrick, "Frames and Brains: Elicitation and Control of Response Tendencies," *Trends in Cognitive Sciences*, 11 (2007), pp. 45–6.

Kalanithi, P., *When Breath Becomes Air*, New York: Random House (2016).

Kamins, M., and C.S. Dweck, "Person vs. Process Praise and Criticism: Implications for Contingent Self-Worth and Coping," *Developmental Psychology*, 35 (1999), pp. 835–47.

Kauber, P., "The Foundations of James's Ethics of Belief," *Ethics*, 84, 2 (Jan 1974), pp. 151–66.

Keijzer, F.A., M. Van Duijn, and P. Lyon, "What Nervous Systems Do: Early Evolution, Input-Output, and the Skin Brain Thesis," *Adaptive Behavior*, 21, 2 (2013), pp. 67–85.

Kellet, W.M., D.D. Wagner, and T.F. Heatherton, "In Search of a Human Self-Regulation System," *Annual Review of Neuroscience*, 38 (2015), pp. 389–411.

Kelly, T., "The Rationality of Belief and Some Other Propositional Attitudes," *Philosophical Studies*, 110 (2002), pp. 163–96.

Kenny, A.J.P., *The Metaphysics of Mind*, Oxford: Oxford University Press (1989).

Keren, G., and Y. Schul, "Two is Not Always Better Than One: A Critical Evaluation of Two-System Theories," *Perspectives on Psychological Science*, 4 (2009), pp. 533–50.

Keven, N., and K.A. Akins, "Neonatal Imitation in Context: Sensory-Motor Development in the Prenatal Period," *Behavioral and Brain Sciences* (2016), pp. 1–107; doi:10.1017/S0140525X160009111.

Kim, D.H., "The Unexamined Frontier: Dewey, Pragmatism and America Enlarged," in C. Kautzer and E. Mendenieta (eds.), *Pragmatism, Nation and Race: Community in the Age of Empire*, Bloomington, IN: Indiana University Press (2009), pp. 46–72.

Kim, D.Y., "Voluntary Controllability of the Implicit Association Test (IAT)," *Social Psychology Quarterly*, 66 (2003), pp. 83–96.

King, S.L., and V.M. Janik, "Bottlenose Dolphins Can Use Learned Vocal Labels to Address Each Other," *Proceedings of the National Academy of Sciences, USA*, 110 (2013), pp. 13216–21.

King, S.L., L.S. Sayigh, R.S. Wells, W. Fellner, and V.M. Janik, "Vocal Copying of Individually Distinctive Signature Whistles in Bottlenose Dolphins," *Proceedings of the Royal Society B*, 280, 1757 (April 2013), pp. 1–9.

Kitayama, S., H.R. Marcus, H. Matsumoto, and V. Norasakkundit, "Individual and Collective Process in the Construction of the Self: Self-Enhancement in the U.S. and Self-Criticism in Japan," *Journal of Personality and Social Psychology*, 72 (1997), pp. 1245–67.

Kneale, W., *Probability and Induction*, Oxford: Clarendon (1949).

Knoblich, G., and T.T.J. Kircher, "Deceiving Oneself about Being in Control: Conscious Detection of Changes in Visuomotor Coupling," *Journal of Experimental Psychology: Human Perception and Performance*, 30 (2004), pp. 657–66.

Koechlin, E., and C. Summerfield, "An Information Theoretical Approach to Prefrontal Executive Function," *Trends in Cognitive Sciences*, 11, 6 (2007), pp. 229–35.

Konecni, V.J., "A Positive Illusion about 'Positive Illusions'?" *Behavioral and Brain Sciences*, 32, 6 (2009), pp. 524–5.

Kornblith, H., *On Reflection*, Oxford: Oxford University Press (2012).

Korsgaard, C., "Skepticism about Practical Reason," *Journal of Philosophy*, 83, 1 (1986), pp. 5–25.

Kripke, S., "A Puzzle about Belief," in N. Salmon and S. Soames (eds.), *Propositions and Attitudes*, New York: Oxford University Press (1988), pp. 102–48;

reprinted from A. Margalit (ed.), *Meaning and Use*, Dordrecht: D. Reidel (1979), pp. 239–83.

Kruger, J., S. Chan, and N. Roese, "(Not so) Positive Illusions," *Behavioral and Brain Sciences*, 32, 6 (2009), pp. 526–7.

Kruglansk, A.W., and E. Orehek, "Partitioning the Domain of Social Inference: Dual Mode and Systems Models and their Alternatives," *Annual Review of Psychology*, 58 (2007), pp. 291–316.

Kubota, J.T., M.R. Banaji, and E.A. Phelps, "The Neuroscience of Race," *Nature Neuroscience*, 15, 7 (2012); 10.1038/nn.3136. doi:10.1038/nn.3136.

Kuhn, T., *The Structure of Scientific Revolutions*, Chicago: University of Chicago Press (1962/2012).

Kummer, H., and J. Goodall, "Conditions of Innovative Behaviour in Primates," *Philosophical Transactions of the Royal Society of London*, Series B, 308 (1985), pp. 203–14.

Kvart, I., "Beliefs and Believing," *Theoria*, 9, 3 (1986), pp. 129–45.

Langdon, R., and M. Coltheart, "The Cognitive Neuropsychology of Delusions," *Mind and Language*, 15, 1 (2000), pp. 183–216.

Langland-Hassan, P., "Pretense, Imagination and Belief: The Single Attitude Theory," *Philosophical Studies*, 159, 2 (2012), pp. 155–79.

Lau, H., "Volition and the Function of Consciousness," in M. Gazzaniga (ed.), *The Cognitive Neurosciences*, 4th Edition, Cambridge, MA: MIT Press/Bradford (2009), pp. 1191–1200.

Lawson, B.E., and D.F. Koch, "Introduction," in Lawson and Koch (eds.), *Pragmatism and the Problem of Race*, Bloomington, IN: Indiana University Press (2004), pp. 1–7.

Leslie, A., "Pretense and Representation: The Origins of 'Theory of Mind'," *Psychological Review*, 94 (1987), pp. 412–26.

Lessig, L., "The Regulation of Social Meaning," *The University of Chicago Law Review*, 62, 3 (1995), pp. 943–1045.

Levy, N., "Resisting 'Weakness of the Will'," *Philosophy and Phenomenological Research*, LXXXII, 1 (2011), pp. 134–55.

Levy, N., "Implicit Attitudes as Patchy Endorsements," *Noûs*, 49, 4 (2015), pp. 800–23.

Levy, N., and T.J. Bayne, "A Will of One's Own: Consciousness, Control and Character," *International Journal of Law and Psychiatry*, 27 (2004), pp. 459–70.

Lewis, D., "A Subjectivist Guide to Objective Chance," in R.C. Jeffrey (ed.), *Studies in Inductive Logic and Probability*, Vol. II, Berkeley, CA: University of California Press (1980); reprinted in D. Lewis (1986), pp. 83–132.

Lewis, D., *Philosophical Papers Volume II*, Oxford: Oxford University Press (1986).

Lewis, D., "Humean Supervenience Debugged," *Mind*, 103 (1994), pp. 473–90; reprinted in D. Lewis, *Papers in Metaphysics and Epistemology*, Cambridge: Cambridge University Press (1999), pp. 224–47.

Libet, B., "Unconscious Cerebral Initiative and the Role of Conscious Will in Voluntary Action," *Behavioral and Brain Science*, 6 (1985), pp. 529–66.

Lichtneckert, R., and H. Reichert, "Origin and Evolution of the First Nervous System," in G.F. Striedter and J.L.R. Rubinstein (eds.), *Evolution of Nervous Systems, Volume 1: Theories, Development, Invertebrates*, Amsterdam: Elsevier (2007), pp. 289–315.

Lieberman, M.D., A. Hariri, J.M. Jarcho, N.I. Eisenberger, and S.Y. Bookheimer, "An fMRI Investigation of Race-Related Amygdala Activity in African-American and Caucasian-American Individuals," *Nature Neuroscience*, 8, 6 (2005), pp. 720–2.

Loar, B., "Social Content and Psychological Content," in R. Grimm and D. Merrill (eds.), *Contents of Thought*, Tucson: University of Arizona Press (1988).

Lofting, H., *The Story of Dr. Dolittle*, Mineola, NY: Dover (1920/2004).

Lovato, D., I. Salmanzadeg, S.H. Kotecha, and M.K. Sandberg, "Confident," on D. Lovato, *Confident*, Warner/ChappellMusic, Inc., Universal Music Publishing Group (2015).

Lovejoy, A.O., "The Thirteen Pragmatisms," *The Journal of Philosophy, Psychology and Scientific Methods*, 5, 1 (1908), pp. 5–12.

Lugones, María C., "Playfulness, World-Traveling, and Loving Perception," *Hypatia*, 2, 2 (1987), pp. 3–19.

Lyons, J., *Perception and Basic Beliefs: Zombies, Modules, and the Problem of the External World*, New York: Oxford University Press (2009).

Maguire, E.A., and D. Hassabis, "Role of the Hippocampus in Imagination and Future Thinking," *Proceedings of the Natural Academy of Sciences*, 108 (2011), p. E39.

Maher, P., *Betting on Theories*, Cambridge: Cambridge University Press (1993).

Maia, T.V., and J.L. McClelland, "A Reexamination of the Evidence for the Somatic Marker Hypothesis: What Participants Really Know in the Iowa Gambling Task," *Proceedings of the National Academy for Science* (USA), 101, 45 (2004), pp. 16075–80.

Maia, T.V., and J.L. McClelland, "The Somatic Marker Hypothesis: Still Many Questions but No Answers," *Trends in Cognitive Science*, 9, 4 (2005), pp. 162–4.

Malcolm, N., "Thoughtless Brutes," *Proceedings and Addresses of the American Philosophical Association*, XLVI (1973), pp. 5–20.

Malebranche, N., *The Search After Truth*, T.M. Lennon and P.J. Olscamp (trans.), Cambridge: Cambridge University Press (1674–5/1997).

Malinowski, B., *Magic, Science and Religion and Other Essays*, Boston, MA: Beacon (1948).

Mandelbaum, E., "Attitude, Inference, Association," *Noûs*, 50, 3 (2016), pp. 629–58.

Maner, J.K., D.T. Kendirck, S.L. Neurberg, D.V. Becker, T. Robertson, B. Hofer, A. Delton, J. Butner, and M. Schaller, "Functional Projection: How Fundamental Social Motives Can Bias Interpersonal Perception," *Journal of Personality and Social Psychology*, 88 (2005), pp. 63–78.

Marcus, R.B., "Some Revisionary Proposals about Belief and Believing," *Philosophy and Phenomenological Research*, 50, Supplement (1990), pp. 133–53.

Marshall, M.A., and J.D. Brown, "On the Psychological Benefits of Self-Enhancement," in E. Chang (ed.), *Self- Enhancement and Self-Criticism: Theory, Research, and Clinical Implications*, Washington, DC: American Psychological Association (2007), pp. 19–35.

Martin, A., "Circuits in Mind: The Neural Foundations for Object Concepts," in M. Gazzaniga (ed.), *The Cognitive Neurosciences*, 4th Edition, Cambridge, MA: MIT Press/Bradford (2009), pp. 1031–45.

Marx, K., *Capital*, F. Engels (ed.), S. Moore and E. Averling (trans.), Volume 1, New York: International Publishers (1867/1967).

Matsuzawa, T., "Field Experiments on Use of Stone Tools by Chimpanzees in the Wild," in R.W. Wrangham, W.C. McGrew, F.B.M. de Waal, and P. Heltne (eds.), *Chimpanzee Cultures*, Cambridge, MA: Harvard University Press (1994).

Mayo, B., "Belief and Constraint," *Proceedings of the Aristotelian Society*, New Series, 64 (1963–4), pp. 139–56.

McCann, H., "Conative Intuitionism," in J. Graper (ed.), *The New Intuitionism*, London: Continuum (2001), pp. 29–47.

McClelland, J., T.T. Rogers, K. Patterson, K. Dilkina, and M.L. Ralph, "Semantic Cognition: Its Nature, Its Development, and Its Neural Basis," in M. Gazzaniga (ed.), *The Cognitive Neurosciences*, 4th Edition, Cambridge, MA: MIT Press/Bradford (2009), pp. 1047–66.

McDowell, J., *Mind and World*, Cambridge, MA: Harvard University Press (1994).

McKay, R.T., and D.C. Dennett, "The Evolution of Misbelief," *Behavioral and Brain Sciences*, 32, 6 (2009), pp. 493–561.

Medina, J., *The Epistemology of Resistance: Gender and Racial Oppression, Epistemic Injustice and Resistant Imaginations*, Oxford: Oxford University Press (2013).

Mele, A.R., *Self-Deception Unmasked*, Princeton, NJ: Princeton University Press (2001).

Mele, A.R., *Effective Intentions*, Oxford: University Press (2009).

Mellor, H., "Conscious Belief," *Proceedings of the Aristotelian Society*, New Series, LXXXVIII (1977–78), pp. 87–101.

Mellor, H., "Consciousness and Degrees of Belief," in D.H. Mellor (ed.), *Prospects for Pragmatism: Essays in Memory of F. P. Ramsey*, Cambridge: Cambridge University Press (1991), reprinted in H. Mellor, *Matters of Metaphysics*, Cambridge: Cambridge University Press (1991), pp. 30–60.

Menand, L., *The Metaphysical Club: A Story of Ideas in America*, New York: Farrar, Straus and Giroux (2001).

Mendell, M., "The Problem of the Origin of Pragmatism," *History of Philosophy Quarterly*, 12, 1 (1995), pp. 111–31.

Metcalfe, J., and W. Mischel, "A Hot/Cool Analysis of Delay of Gratification: Dynamics of Willpower," *Psychological Review*, 106 (1999), pp. 3–19.

Metzoff, A.N., and M.K. Moore, "Explaining Facial Imitation: A Theoretical Model," *Early Development and Parenting*, 6 (1997), pp. 179–92.

Mikkleson, D., "Inscrutable Cookie," www.snopes.com/food/origins/fortune.asp (2016).

Miller, E.K., "The Prefrontal Cortex and Cognitive Control," *Nature Reviews Neuroscience*, 1 (2000), pp. 59–65.

Millikan, R.G., "Pushmi-Pullyu Representations," *Philosophical Perspectives*, 9 (1995), pp. 185–200.

Millikan, R.G., "Styles of Rationality," in S. Hurley and M. Nudds (eds.), *Rational Animals?* Oxford: University Press (2006), pp. 117–26.

Mill, J.S., *On Liberty*, K. Casey (ed.), Mineola, NY: Dover (1859/2002).

Mill, J.S., "Utilitarianism," in J. Schneewind and D.E. Miller (eds.), *The Basic Writings of John Stuart Mill*, New York: Random House (1863/2002), pp. 230–301.

Mills, C.W., "White Ignorance," in S. Sullivan and N. Tuana (eds.), *Race and Epistemologies of Ignorance*, Albany, NY: SUNY Press (2007), pp. 13–38.

Mithen, M., *The Prehistory of Mind*, London: Thames and Hudson (1996).

Mole, C., *Attention is Cognitive Unison: An Essay in Philosophical Psychology*, New York: Oxford University Press (2013).

Monsell, S., and J. Driver (eds.), *Attention and Performance XVIII: Control of Mental Processes*, Cambridge, MA: MIT Press (2000).

Montmarquet, J., "The Voluntariness of Belief," *Analysis*, 46 (1986), pp. 49–53.

Moore, J., and P. Haggard, "Awareness of Action: Inference and Prediction," *Consciousness and Cognition*, 17, 1 (2008), pp. 136–44.

Moran, R., "Problems of Sincerity," *Proceedings of the Aristotelian Society*, New Series, 105 (2005), pp. 325–45.

Moran, T., and Y. Bar-Anan, "The Effect of Object–Valence Relations on Automatic Evaluation," *Cognition and Emotion*, 27, 4 (2013), pp. 743–52.

Morgan, C.L., *An Introduction to Comparative Psychology*, London: Walter Scott (1894).

Moskowitz, G.B., P.M. Gollwitzer, W. Wasel, and B. Schaal, "Preconscious Control of Stereotype Activation through Chronic Egalitarian Goals," *Journal of Personality and Social Psychology*, 77 (1999), pp. 167–84.

Moskowitz, G. B., A.R. Salomon, and C.M. Taylor, "Preconsciously Controlling Stereotyping: Implicitly Activated Egalitarian Goals Prevent the Activation of Stereotypes," *Social Cognition*, 18 (2000), pp. 151–77.

Mueller, C.M., and C.S. Dweck, "Intelligence Praise Can Undermine Motivation and Performance," *Journal of Personality and Social Psychology*, 75 (1998), pp. 33–52.

Murphy, J.P., *Pragmatism: From Peirce to Davidson*, Boulder, CO: Westview Press (1990).

Murray, S.L., J.G. Holmes, and D.W. Griffin, "The Benefits of Positive Illusions: Idealization and the Construction of Satisfaction in Close Relationships," *Journal of Personality and Social Psychology*, 70 (1996), pp. 79–98.

Nagel, T., "Brain Bisection and the Unity of Consciousness," in T. Nagel, *Mortal Questions*, Cambridge: Cambridge University Press (1979), pp. 147–64.

Nagel, T., *The Possibility of Altruism*, Princeton, NJ: Princeton University Press (1979).

Nanay, B., *Between Perception and Action*, Oxford: Oxford University Press (2013).

Navarette, C.D., D.M.T. Fessler, and S.J. Eng, "Increased Ethnocentrism in the First Trimester of Pregnancy," *Evolution and Human Behavior*, 28 (2007), pp. 60–5.

Nelson, L.H., *Who Knows: From Quine to a Feminist Empiricism*, Philadelphia: Temple University Press (1990).

Newman, J.H., *An Essay in Aid of a Grammar of Assent*, South Bend, IN: University of Notre Dame Press (1870/1992).

Newstead, S.E., "Are There Two Different Types of Thinking?" *Behavioral and Brain Sciences*, 23 (2000), pp. 690–1.

Nichols, S., "Just the Imagination: Why Imagining Doesn't Behave Like Believing," *Mind and Language*, 21 (2006a), pp. 459–474.

Nichols, S., "Introduction," in S. Nichols (ed.), *The Architecture of the Imagination*, Oxford: Oxford University Press (2006b), pp. 1–18.

Nichols, S., and S. Stich, "A Cognitive Theory of Pretense," *Cognition*, 74 (2000), pp. 115–47.

Nichols, S., and S. Stich, *Mindreading: An Integrated Account of Pretense, Self-Awareness, and Understanding Other Minds*, Oxford: Clarendon (2003).

Nielsen, T.I., "Volition: A New Experimental Approach," *Scandinavian Journal of Psychology*, 4 (1963), pp. 225–30.

Nielsen, T.I., *Acts: Analyses and Syntheses of Human Acting, concerning the Subject and from the Standpoint of the Subject*, Forlag, Copenhagen: Dansk Psykologisc (1978).

Nielsen, T.I., N. Praetorius and R. Kuschel, "Volitional Aspects of Voice Performance: An Experimental Approach," *Scandinavian Journal of Psychology*, 6 (1965), pp. 201–8.

Noad, M., D. Cato, M. Bryden, M. Jenner, and K. Jenner, "Cultural Revolution in Whale Songs," *Nature*, 408 (2000), p. 537.

Norman, D.A., and T. Shallice, "Attention to Action: Willed and Automatic Control of Behavior," *Center for Human Information Processing Technical Report No. 99*, reprinted with revisions in R.J. Davidson, G.E. Schwartz, and D. Shapiro (eds.), *Consciousness and Self-Regulation*, IV, New York: Plenum (1986), pp. 1–18.

Obama, U.S. President B., Memorial Speech, Dallas, Texas, July 12, 2016.

O'Connor, D.J., "Beliefs, Dispositions and Actions," *Proceedings of the Aristotelian Society*, 69 (1968–9), pp. 1–16.

O'Connor, A.R., and C.J.A. Moulin, "Recognition without Identification: Erroneous Familiarity and Déjà Vu," *Current Psychiatry Reports*, 12 (2010), pp. 165–73.

Olsson, A., K.I. Nearing, and E.A. Phelps, "Learning Fears by Observing Others: The Neural Systems of Social Fear Transmission," *Social Cognitive Affective Neuroscience*, 2, 3 (2007), pp. 3–11.

Osman, M., "An Evaluation of Dual-Process Theories of Reasoning," *Psychonomic Bulletin and Review*, 11 (2004), pp. 988–1010.

Ouellette, J.A., and W. Wood, "Habit and Intention in Everyday Life: The Multiple Processes by Which Past Behavior Predicts Future Behavior," *Psychological Bulletin*, 124, 1 (1998), p. 54.

Owens, D., "Does Belief Have an Aim?" *Philosophical Studies*, 115 (2003), pp. 283–305.

Pacherie, E., "The Phenomenology of Action: A Conceptual Framework," *Cognition*, 107 (2008), pp. 179–217.

Papineau, D., "Choking and the Yips," *Phenomenology and Cognitive Science*, 14 (2015), pp. 295–308.

Papineau, D., and C. Heyes, "Rational or Associative? Imitation in Japanese Quail," in S. Hurley and M. Nudds (eds.), *Rational Animals?* Oxford: Oxford University Press (2006), pp. 187–96.

Peacocke, C., *Being Known*, Oxford: Oxford University Press (1999).

Peirce, C.S., "Some Consequences of Four Incapacities," *Journal of Speculative Philosophy*, 2 (1868), pp. 140–57.

Peirce, C.S., "The Fixation of Belief," *Popular Science Monthly*, 12 (November 1877), pp. 1–15.

Peirce, C.S., *Collected Papers of Charles Sanders Peirce*, Vols. 1–IV, C. Hartshorne and P. Weiss (eds.), Cambridge, MA: Harvard University Press (1931–5).

Pepperberg, I.M., "Grey Parrot (*Psittacus erithacus*) Numerical Abilities: Addition and Further Experiments on a Zero-like Concept," *Journal of Comparative Psychology*, 120, 1 (2006a), pp. 1–11.

Pepperberg, I.M., "Ordinality and Inferential Abilities of a Grey Parrot (*Psittacus erithacus*)," *Journal of Comparative Psychology*, 120, 3 (2006b), pp. 205–16.

Pepperberg, I.M., and J.D. Gordon, "Number Comprehension by a Grey Parrot (*Psittacus erithacus*), Including a Zero-like Concept," *Journal of Comparative Psychology*, 119, 2 (2005), pp. 197–209.

Pepperberg, I.M., A. Koepke, P. Livingston, M. Girard, and L.A. Hartsfield, "Reasoning by Inference: Further Studies on Exclusion in Grey Parrots (*Psittacus erithacus*)," *Journal of Comparative Psychology*, 127, 3 (2013), pp. 272–81.

Perner, J., "Dual Control and the Causal Theory of Action: The Case of Non-Intentional Action," in J. Roessler and N. Eilan (eds.), *Agency and Self-Awareness*, Oxford: Clarendon (2003), pp. 218–43.

Petersen-Steglich, A., "No Norm Needed: On the Aim of Belief," *The Philosophical Quarterly*, 56 (2006), pp. 499–516.

Peterson, S.E., and M.I. Posner, "The Attention System of the Human Brain: 20 Years After," *Annual Review of Neuroscience*, 35 (2012), pp. 73–89.

Petty, R.E., R.H. Fazio, and P. Briñol (eds.), *Attitudes: Insights from the New Implicit Measures*, New York: Taylor and Francis (2009).

Piaget, J., *The Construction of Reality in the Child*, New York: Basic Books (1954).

Pickering, M.J., and V.S. Ferreira, "Structural Priming: A Critical Review," *Psychological Bulletin*, 134, 3 (2008), pp. 427–59.

Pisella, L., H. Grea, C. Tilikete, A. Vighetto, M. Desmurget, G. Rode, D. Boisso, and Y. Rossetti, "An 'Automatic Pilot' for the Hand in Human Posterior Parietal Cortex: Toward Reinterpreting Optic Ataxia," *Nature Neuroscience*, 3 (2000), pp. 729–36.

Pojman, L., "Believing and Willing," *Canadian Journal of Philosophy*, 15, 1 (1985), pp. 37–55.

Posner, M.I., and C.R. Snyder, "Attention and Cognitive Control," in R.L. Solso (ed.), *Information Processing and Cognition*, Hillsdale, NJ: Erlbaum (1975), pp. 55–85.

Premack, D., "Human and Animal Cognition: Continuity and Discontinuity," *Proceedings of the National Academy of Sciences USA*, 104 (2007), pp. 13861–7.

Price, H.H., *Belief*, London: George Allen and Unwin (1969).

Prinz, W., "How Do We Know about Our Own Actions?" in S. Maasen, W. Prinz and G. Roth (eds.), *Voluntary Actions: Brains, Minds and Society*, New York: Oxford University Press (2003), pp. 21–33.

Pronin, E., "How We See Ourselves and How We See Others," *Science*, 320, 5880 (2008), pp. 1177–80.

Pronin, E., D. Lin, and L. Ross, "The Bias Blind Spot: Perceptions of Bias in Self Versus Others," *Personality and Social Psychology Bulletin*, 28, 3 (2002), pp. 369–81.

Proust, J., "The Representational Structure of Feelings," in T. Metzinger and J.M. Windt (eds.), *Open MIND*: 31, Frankfurt am Main: MIND Group (2015a), pp. 1–26; doi: 10.15502/9783958570047.

Proust, J., "Time and Action: Impulsivity, Habit, Strategy," *The Review of Philosophy and Psychology*, 6 (2015b), pp. 717–43.

Purcell Jr., E. A., "On the Complexity of 'Ideas in America': Origins and Achievements of the Classical Age of Pragmatism," *Law and Social Inquiry*, 27, 4 (Autumn 2002), pp. 967–99.

Putnam, H., *Mind, Language and Reality: Philosophical Papers Volume 1*, Cambridge: Cambridge University Press (1975a).

Putnam, H., "The Meaning of 'Meaning'," in K. Gunderson (ed.), *Language, Mind and Knowledge*, Minneapolis: University of Minnesota Press (1975b), pp. 131–93; reprinted in H. Putnam, *Mind, Language and Reality: Philosophical Papers Volume 1*, Cambridge: Cambridge University Press (1975b), pp. 362–85.

Putnam, H., *Reason, Truth and History*, Cambridge: Cambridge University Press (1982).

Quine, W.V.O., *Word and Object*, Cambridge, MA: MIT Press (1960/2015).

Quinn, W., "Putting Rationality in Its Place," in his *Morality and Action*, Cambridge: Cambridge University Press (1993), pp. 228–55; originally published in R.G. Frey and C. Morris (eds.), *Value, Welfare and Morality*, Cambridge: Cambridge University Press (1993), pp. 26–50.

Rachels, J., *Created from Animals: The Moral Implications of Darwinism*, Oxford: Oxford University Press (1990).

Radvansky, G.A., and D.E. Copeland, "Walking through Doorways Causes Forgetting," *Memory and Cognition*, 34 (2006), pp. 1150–6.

Radvansky, G.A., S.A. Krawietz, and A.K. Tamplin, "Walking through Doorways Causes Forgetting: Further Explorations," *The Quarterly Journal of Experimental Psychology*, 64, 8 (2011).

Raiffa, H., *Decision Analysis: Introductory Lectures on Choices Under Uncertainty*, Reading, MA: Addison Wesley (1968).

Ramsey, F. P. (with G. E. Moore), "Symposium: Facts and Propositions." *Proceedings of the Aristotelian Society, Supplementary Volume 7* (1927), pp. 153–206.

Ramsey, F., "Truth and Probability," in R.B. Braithwaite (ed.), *The Foundations of Mathematics*, London: Routledge and Keegan Paul (1931), pp. 156–98.

Ransom, M., S. Fazelpour, and C. Mole, "Attention in the Predictive Mind," *Consciousness and Cognition*, (Jul 4, 2016), prepublication doi: 10.1016/j.concog.2016.06.011.

Reader, S.M., and K.N. Laland (eds.), *Animal Innovation*, Oxford: Oxford University Press (2003).

Reber, A., *Implicit Learning and Tacit Knowledge: An Essay on the Cognitive Unconscious*, Oxford: Oxford University Press (1993).

Reber, R., and E.G. Slingerland, "Confucius Meets Cognition: New Answers to Old Questions," *Religion, Brain and Behavior*, 1, 2 (2011), pp. 135–45.

Recanati, F., "Can We Believe What We Do Not Understand?" *Mind and Language*, 12, 1 (1997), pp. 84–100.

Redmayne, M., "Exploring the Proof Paradoxes," *Legal Theory*, 14 (2008), pp. 281–309.

Reed, N., P. McLeod, and Z. Dienes, "Implicit Knowledge and Motor Skill: What People Who Know How to Catch Don't Know," *Consciousness and Cognition*, 19 (2010), pp. 63–76.

Reisner, A., "Weighing Pragmatic and Evidential Reasons for Belief," *Philosophical Studies*, 138 (2008), pp. 17–27.

Reisner, A., "The Possibility of Pragmatic Reasons for Belief and the Wrong Kind of Reasons Problem," *Philosophical Studies*, 145 (2009), pp. 257–72.

Rendell, L., and H. Whitehead, "Culture in Whales and Dolphins," *Behavioral and Brain Sciences*, 24 (2001), pp. 309–24.

Rescorla, M., "Chrysippus' Dog as a Case Study in Non-Linguistic Cognition," in R. Lutz (ed.), *The Philosophy of Animal Minds*, New York: Cambridge (2009).

Richard, M., "Marcus on Belief and Belief in the Impossible," *Theoria*, 28, 3 (September 2013), pp. 407–20.

Richardson, A., "Carnapian Pragmatism," in M. Friedman and R. Creath, *The Cambridge Companion to Carnap*, Cambridge: Cambridge University Press (2007), pp. 295–315.

Riddoch, M.J., M.G. Edwards, G.W. Humphreys, R. West, and T. Heafield, "Visual Affordances Direct Action: Neuropsychological Evidence from Manual Interference," *Cognitive Neuropsychology*, 15 (1998), pp. 645–84.

Riddoch, M.J., G.W. Humphreys, and M.G. Edwards, "An Experimental Analysis of Anarchic Lower Limb Action," *Neuropsychologia*, 39 (2001), pp. 574–9.

Roediger, D.R. (ed.), *Black on White: Black Writers on What It Means to Be White*, New York: Schocken Books (1998).

Rorty, R., "Is Natural Science a Natural Kind?" in E. McMullin (ed.), *Construction and Constraint: The Shaping of Scientific Rationality*, Notre Dame, IN: Notre Dame University Press (1988), pp. 49–74.

Rorty, R., "Pragmatism as Anti-Representationalism," in J.P. Murphy, *Pragmatism: From Peirce to Davidson*, Boulder, CO: Westview Press (1990), pp. 1–6.

Rose, D., W. Buckwalter, and J. Turri, "When Words Speak Louder than Actions: Delusion, Belief and the Power of Assertion," *Australasian Journal of Philosophy*, 92, 4 (2014), pp. 683–700.

Rowbottom, D.P., "'In-Between Believing' and Degrees of Belief," *Teorema*, 26 (2007), pp. 131–7.

Rubio-Fernández, P., and B. Geurts, "How to Pass the False Belief Test Before Your Fourth Birthday," *Psychological Science*, 24 (2013), pp. 27–33.

Ruskin, J., *Modern Painters*, III (1856); available online from the Ruskin Library and Research Center at Lancaster University: http://www.lancaster.ac.uk/fass/ruskin/.

Russell, B., *The Analysis of Mind*, New York: Allen and Unwin (1921).

Russell, B., *Logic and Knowledge*, R. Marsh (ed.), New York: Putnam (1971).

Ryan, S., "Doxastic Compatibilism and the Ethics of Belief," *Philosophical Studies*, 114 (2003), pp. 47–79.

Ryle, G., *The Concept of Mind*, New York: Barnes and Noble (1949/2012).

Safina, C., *Beyond Words: What Animals Think and Feel*, New York: Henry Holt (2015).

Sapolsky, R.M., "Social Cultures among Nonhumans," *Current Anthropology*, 47, 4 (2006), pp. 641–56.

Sartre, J.P., *Being and Nothingness: An Essay on Phenomenological Ontology*, H.E. Barnes (trans.), New York: Philosophical Library (1943/1956).

Saujani, R.M., "The Implicit Association Test: A Measure of Unconscious Racism in Legislative Decision-Making," *Michigan Journal of Race and Law*, 8, 395 (2002–3), pp. 395–423.

Savage, L.J., *The Foundations of Statistics*, New York: Dover (1954).

Savage-Rumbaugh, S., S.G. Shanker, and T.J. Taylor, *Apes, Language and the Human Mind*, Oxford: Oxford University Press (1998).

Schneider, S., *The Language of Thought: A New Philosophical Direction*, Cambridge, MA: MIT Press (2011).

Schneider, W., and R. Shiffrin, "Controlled and Automatic Human Information Processing I: Detection, Search and Attention," *Psychological Review*, 84 (1977a), pp. 1–66.

Schneider, W., and R. Shiffrin, "Controlled and Automatic Human Information Processing II: Perceptual Learning, Automatic Attending and a General Theory," *Psychological Review*, 84 (1977b), pp. 127–89.

Schoenfield, M., "Permission to Believe: Why Permissivism is True and What It Tells Us about Irrelevant Influences on Belief," *Noûs*, 48, 2 (2014), pp. 193–218.

Schroeder, T., and C. Matheson, "Imagination and Emotion," in S. Nichols (ed.), *The Architecture of Imagination*, Oxford: Oxford University Press (2006), pp. 19–40.

Schusterman, R.J., C. Reichmuth Kastak, and D. Kastak, "Equivalence Classification as an Approach to Social Knowledge: From Sea Lions to Simians," in F.B.M. de Waal and P.L. Tyack (eds.), *Animal Social Complexity*, Cambridge, MA: Harvard University Press (2003), pp. 179–206.

Schwarz, A., *ADHD Nation: Children, Doctors, Big Pharma and the Making of an American Epidemic*, New York: Scribner (2016).

Schwitzgebel, E., "A Phenomenal, Dispositional Account of Belief," *Noûs*, 36 (2001a), pp. 249–75.

Schwitzgebel, E., "In-Between Believing," *Philosophical Quarterly*, 51 (2001b), pp. 76–82.

Searle, J., *Intentionality: An Essay in the Philosophy of Mind*, New York: Cambridge University Press (1983).

Seigfried, C.H., "John Dewey's Pragmatist Feminism," in L.A. Hickman (ed.), *Reading Dewey: Interpretations for a Postmodern Generation*, Bloomington, IN: Indiana University Press (1989), pp. 149–65.

Shah, N., "How Truth Governs Deliberation," *Philosophical Review*, 112 (2003), pp. 447–82.

Shapiro, J.R., J.M. Ackerman, S.L. Neuberg, J.K. Maner, D.V. Becker, and D.T. Kenrick, "Following in the Wake of Anger: When Not Discriminating is Discriminating," *Personality and Social Psychology Bulletin*, 35 (2009), pp. 1356–67.

Sheets-Johnstone, M., "Taking Evolution Seriously," *American Philosophical Quarterly*, 29, 4 (1992), pp. 343–52.

Sherman, J.W., K. Gonsalkorale, T.J. Allen, B. Gawronski, K. Hugenberg, and C.J. Groom, "The Self-Regulation of Automatic Associations and Behavioral Impulses," *Psychological Review*, 115, 2 (2008), pp. 314–35.

Shettleworth, S.J., *Cognition, Evolution and Behavior*, 2nd Edition, Oxford: Oxford University Press (2010).

Shettleworth, S.J., "Modularity, Comparative Cognition and Human Uniqueness," *Philosophical Transactions of the Royal Society B*, 367 (2012), pp. 2794–2802.

Shoemaker, S., *Identity, Cause and Mind: Philosophical Essays*, Oxford: Oxford University Press (1984/2003).

Siegel, S., "How is Wishful Seeing Like Wishful Thinking?" *Philosophy and Phenomenological Research* (Feb 2016); online version DOI: 10.1111/phpr.12273.

Silk, J.B., "The Form and Function of Reconciliation in Primates," *Annual Review of Anthropology*, 31 (2002), pp. 21–44.

Silva, J.A., G.B. Leong, R. Weinstock, and C.L. Boyer, "Capgras Syndrome and Dangerousness," *Bulletin of the American Academy of Psychiatry and the Law*, 17 (1989), pp. 5–14.

Simpson, J.A., S.W. Gangestad, and M. Lerma, "Perception of Physical Attractiveness: Mechanisms Involved in the Maintenance of Romantic Relationships," *Journal of Personality and Social Psychology*, 59 (1990), pp. 1192–201.

Singer, P., *Animal Liberation*, 2nd Edition, New York: New York Review of Books (1990).

Slachewsky, A., B. Pillon, P. Fourneret, P. Pradat-Diehl, M. Jeannerod, and B. Dubois, "Preserved Adjustment but Impaired Awareness in a Sensory-Motor Conflict Following Prefrontal Lesions," *Journal of Cognitive Neuroscience*, 13 (2001), pp. 332–40.

Smith, A., "Responsibility for Attitudes: Activity and Passivity in Mental Life," *Ethics*, 115 (January 2005), pp. 236–71.

Smith, S.M., "Looking at One's Self through the Eyes of Others: W.E.B. Du Bois's Photographs for the 1900 Paris Exposition," in D. Hubbard (ed.), *The Souls of Black Folk: One Hundred Years Later*, Columbia: University of Missouri Press (2003), pp. 189–217.

Smith, D.W., and G. Ferguson, *Decade of the Wolf: Returning the Wild to Yellowstone*, Guilford, CT: Lyons Press (2005).

Smith, E. R., and J. DeCoster, "Dual Process Models in Social and Cognitive Psychology: Conceptual Integration and Links to Underlying Memory Systems," *Personality and Social Psychology Review*, 4 (2000), pp. 108–31.

Sober, E., "Comparative Thinking Meets Evolutionary Biology: Morgan's Canon and Cladistic Parsimony," in L. Datson and G. Mitman (eds.), *Thinking with Animals: New Perspectives on Anthropomorphism*, New York: Columbia University Press (2005), pp. 85–99.

Sorabji, R., *Emotion and Peace of Mind: from Stoic Agitation to Christian Temptation*, Oxford: Oxford University Press (2000).

Spangler, W.D., "Validity of Questionnaire and TAT Measures of Need for Acheivement: Two Meta-Analyses," *Psychological Bulletin*, 112 (1992), pp. 140–54.

Spelke, E.S., "Initial Knowledge: Six Suggestions," *Cognition*, 50 (1994), pp. 431–45.

Spelke, E.S., and K.D. Kinzler, "Core Knowledge," *Developmental Science*, 10 (2007), pp. 89–96.

Sperber, D., "Apparently Irrational Beliefs," in S. Lukes and M. Hollis (eds.), *Rationality and Relativism*, Oxford: Blackwell (1982), pp. 149–80.

Sperber, D., "Intuitive and Reflexive Beliefs," *Mind and Language*, 12, 1 (1997), pp. 67–83.

Stalnaker, R., *Inquiry*, Cambridge, MA: MIT (1984).

Stanley, J., *Knowing How*, Oxford: Oxford University Press (2011).

Stanley, J., and J. W. Krakauer, "Motor Skill Depends on Knowledge of Facts," *Frontiers in Human Neuroscience*, 7 (2013), p. 503.

Stanovich, K., *Who Is Rational? Studies of Individual Differences in Reasoning*, Mahwah, NJ: Lawrence Erlbaum (1999).

Steele, C., *Whistling Vivaldi: How Stereotypes Affect Us and What We Can Do*, New York: W.W. Norton (2010).

Steglich-Petersen, A., "Weighing the Aim of Belief," *Philosophical Studies*, 145, 3 (2009), pp. 395–405.

Steiner, G., *Anthropocentricism and Its Discontents: The Moral Status of Animals in the History of Western Philosophy*, Pittsburgh: PA: University of Pittsburgh Press (2005).

Steiner, G., *Animals and the Moral Community*, New York: Columbia University Press (2008).

Stich, S.P., "Do Animals Have Beliefs?" *Australasian Journal of Philosophy*, 57 (1978), pp. 15–28.

Stone, T., and A.W. Young, "Delusions and Brain Injury: The Philosophy and Psychology of Belief," *Mind and Language*, 12 (1997), pp. 327–64.

Strawson, G., "Realistic Monism: Why Physicalism Entails Panpsychism," in D. Skrbina (ed.), *Mind that Abides: Pansychism in the New Millenium, Advances in Consciousness Research*, 75, Amsterdam: John Benjamins (2009), pp. 33–57.

Strawson, P.F., "Freedom and Resentment," *Proceedings of the British Academy*, 48, 1 (1962), pp. 1–25.

Suddendorf, T., *The Gap: The Science of What Separates Us from Other Animals*, New York: Basic Books (2013).

Suddendorf, T., and M.C. Corballis, "Mental Time Travel and the Evolution of the Human Mind," *Genetic, Social and General Psychology Monographs*, 123 (1997), pp. 133–67.

Suddendorf, T., D.R. Addis, and M. Corballis, "Mental time Travel and the Shaping of the Human Mind," *Philosophical Transactions of the Royal Society B: Biological Sciences*, 364 (2009), p. 1317.

Sullivan, S., "From the Foreign to the Familiar: Confronting Dewey Confronting Racial Prejudice," *Journal of Speculative Philosophy*, 18, 3 (2004), pp. 193–202.

Taylor, B.L., "An Alternative Strategy for Adaptation in Bacterial Behavior," *Journal of Bacteriology*, 186 (2004), pp. 3671–3.

Taylor, S.E., *Positive Illusions: Creative Self-Deception and the Healthy Mind*, New York: Basic Books (1989).

Taylor, S.E., and J.D. Brown, "Illusion and Well-Being: A Social Psychological Perspective on Mental Health," *Psychological Bulletin*, 103, 2 (1988), pp. 193–210.

Taylor, A.H., G.R. Hunt, J.C. Holzhaider, and R.D. Gray, "Spontaneous Metatool Use by New Caledonian Crows," *Current Biology*, 17 (2007), pp. 1504–7.

Tejada, J., and S. Shenolikar (eds.), *Pro Files: Baseball—Intel on Today's Biggest Stars and Tips on How to Play Like Them*, New York: Time Home Entertainment (2012).

Thayer, H.S., "Pragmatism: A Reinterpretation of the Origins and Consequences," in R.J. Mulvaney and P.M. Zeltner, *Pragmatism: Its Sources and Prospects*, Columbia, SC: University of South Carolina Press (1981), pp. 1–20.

Tibbets, P., "The Concept of Voluntary Motor Control in the Recent Neuroscientific Literature," *Synthese*, 141, 2 (August 2004), pp. 247–76.

Tomasello, M., *A Natural History of Human Thinking*, Cambridge, MA: Harvard University Press (2014).

Traynor, M., and J. Kasher, "No" on *Thank You*, Epic Records, Sony/ATV Music Publishing LLC, Warner/Chappell Music Inc. (2016).

Turner, M., and M. Coltheart, "Confabulation and Delusion: A Common Monitoring Framework," *Cognitive Neuropsychiatry*, 15 (2010), pp. 346–76.

Uhlmann, E.L., V.L. Brescoll, and E. Machery, "The Motives Underlying Stereotype-Based Discrimination against Members of Stigmatized Groups," *Social Justice Research*, 23, 1 (2010), pp. 1–16.

Vahid, H., "Aiming at Truth: Doxastic vs. Epistemic Goals," *Philosophical Studies*, 131 (2006), pp. 499–516.

Vahid, H., "Rationalizing Beliefs: Evidential vs. Pragmatic Reasons," *Synthese*, 176, 3 (2010), pp. 447–62.

Vail, A.L., A. Manica, and R. Bshary, "Fish Choose Appropriately When and with Whom to Collaborate," *Current Biology*, 24, 17 (2014), R791–3.

van de Waal, E., C. Borgeaud, and A. Whiten, "Potent Social Learning and Conformity Shape a Wild Primate's Foraging Decisions," *Science*, 340 (2013), pp. 483–5.

van Duijn, M., F. Keijzer, and D. Franken, "Principles of Minimal Cognition: Casting Cognition as Sensorimotor Coordination," *Adaptive Behavior*, 14, 2 (2006), pp. 157–70.

van Fraassen, B.C., "Belief and the Will," *The Journal of Philosophy*, 81, 5 (1984), pp. 235–56.

van Leeuwen, E.J.C., K.A. Cronin, and D.B.M. Haun, "A Group-Specific Arbitrary Tradition in Chimpanzees (*Pan troglodytes*)," *Animal Cognition*, 17 (2014), pp. 1421–5.

Vanman, E.J., J.P. Ryan, W.C. Pederson, and T.A. Ito, "Probing Prejudice with Startle Eyeblink Modification: A Marker of Attention, Emotion or Both?" *International Journal of Psychological Research*, 6 (2013), pp. 30–41.

van Schaik, C.P., L. Damerius, and K. Isler, "Wild Orangutan Males Plan and Communicate Their Travel Direction One Day in Advance," *PLoS ONE*, 8, 9 (2013), p. e74896.

Velleman, J.D., *Practical Reflection*, Stanford, CA: CSLI Publications (1989).

Velleman, J.D., *The Possibility of Practical Reason*, Oxford: Oxford University Press (2000).

Verbeek, P., "Peace Ethology," *Behavior*, 145, 11 (Nov 2008), pp. 1497–1524.

Vincent, A., R. Ring, and K. Andrews, "Normative Practices of Other Animals," in A. Zimmerman, K. Jones, and M. Timmons (eds.), *The Routledge Handbook of Moral Epistemology*, New York: Routledge (forthcoming).

von Hippel, W., and R. Trivers, "The Evolution and Psychology of Self-Deception," *Behavioral and Brain and Sciences*, 34 (2011), pp. 1–56.

Walton, K., *Mimesis as Make-Believe: on the Foundations of the Representational Arts*, Cambridge, MA: Harvard University Press (1990).

Watson, G., "Free Agency," *The Journal of Philosophy*, 72, 8 (1975), pp. 205–20.

Wegner, D., *The Illusion of Conscious Will*, Cambridge, MA: MIT Press (2002).

Weil, S., "Draft for a Statement of Human Obligations," in R. Hathaway (ed.), *Two Moral Essays by Simone Weil*, Pendle Hill Pamphlet #240, Wallingford, PA: Pendle Hill (1943/1981); online at http://www.pbs.org/wgbh/questionofgod/voices/weil.html

Weinberg, J., and A. Meskin, "Puzzling Over the Imagination: Philosophical Problems, Architectural Solutions," in S. Nichols (ed.), *The Architecture of Imagination*, Oxford: Oxford University Press (2006), pp. 175–204.

West, C., *The American Evasion of Philosophy: A Genealogy of Pragmatism*, Madison, WI: University of Wisconsin Press (1989).

White, E.G., *Justice Oliver Wendell Holmes: Law and the Inner Self*, New York: Oxford University Press (1993).

White, M., *The Philosophy of the American Revolution*, New York: Oxford (1978).

Whiten, A., V. Horner, and F.B.M. de Waal, "Conformity to Cultural Norms of Tool Use in Chimpanzees," *Nature*, 437 (2005), pp. 737–40.

Wiener, Philip P., "Peirce's Metaphysical Club and the Genesis of Pragmatism," *Journal of the History of Ideas*, VII (1946), pp. 218–33.

Wilde, O., "Intentions," in J.M. Guy (ed.), *The Complete Works of Oscar Wilde, Volume 4: Criticism*, Oxford: Oxford University Press (2007), pp. 71–230.

Wilkes, K.V., "Talking to Cats, Rats and Bats," in J. Preston (ed.), *Thought and Language: Royal Institute of Philosophy Supplement 42*, Cambridge: Cambridge University Press (1997), pp. 177–95.

Williams, B., "The Idea of Equality," in Laslett and Runciman (eds.), *Politics, Philosophy and Society II*, Oxford: Blackwell (1962), reprinted in B. Williams, *Problems of the Self*, Cambridge: Cambridge University Press (1973), pp. 230–49.

Williams, B., "Deciding to Believe," in Kiefer and Munitz (eds.), *Language, Belief and Metaphysics*, Albany, NY: SUNY Press (1970), pp. 95–11; reprinted in B. Williams, *Problems of the Self*, Cambridge: Cambridge University Press (1973), pp. 136–51.

Williams, B., *Problems of the Self*, Cambridge: Cambridge University Press (1973).

Williams, B., *Truth and Truthfulness*, Princeton, NJ: Princeton University Press (2002).

Wilson, T.D., and E.W. Dunn, "Self-Knowledge: Its Limits, Value and Potential for Improvement," *Annual Review of Psychology*, 55 (2004), pp. 493–518.

Winters, B., "Believing at Will," *The Journal of Philosophy*, 76, 5 (1979), pp. 243–56.

Wittenbrink, B., and N. Schwarz (eds.), *Implicit Measures of Attitudes*, New York: Guilford (2007).

Wu, W., *Attention*, Abingdon, UK: Routledge (2014).

Wu, W., "Experts and Deviants: The Story of Agential Control," *Philosophy and Phenomenological Research*, XCIII, 1 (2015), pp. 101–26.

Yerkes, R.M., *Almost Human*, New York: Century (1925).

Young, A., "Wondrous Strange: The Neuropsychology of Abnormal Beliefs," *Mind and Language*, 15, 1 (2000), pp. 47–73.

Zackariasson, U., "Pragmatism and Moral Critique of Religion," *American Journal of Theology and Philosophy*, 31, 1 (2010), pp. 3–14.

Zimmerman, A., *Directly in Mind: A Defense of First-Person Authority*, Cornell University, Ph.D. dissertation (2002).

Zimmerman, A., "Self-Verification and the Content of Thought," *Synthese*, 149 (2006), pp. 59–75.

Zimmerman, A., "The Nature of Belief," *Journal of Consciousness Studies*, 14, 11 (2007a), pp. 61–82.

Zimmerman, A., "Against Relativism," *Philosophical Studies*, 133 (2007b), pp. 313–48.

Index

0-six 44–6, 71–2

acceptance 32
Ackerman, J.M. 131
acting on stage 86–8
action defined as sensorimotor
    coupling 5, 9
Alfano, M. 114–15
alief 30n11, 102–3, 102n8
Anscombe, G.E.M. 45
anthropodenial 51
Aristotle 17, 20, 86n5
association 51, 101–2, 102–3n8, 104–5
assumption as distinct from belief 20
attention 1–5, 26n6, 27–8, 28n9,
    29–41, 42
    divided 3–5, 27, 75
    dissociated from self-control 4–5
    importance for self-control 9–10
attention deficit hyperactivity disorder 123
automaticity 2–4, 14
autonomy 122

bacteria 75n51
Bain, A. xi–xiii, 7–8, 12, 16n13, 38, 41,
    73, 75–8, 77n53, 83, 85n4, 87n7, 89,
    97, 112, 120n26, 126, 128, 130–1,
    136n10, 137, 139
    on association 113
    on bias 107–8
    definition of belief 1, 75, 77–8, 81
    definition of self 17
    on emotional belief 83
    on habit 7–9
    metaphysics of mind xiin2
    origins of belief 70
    on self-control 18, 112, 126
    taxonomy of the mind 11, 97
    on varieties of religious belief 62
baseball cognition 40–1, 106
Bauby, J.-D. 15
Bayesianism 84, 136n10, 138
belief
    actively formed 83–4, 128–40

aim of 20, 43, 46n7
animal 42–80
    definition of 1–3, 22, 98, 102,
        104–5
    false belief concept 48–9
    irrational 84–5, 89–96, 108–9,
        128–40
    moral 60–1, 63
    non-propositional 20, 44, 46n7,
        57–8, 72
    origins of 75
    partial 20, 89–91
    passivity of 42–3, 81–4
    religious 62–4, 84, 140
Bermudez, J. 65, 65n38
Brown, J.D. 130
Burge, T. 46n7, 59n28, 101n3, 129

Camp, E. 59n30, 71n47
Candy, J. 69n44
Capgras syndrome 20, 89–96
Carnap, R. 67, 124, 124nn28–9
Carruthers, P. 70n45, 71n47, 72
central executive 28
Chalmers, D. 74, 116n21
character 114
Clark, A. 116n21
cognitive neuroscience 2–5, 7–9, 28
cognitive penetration 120n26
Cohen, L.J. 19, 25n5, 32n14
concepts 58–65, 61n33
Confucius 41, 41n27
conservatism, intellectual 63
credence; see degree of belief
culture, animal 46–7

Darwin, C. 18, 50, 73–4
    on guilt and remorse 54
    on human morality 52
    on reflection 53
Davidson, D. 43, 59n29, 84n3
Declaration of Independence 60
deference to experts 20–1, 35–7, 63,
    98–101, 119–27

degree of belief 22, 33–4
  differentiated from degree of
    assimilation 22–3
  measured by entrenchment 26
  measured by willingness to risk 23–4,
    32–3, 137–9
  phenomenological measures of 24–5
déjà vu 91n11
delusion 20, 88–96
Dennett, D.C. 32n14, 68n43, 71n46,
    73–4, 90n10, 130, 134
Descartes, R. xi, 44n4, 55n21, 73, 82, 134
de Sousa, R. 32–4, 71n46, 90n10
desire 20, 78–80
  as evaluative judgment 20, 78–80
  partial contrast with belief 20, 78–80
determinacy; see indeterminacy
de Waal, F. 47–9, 51–2, 54–5, 69, 71,
    76, 92
Dewey, J. xiii, 76, 124–5, 131
Diagnostic and Statistical Manual of
    Mental Disorders 123
dispositions related to belief 20, 75–7,
    85–7
Douglas, F. 60
doxastic commitment 136–7
Du Bois, W.E.B. 107, 107n14
Dummett, M. 55n21, 59n29
Dunn, E. 109
Dunning, D. 131
Durkheim, E. 63
Dweck, C. 133, 134n9

egalitarianism, racial 102–27
emotion 30–2, 41, 50
empirical equivalence 103
entitlement 133–4
epistemic authority 36–7, 97–127
epistemic decision theory 138
ethology 19, 42–8
evidentialism 21, 43n3
executive function 28, 116
existentialism 124–5
expectation 33, 57–8, 70, 72
explicit/implicit distinction 110–11
externalism 28n7, 116n21

face recognition 89–91
Field, H. 60n32
Fisch, M.H. xiii
Fodor, J. xiin1, 71

folk psychology 1, 26, 98–101
Foster, C. 69, 96
Fourneret, P. 4–5
Frankfurt, H. 80n56
Frankish, K. 19, 32–5, 71n46, 90n10
  on ambiguity of "belief," 32
  defense of "two systems" theory of
    belief 32–5
  distinction between mind and
    supermind 32–4
  distinction between personal and
    subpersonal 35, 35n19
Frege, G. 46n7, 67
Frith, C.D. 6

Garzón, P.C. 127
Gazzaniga, M. 9n5, 16n12
Gendler, T. 30n11, 102, 102n7, 136n10
Gilbert, D. 38n23
Glock, H.J. 59
good, guise of 79
Greenwald, A. 35n18, 105, 105n12

habit 2–3, 51
  accordance with belief 2–3, 22–3
  discordance with belief 3–4, 22–3,
    104–5
Haidt, J. 40
harm principle 118
Holmes, O.W. xii, 65n37
hope 140
Hume, D. xii, 37, 44, 57, 78n54, 81–2,
    88–9, 114

imagination 86–9, 91–6
implicit associations 34–5, 101–5, 116–22
implicit association test 34–5, 101–5,
    116–19
implicit attitudes 111–13
indeterminacy 55–8
  of animal thought 55–9
  of human thought 60–73, 61n33
  of legal interpretation 63–5
  of neurological representation 64–5
information 1–2, 26n6, 28
  assimilation of 2, 22–6
  guidance by 1, 26n6, 42
  format of 27, 71–3
innovation, animal 45, 45n5
instinct 12–13, 39, 51, 73–5, 75n52, 81
intellectualism 19–20, 43–4, 67–9, 79

intention in action 43n3, 44–6, 45n6,
    70n45
interpretation 63–6, 101–3
    accordance with belief 2–3, 22–3
    arguments against 42–80
intuition 31
Iowa Gambling Task 31n13

James, W. xii–xiv, 1, 5n3, 7, 9n5, 11, 13,
    21, 38, 46n7, 84, 97, 111, 126–7,
    129, 132, 139
    definition of belief 1
    on habit 7, 111
    identification of attention and
        control 5n3
Jeannerod, M. 4–5, 7–9
Jefferson, T. 60, 60n32, 65
Jeffery, R. 32n15
Johnson, J.W. 106
judgment, burdens of 82–3, 85–6

Kahneman, D. 19, 35–9, 120
    defense of "two systems" theory 37–9
Kalanithi, P. 136
Kant, I. xiiin3, 85, 84n3, 114–16
Kasher, J. 132
Keijzer, F. 127
Keren, G. 30–2
King Jr., M.L. 116
Konecni, V.J. 134n8
Kornblith, H. 38n23, 39n25
Korsgaard, C. 84n3
Kripke, S. 67n41
Kuhn, T. 125n30

language 33, 52
    animal 48, 49n13, 57, 58n25
    dissociation from attention and
        control 31–3, 38–9
    dissociation from belief 44, 57–8,
        57n24, 70–1
language of thought 71–2
Levy, N. 6–7, 17n14, 29n10, 45n6,
    102–3n8
Lewis, C.I. 124
Lewis, D. xiin1, 137–8
Lewis, D.D. 88
liberalism 118
Libet, B. 6
locked-in syndrome 15
locked-out syndrome 15–16

locomotion 12–13
Lovato, D. 131

Malebranche, N. 55n21
Mandelbaum, E. 102n8
Marcus, R.B. 66–7, 66n40
Marx, K. 70n45
Maudsely, H. 7
May, J. 17n14
McIntyre, R. 45
McKay, R.T. 130, 134
memory 3–4, 33, 57–8, 72, 101
Menand, L. xiiin3
metacognition in animals 44–6
Mill, J.S. xiiin3, 80, 118, 118nn23–4
Mills, C. 108n16, 111n18
mind 1, 11
    equated with nervous system 1, 18n15, 28
    Frankish's conception of 33
    modularity 72, 120n26
    moral belief 63, 140
    moral fiber 116
Moran, R. 56–7
Morgan, C.L 50–1

Nagel, T. 16n12, 74, 80n56
neobeaviorism 75–7
Nichols, S. 91–2

Obama, B. 119
O'Connor, D.J. 61, 70
other minds 57n24
overconfidence 132–3

Pacherie, E. 7
panpsychism 73–5
partial belief 20, 89–91
Peacocke, C. 38n22
Peirce, C.S. xii, 27, 76, 82, 87
    definition of belief 22
    definition of pragmatism xii, 124
phototropism 73
play 86–8, 91–4
Pluto 100–1
positive illusions 21, 130–40
post-traumatic stress syndrome 116–17
pragmatism xii–xiii
    meta-level 97–8, 119–27
    origins in Bain's definition of
        belief xii–xiii
    relation to liberalism 118

prescriptive authority 123
pretense 20, 81–96
  as distinct from belief 20, 81–96
primitive credulity 38
principal pinciple 137–8, 138n11
Prinz, W. 6
probability, subjective 31, 32n15, 136–9
prospection 53n19
prudence 79–80
Pujols, A. 40–1
Putnam, H. xiin1, 97–8, 101n3

Quine, W.V.O. 60n32

race xivn4, 103–5
racial profiling 112n19, 136n10
racism xivn4, 60, 65n37, 101–22
rape 132n5
reactions 116–22
reactive attitudes 113–16
reasoning, by animals 44n4, 48
reference class problem 116n22
reflection 53
religious belief 61–3
responsibility, moral 10, 52–3, 113–22
Ramsey, F. 19, 23–4, 23n3, 25n5, 65–6,
  66n39, 87n7, 129, 137
Reisner, A. 128n1, 139
Richard, M. 67
Rorty, R. xiiin3, 120n26
Russell, B. 46n7, 87n7
Ryle, G. 2, 5n3, 73, 75

Safina, C. 44–7
St. John Green, N. xii
Sartre, J.P. 5n3
Saujani, R. 117–18
Schlick, M. 124n28
Schneider, G.H. 7
Schoenfeld, M. 138n12
Schul, Y. 30–2
Schwitzgebel, E. 75–6, 102n8, 110n17
scientific belief 137–40
Searle, J. 8
self 17–18, 34–5
  definition of 17–18
  conceptualized as "deep," 115–17
self-control 1–5, 9–10, 17–18, 26n6, 28,
  28n9, 29–41, 42, 79–80
  as motor control 17–18
  connected to attention 9–10
  dissociated from attention 4–5
self-deception 105–11, 135–40

self-promoting beliefs 128–30
self-verification 129, 134–5
sensorimotor coupling 9
Siegel, S. 132–3n6, 136n10
sincerity 56–7, 101–2, 101n5
skepticism
  with regard to animal minds 44n4,
    55n21, 57n24
  with regard to the senses 81–3
  with regard to the will 6–10, 29
skill 11–12, 39–41
  belief's role in 12–14, 39–41
  importance of attention and control
    for 11–12
Smith, A. 115–16
Socrates 1, 63, 79
Sperber, D. 61
Spielberg, S. 88
Spinoza, B. 38n23
spontaneity 75–7
spying 88–9
Steglich-Petersen, A. 131
Steiner, G. 55n21, 59n29, 69
Stich, S. 91–2
Stoicism 41, 41n27, 55n21
Strawson, G. 74
Strawson, P.F. 113n20
subpersonal 35, 105–6
suicide 84–5
Sullivan, S. 107

thematic apperception test 121n27
Traynor, M. 132
trinity, belief in 61–3
Trump, D.J. 112n19, 133
trust 140
truth 20
  not the "constitutive" aim of
    belief 20, 43, 46n7, 49, 56n22,
    67–8, 78–80, 78n54, 83–4,
    84n3, 139–40
  normative importance of 139–40
  in a post-truth society 139–40
Turing machine functionalism xi
two systems models of cognition 29–41
  history of 29n10

value, representation of 78–80
Velleman, D. 20, 43, 43n3, 46n7, 56n21,
  84n3, 104–5n11, 131
Verbeek, P. 55
volition 5n3, 76–7, 77n53
voluntarism 85–6

Watson, G. 80n56
Wegner, D. 6
Weil, S. 127
West, C. xiiin3, 140
Wilde, O. 76
Wilkes, K. 60-1
will 5-10
  as complex 5
  skepticism about 6-10, 29
  unity of 10
  to believe 21, 128-40

Williams, B. 20, 43, 43n3, 55-6, 86, 110,
  131, 134
willpower 17-18, 79-80
  exhibited by animals
  18-19n16
Wilson, T. 109
Wittgenstein, L. 124n28
working memory 28n8

Zimmerman, A. 65-6n38, 102, 120n26,
  122, 133-4

Respect for NORMS — truth